# Talking in Class

# Talking in Class

## Using Discussion to Enhance Teaching and Learning

**Thomas M. McCann**
Elmhurst Community Unit School District, Elmhurst, Illinois

**Larry R. Johannessen**
Northern Illinois University

**Elizabeth Kahn**
James B. Conant High School, Hoffman Estates, Illinois

**Joseph M. Flanagan**
York Community High School, Elmhurst, Illinois

National Council of Teachers of English
1111 W. Kenyon Road, Urbana, Illinois 61801-1096

Staff Editor: Bonny Graham

Manuscript Editor: Amy Bauman

Interior Design: Doug Burnett

Cover Design: Pat Mayer

NCTE Stock Number: 50012

**Library of Congress Cataloging-in-Publication Data**

Talking in class : using discussion to enhance teaching and learning /
Thomas M. McCann . . . [et al.].
     p. cm.
  Includes bibliographical references and index.
  ISBN 0-8141-5001-2 (pbk.)
1. English language—Study and teaching (Secondary) 2. Literature—
Study and teaching (Secondary) 3. Communication in education.
4. Discussion. I. McCann, Thomas M.
  LB1631.T263 2006
  428'.0071'2—dc22

                             2006001303

*This book is dedicated to all of those who have taught us how complex and important discussion is in teaching and learning—our students, colleagues, and teachers, especially George Hillocks, Jr., who taught us what authentic discussion is and how to enact it in the classroom.*

# Permission Acknowledgments

**Chapter 1:** An earlier version of this chapter appeared as an article in *English Leadership Quarterly*, Volume 26, Number 1 (August 2003), reprinted here by permission of the National Council of Teachers of English.

**Chapter 2:** An earlier version of this chapter appeared as an article in the *Illinois English Bulletin*, Volume 85, Number 3 (Spring 1998), reprinted here by permission of the Illinois Association of Teachers of English.

**Chapter 3:** An earlier version of this chapter appeared as an article in *English Journal*, Volume 92, Number 6 (July 2003), reprinted here by permission of the National Council of Teachers of English.

**Chapter 7:** "Base Details" by Siegfried Sassoon. Copyright Siegfried Sassoon by kind permission of Mr George Sassoon. From COLLECTED POEMS OF SIEGFRIED SASSOON by Siegfried Sassoon, copyright 1918, 1920 by E. P. Dutton. Copyright 1936, 1946, 1947, 1948 by Siegfried Sassoon. Used by permission of Viking Penguin, a division of Penguin Group (USA) Inc.

Figure 7.1: Question-answer relationships (QAR). Reprinted by permission from Taffy E. Raphael, "Question-Answering Strategies for Children." *The Reading Teacher* 36 (1982): 186-90. Copyright © 1982 by the International Reading Association.

**Chapter 8:** An earlier version of this chapter appeared as an article in the *Illinois English Bulletin*, Volume 87, Number 3 (Spring 2000), reprinted here by permission of the Illinois Association of Teachers of English.

**Chapter 12:** An earlier version of this chapter appeared as an article in the *Illinois English Bulletin*, Volume 86, Number 3 (Spring 1999), reprinted here by permission of the Illinois Association of Teachers of English.

# Contents

# Foreword

George Hillocks, Jr.
Professor Emeritus, University of Chicago

Over the past forty years, many writers and researchers have turned their attention to the nature of classroom talk, some making detailed studies of the kinds of talk present in hundreds of hours of observed classrooms, some analyzing the role of questions in generating different kinds of student response, some charting the ways in which teacher talk hinders or encourages response and discussion, some examining the ways in which a teacher's epistemological stance and attitudes toward students affect student response and achievement, several examining the typology of questions, and many addressing a multitude of other concerns.

I know of no previous study that has addressed what might be called the ecology of talk in the classroom. Most studies and most papers making recommendations for teachers have examined only one or, at most, a few of the factors responsible for the nature of classroom talk over extended periods of time. *Talking in Class* by McCann, Johannessen, Kahn, and Flanagan is a first in going beyond the superficial conditions of question asking and teacher behavior to examine the conditions of pedagogy and curriculum that are most conducive to the development and maintenance of discussion and inquiry resulting in deep learning over long periods of time. This is an extremely valuable book for readers who hope to develop learning environments that engage students daily in discussions promoting insight and learning.

The writers begin with a chapter on relatively simple pedagogical methods for increasing the possibility of student response: asking authentic questions, avoiding teacher talk that tends to end discussion, and giving students opportunities to process complex questions through "wait time," response logs, and the use of "uptake." However, they realize that good classroom discussions will not occur serendipitously on a daily basis even with the use of these pedagogical tips. For the level of discussion to be consistently high, many discussions must be planned in advance, planned in the sense that the curricular conditions are in place to engender discussion, conditions that help students reconceive their own roles from passive recipient to active participant in the development of knowledge. The authors present a series of types of structures to ensure that discussion occurs: opinionnaires, scenarios, case studies, and role-playing simulations. They attend to how to make discussion relevant in the contexts of teaching both literature and composition. From these activities, the authors move to the development of larger curricular structures (units and yearlong programs) that will engage students in continuous critical thinking and inquiry in their reading and writing, activities known to promote higher levels of achievement. Finally, they attend to the relevance of discussion to diverse communities and to the ideals of democracy.

The authors have brought their combined seventy-plus years of classroom experience to bear on making this book an important and delightful read. Whether you are a neophyte or an experienced professional teacher, you will find great value in this book. I believe it is one you will want to keep on your desk for ready reference. I am certain that, if you are concerned with good discussion in your classes, you will want to try some of the many fascinating, sure-fire materials and activities included. The book is a must-read for every teacher, neophyte or pro, concerned with discussion, whatever the subject matter.

# Preface

While it is common to think of a typical English classroom as one in which a teacher engages students in engrossing discussions about the stories and poems that they have read, current research reveals that seldom does authentic discussion occur in middle school and high school English classes. In our preparation, inservice training, and supervision of teachers, we have come to recognize how difficult it is to engage students in the kind of discussion that represents an open exploration of ideas rather than a simple recitation.

To be an effective facilitator of discussion requires some developed skill. It also requires time and diligence to prepare instructors to be good at the craft of facilitating discussion. It appears to us that specific work in the craft of initiating and managing discussions is only a small part of methods education, if it is a component of the methods class at all. We have seen only slim evidence that anyone in teacher education programs attempts to develop teachers further in the craft of discussion, and we have not seen the topic elevated as a priority in any school.

We know that we have often left our own classrooms with a self-confident feeling that we had just had a "great discussion" with our class; but when we reflected on what had actually happened, we were forced to admit that the "great discussion" seemed so satisfying to us only because we dominated the talk. As a means to reflect on classroom discussions, we have gotten into the habit of recording discussions on audiotape or videotape or having a colleague take notes in order to produce transcripts that reveal what actually occurred in large-group and small-group forums. In the chapters of this book, we share some of the transcript data that we have collected to help to distinguish the rote recitation of recall from discussion that represents an analytical exploration of concepts, issues, and policies. The classroom discussion transcripts also show the kind of thinking that the interchanges among peers stimulates and how this thinking transfers to subsequent learning.

It would not matter much whether students engaged in authentic discussion if their participation did not have such a positive impact on their learning. If students rarely engage in authentic discussion, as the current research shows, they are losing the valuable learning experiences they could have if such discussions were more frequent.

We have to acknowledge that the art of facilitating authentic discussion is not easily acquired. In the best of all possible worlds, an apprentice teacher would learn some basic principles, would see master teachers model the process, and would have numerous occasions to practice and refine the craft under the insightful and sensitive supervision of a recognized expert. If anyone has experienced such training, we envy you. For most teachers, the methods class was a whirlwind of theories, examples, and explanations that were intended to equip the novice for the rigors of practice teaching. For those who did not see the attention to discussion as part of the methods class or were absent that day, this book can provide some guidelines. It offers an extensive look at the concept of authentic classroom discussion.

The chapters of this book are organized in a way that should support preparation in the craft of facilitating discussion. First we make a case for the importance of providing opportunities for students to engage in purposeful talk in their English classes. The earlier chapters of the book introduce the reader to some basic considerations for planning and managing large-group and small-group discussions. Subsequent chapters illustrate the ways that discussion prepares students for other learning. The later chapters explore some broader issues related to the importance of discussion: how it can connect many phases and components of the curriculum, how it promotes and supports critical thinking, and how it connects students to issues that are important to them and to a world of thinkers.

Throughout the book, we provide examples of prompts, structures, and activities that encourage students to participate in authentic discussion, and we illustrate their effect by reproducing samples of in-class and online dialogues. We invite readers to experiment with some of the examples, to analyze the dialogues, to design activities for their own students, and to discuss their effects with colleagues to validate which activities, practices, and behaviors involve students in the kind of discussion that promotes learning.

# Acknowledgments

First, we acknowledge our indebtedness to George Hillocks, who is the primary influence on our thinking about the effect of purposeful discussion on learning. Long ago, George, more than anyone else, shaped our thinking about teaching, especially by emphasizing the critical role that peer interaction plays in learning. More recently, he generously examined early versions of this book and provided suggestions that helped to shape it into a more sensible and readable text.

We are also indebted to several of our colleagues who over the years have helped to shape our thinking about the kind of dynamic classroom environments that would support frequent peer interactions that foster learning. Among these cherished partners are Julianna Cucci, Steve Gevinson, Jane Feeney Kade, Steve Kern, Jamie Kowalczyk, Peter Smagorinsky, Michael Smith, Carolyn Walter, and Jeff Wilhelm.

We are grateful to Jeff Kargol and Judy Minor who assisted us in looking into what actually happens in the classroom when teachers attempt to engage students in discussion. Jeff and Judy allowed us to observe in their classrooms and assisted us in the analysis of transcripts and related artifacts to speculate on the effect that purposeful discussion has on learning.

Our colleagues Susan Callahan, Dianne Chambers, John V. Knapp, and Judy Pokorny have supplied us with cautions, insights, and constructive suggestions as we have attempted to articulate the teaching practices that prompt extended discussions to promote learning. We have relied on their general support and partnership as we have worked through this current project and others.

We acknowledge a special debt to our many students. From our work with them over dozens of years, we have learned much about classroom discussion. The pages that follow contain several transcripts and writing samples that represent the voices of our students, who generously allowed us to represent them for the benefit of other teachers.

We appreciate the general assistance we have received from Colleen Braun, Ann Bruno, Lori Hall, and Ellen Walsh. Their constant help allowed us to advance this project in a timely fashion.

We have depended on the painstaking editorial work of Amy Bauman, who guided us toward producing a more refined and readable text. Throughout the process of preparing the manuscript for printing, she has guided and encouraged us, and in many instances prompted us to reflect more closely on the expression of our ideas.

At NCTE, Production Editor Bonny Graham has provided steady leadership in guiding this project into print. Her care and attention to detail have been steady supports and reliable assistance. We also appreciate the unwavering encouragement and generous guidance of NCTE Senior Editor Zarina Hock, whose vision has moved this project forward from rough proposal to finished product.

# 1 Talking in Class

## Some of Us Are Trying to Teach

When Larry began teaching in a large suburban high school outside of Chicago, he commonly organized small-group discussions and infused the conversations with the kind of controversies that would stimulate lively talk. One was likely to hear animated voices emanating from his classroom. Larry recalls one occasion when the class was embroiled in vigorous debates about the relative moral sense of Huckleberry Finn and Jim. Surveying the room and seeing the students challenging each other, referring to the text, citing rules, making analogies, and contending with multiple perspectives, Larry was delighted to think that his students were deeply engaged in exploring a significant critical question and applying it to an important work of literature. Then a sharp tap at the door attracted Larry's attention. When he looked toward the door, he saw the granite face of Ms. Hufflocher (not her real name), another English teacher, who labored in a classroom across the hall. Larry accommodated his colleague by moving into the hall for a brief colloquy. Ms. Hufflocher faced Larry and announced: "Mr. Johannessen, could you regain order in your classroom? Some of us are trying to *teach!*"

Besides exposing the fact that Larry was clearly a rabble-rouser when he began teaching, the scenario reveals that in the late 1970s, a teacher who encouraged students to talk in class was a bit suspect, and the instructional mode of choice at the time designated that the teacher did most of the talking and the students did most of the listening and noting. Of course, Larry's school was not the exception.

Anyone who has been an English major in college will recall professors who assigned reading and expected students to read the assignment insightfully and to be prepared for discussions about it in class. Some of those discussions were painful to sit through when few class members had actually read and understood the text and the professor had no clue about ways to initiate discussion that would invite wide and thoughtful participation. Anyone who has supervised English teachers and observed in their classrooms will recall witnessing new and

An earlier version of this chapter appeared as an article in *English Leadership Quarterly* 26(1). It is reprinted here by permission of the National Council of Teachers of English.

veteran teachers alike prompting students to respond orally to a series of questions from a "study guide" under the misconception that this routine was a "discussion."

The prevailing practices reveal that meaningful discussions seldom take place in English classes. This seems impossible when experience would suggest that discussion is an essential mode of learning in English classes, and current conceptions of best practices in the teaching of English would underscore the idea that discussion is a powerful tool for preparing students to write and to understand the literature that they study (Applebee 1996; Hillocks 1999, 2002; Langer 2001a). Although the initiation and development of lively and meaningful discussion might appear to be rudimentary and common tasks, it is not easy to engage adolescent learners in purposeful discussions. Probably the most influential resource that prospective English teachers have for learning how to facilitate discussion is the years of watching their own English teachers trying to lead discussions. In fact, Lortie (1975), Grossman and Richert (1988), and Smagorinsky and Whiting (1995) remind us that there is a tendency on the part of novice teachers to revert to images of their own teachers and of themselves as students as guides for their own behaviors in the classroom. While the important job of engaging students in discussions seems easy, it is an effort that is actually very difficult and remains a neglected part of preservice and inservice training.

## The Dominant Mode of Instruction

In 1984, Goodlad reported that in the classrooms that he studied, a *frontal* style of teaching was the dominant practice, with teachers lecturing and leading large-group discussions, and with the teacher dominating the talk and using the questions in large-group discussions as a means to quiz students on their recall of information. Goodlad (1984) and others (e.g., Boyer 1985; Sizer 1984; NCEE 1983) called for reform to many of the common practices in schools. Since 1984, school reform has taken a variety of shapes, including the adoption of block schedules, the alteration of the school day, the codification of standards, and the proliferation of high-stakes assessments. Applebee (1996, 1999) and Goodlad (2003) remind us, however, that for all the attempts at reform, the behaviors of teachers and the activities of students in the classroom remain essentially the same today as they were when Goodlad looked into schools in 1984. In other words, *recitation*, rather than *authentic discussion*, is the common mode of discourse in most classrooms.

## What Is Authentic Discussion?

Nystrand distinguishes between authentic discussion, which is dialogic, and recitation, which is monologic (Bakhtin 1981; Christoph and Nystrand 2001; Nystrand 1997). With recitation, there are prespecified answers to the teacher's questions. For example, in "discussing" *Romeo and Juliet*, the teacher asks, "Who is hosting the party that Romeo and his friends attend?" "Whom does Romeo hope to see at the party?" The teacher obviously has a specific answer in mind and probes the students until he or she hears the correct answer. In contrast, a teacher might initiate an authentic discussion by asking, "How would you know if Romeo or any adolescent were *really* in love?" The prompt asks the participants in the discussion to identify a series of behaviors and interpret them in some logical fashion. The question invites speculation and encourages several participants to join in the inquiry. The invitation to discuss introduces an authentic problem that has been a focus in the critical tradition that surrounds the play. The teacher would have to admit having some doubts about knowing a definitive answer to the question and would facilitate discussion with an *authentic* openness to exploring possibilities and testing claims.

Simply throwing out an authentic question, however, does not guarantee that an authentic discussion will ensue. The question may be met with blank, silent stares. A student might offer a snide comment, and the class could break up in laughter. In response to the question about signs that a person is in love, a student might say something like, "If they want to be with the person all the time." Additional ideas might be slow in coming forth, however, because there is no easy solution to the question.

## Authentic Discussion Is Rare

Students and teachers seldom engage in authentic discussion (Cristoph and Nystrand 2001; Nystrand 1997; Marshall, Smagorinsky, and Smith 1995). Nystrand and his colleagues (1997) looked into hundreds of classrooms, and they summarize their observations in this way:

> Discussion and small-group work were rare. On average, discussion took 50 seconds per class in eighth grade and less than 15 seconds in grade 9; small-group work, which occupied about half a minute a day in eighth grade, took a bit more than 2 minutes a day in grade 9. (42)

The findings are especially startling after years of teachers' exposure to cooperative learning as a useful tool for discussion, after calls for seeing the curriculum as conversation, and after the claims by many teachers that they are committed to open discussions with broad participation. Christoph and Nystrand (2001) report, "In short, despite teachers' considerable stated allegiance to discussion, Nystrand and colleagues observed little discussion in any classes in the sense of an in-depth exchange of ideas in the absence of teacher evaluation" (251).

## Why Should We Care?

So, despite the claims of many teachers that they are committed to authentic discussions, such discussions seldom occur. But why should we care? Hillocks (1999) points out that teachers' choices about reliance on authentic discussion or recitation reveals different epistemological stances that guide instructional practices. If recitation is the main mode for delivering instruction, the teacher probably conceives of instruction as a process of identifying key information and disseminating it to the students. In contrast, when discussion represents a group inquiry into open questions, the teacher likely sees learning as a process that involves interaction with others and requires the practice of certain habits of mind that go well beyond simple recall. In some instances, teachers may not even be aware of the implications of their instructional choices or their pedagogical habits. Again, several sources (Johannessen 1997b; Grossman and Richert 1988; Lortie 1975) report that it is common for teachers to follow models of teaching by recalling how they were taught themselves. If most instruction has been "frontal," as Goodlad describes it, and most discussion is actually recitation, then the pattern of teachers talking much and assessing often will continue to perpetuate itself unless many teachers make an aggressive shift toward reliance on authentic discussion as an essential element of their instructional practices.

Langer (2001a) reports that language arts programs that promote frequent, meaningful discussion among students will make a significant difference in learning and achievement. Hillocks (2002) reports further that "Research shows that students reach the kinds of goals recommended by the Commission [National Commission on Excellence in Education] best when they are engaged in discussion with their peers and the teacher about complex materials and problems" (3). Zemelman, Daniels, and Hyde (1998), Mitchell and Christenbury (2000) and Jago (2001) offer numerous examples of best practices that rely on meaningful peer interaction. Probst (1988) and Rosenblatt (1995) have long maintained that purposeful discussions among students will support their efforts to make meaning from the texts they encounter. Atwell (1998) and Elbow and Belanoff (1989) describe the essential role that student interaction plays in the students' attempts to develop their writing.

Several influential thinkers see authentic discussion as an essential element in the mission of any school. Authentic discussion promotes critical thinking and allows for the deep examination of enduring themes and essential questions. Nussbaum (1997) observes:

> In order to foster a democracy that is reflective and deliberative, rather than simply a marketplace of competing interest groups, a democracy that genuinely takes thought for the common good, we must produce citizens who have the Socratic capacity to reason about their beliefs. It is not good for democracy when people vote on the basis of sentiments they have absorbed from talk-radio and have never questioned. This failure to think critically produces a democracy in which people talk at one another but never have a genuine dialogue. In such an atmosphere, bad arguments pass for good arguments, and prejudice can all too easily masquerade as reason. To unmask prejudice and to secure justice, we need argument, an essential tool of civic freedom. (19)

Meier (1995) insists that frequent engagement in authentic discussion promotes democratic ideals:

> The habits conducive to free inquiry don't just happen with age and maturity. They take root slowly. And uncertainties, multiple viewpoints, the use of independent judgment, and pleasure in imaginative play aren't luxuries to be grafted on to the mind-set of a mature scholar, suited only to the gifted few, or offered after school on a voluntary basis to the children of parents inclined this way. It's my contention that these are the required habits of a sound citizenry, habits that take time and practice. (81)

Meier reminds us that active, frequent engagement in meaningful discussions not only promotes learning of the skills and substance of a particular subject but fosters an environment of tolerance, critical thinking, and democratic spirit.

## Authentic Discussion, Learning, and Achievement

Cognitive psychologists observe that meaningful interaction among students is not just a philosophically attractive aspect of school; it is essential to learning. Vygotsky (1980) insists that "learning awakens a variety of internal developmental processes that are able to operate only when the child is interacting with people in his environment and in cooperation with his peers. Once these processes are internalized, they become part of the child's independent developmental achievement" (90). To use the language of Bahktin and Nystrand again, the interactions among peers that Vygotsky describes would be dialogic and not the simple recitation of answers or the sharing of responses to fill in blanks on a worksheet.

Smagorinsky and Fly (1993, 1994) report that the behavior of the teacher in leading large-group discussions serves as a powerful model for students as they engage in their own small-group discussions. In other words, if the teacher repeatedly models recitation, then the teacher will convey the message that discussions are essentially the assessments of recall. At the same time, if the teacher commonly poses authentic questions that invite multiple valid responses and that encourage wide participation, and the teacher respectfully acknowledges attempts while challenging students to think fully about their observations, then, over time, students internalize the process, imitate the behaviors of the teacher, and expect discussions to be a dynamic exchange and exploration of ideas.

Nystrand and his colleagues (1997) note that authentic discussions are more likely to occur in the "upper-track" classes of the school. This is discouraging for several reasons, but especially when Nystrand and his colleagues report that "dialogically organized instruction . . . had a strong, positive effect on achievement" (57). This finding would suggest that authentic discussion is not the appropriate practice only for the "gifted students" but for all students in the school. (1) Applebee, Langer, Nystrand, and Gamoran (2003) report that "students whose classroom literacy experiences emphasize discussion-based approaches in the context of high academic demands internalize the knowledge and skills necessary to engage in challenging literacy tasks on their own" (685). This study again suggests that frequent participation in authentic discussion is tied to achievement. Several other authorities (Padron, Waxman, and Rivera 2003; Freeman, Freeman, and Mercuri 2002, 2003) observe that participation in authentic discussion also seems to be essential in making a difference in the achievement of language minority students. The pressures of the No Child Left Behind Act (NCLB) have increased educators' awareness of the achievement gaps between language minority learners and other learners. One can imagine the importance of participating in extended dialogue for language minority learners who are required to have the kind of cognitive academic language proficiency that is necessary in order to perform well on standardized measures of achievement. In short, the more one practices extensively in the use of academic language, the more one is likely to develop proficiency. Providing structures and opportunities for all students to engage in extended dialogues signals the expectation that all learners will meet challenging academic standards.

Delpit (1996) and Lee (2001) suggest that the classroom practices for the upper-track classes, which rely on frequent meaningful discussions, can become the standard for *all* classes. In other words, if authentic discussion supports language learning and critical thinking, promotes tolerance and appreciation of diversity, and fosters empathy and democratic values, it must not be the mode of instruction only for those students who are already high achievers, but it must be the common mode of discourse for all students.

## Where to Begin

Regularly engaging students in authentic discussion is a challenge. Certainly practice will foster improvement, and many text resources exist to guide the practitioner in devising structures and procedures for facilitating small- and large-group discussions (see, for example, Christenbury and Kelly 1983; Kahn, Walter, and Johannessen 1984a, 1984b; Johannessen and McCann 2002; McCann 2003). And for the supervisor or mentor who works with a novice teacher, making authentic discussion a topic of professional conversations would be very valuable: How is authentic discussion different from recitation? Why is authentic discussion an important element in English language arts learning? How is authentic discussion a necessary component of inquiry? A program for engaging teachers in exploring what is involved in becoming capable facilitators of authentic discussion and how to rely on authentic discussion as a frequent component of lessons can be a slow and complicated endeavor. Initially, however, any English teacher will benefit simply from an awareness of the nature and importance of authentic discussion.

# 2 Some Rudiments of Large-Group Discussion

Emglish teachers place a lot of value on *talking* with students, especially about what they were supposed to have read. What is the big deal about talking? Presumably, discussion helps us put thoughts together and sometimes *discover* what we know. In some cases, the kind of discussion that is an open forum for ideas, rather than an inquisition of students suspected of not reading, can lead the way to deeper understanding of the complexity of thought. When one thinks of discussion, and especially the discussion of reading, what images come to mind?

Some teachers might see discussion as the process of leading students down a road to find answers that the teacher already knows (Marshall, Smagorinsky, and Smith 1995). The strategy in this case would involve carefully framing and sequencing the questions to make the path straight and clear, with no detours or distractions. Consider the following example from an interchange about Steinbeck's *The Pearl:*

*Teacher:* How did Kino know that the pearl was valuable?

*Bobby:* It was real big.

*Teacher:* That's right. It was a large pearl, but what else?

*Judy:* It was larger than any other pearl. It was the pearl of the world.

*Teacher:* Yes, but *what else?* . . . [three-second pause] . . . Can you think of something that happens to Kino that tells him that the pearl is valuable?

*Roxanne:* The pearl buyers offer him 1,500 pesos.

*Carl:* But that wouldn't be a lot of money. We talked about that.

*Teacher:* That shows that the pearl is worth something. But *what happens to Kino* to let him know that no matter what the pearl buyers say, his pearl must be worth a lot?

*Roxanne:* Everyone starts coming to see him, like the priest and the doctor.

---

An earlier version of this chapter appeared as an article in the *Illinois English Bulletin* 85(3). It is reprinted here by permission of the Illinois Association of Teachers of English.

*Teacher:* Yes, but *what happens after the visit* to the pearl buyers?
... [three-second pause] ... What happens in Chapter 4?

*Carl:* He gets attacked.

*Teacher: That's right.* He gets attacked; so someone else has
decided that the pearl is worth some risk and will fight Kino
for it.

In this exchange, the teacher begins ostensibly with a question that requires some inferences or interpretation: "How does the reader know
that Kino knows that the pearl is valuable?" When the teacher does not
get the answer that he wants, without saying that the students are exactly wrong, he prompts them to tell him more. He asks, "What else?"
By this time, the students know the nature of the game: Our task is to
tell the teacher the answer that he already has in mind. As the questioning continues, the teacher prompts the students to recall a specific event
that is described in a particular chapter: "What happens in Chapter 4?"
The teacher is not entertaining various interpretive hypotheses; he is
looking for a specific correct answer. This line of questioning does not
encourage students to participate. Everyone knows that there is a specific correct answer. If you dare to attempt the answer, you might earn
praise, or you might fail and embarrass yourself before the whole class.
Why would anyone be eager to join the conversation?

Another image of discussion involves the posing of a question
about which everyone, including the teacher, has some ideas *and* some
doubts. In the second instance, the teacher simply sounds the first note
in a freewheeling jam session, where everyone contributes and no one's
contributions are any better than anyone else's. Smith (Marshall,
Smagorinsky, and Smith 1995) notes that this is a common mode of conversation among adult reading groups, when there is no formal agenda
and no instructional leader trying to advance particular educational
goals. Unlike a pathfinder metaphor that Marshall (Marshall, Smagorinsky, and Smith 1995) reports is a common image to guide literature teachers, the second scenario allows for discussion that could me-
ander in many different directions, sometimes far away from the topic
that was the initial focus. The discussion can proceed without any attention to an existing critical tradition related to the text.

Perhaps the descriptions above represent two extremes for facilitating large-group discussions: One is narrowly focused and controlled;
the other is wide-open and unstructured. Another useful image of classroom discussion lies somewhere between the two models described
above. The teacher has some instructional objectives and hopes that the
students have recall of some content, but there are also opportunities

for sharing opinions about the sense that individuals make of the texts and ideas. In a discussion about literature, the interaction includes the text, the teacher, and the many readers. The discussion becomes an exploration of the possible readings of the text, and the process includes the attention to, and assessment of, the opinions, the feelings, and the analyses of others.

In contrast to the brief discussion that we reproduce above, imagine that a teacher frames a question in a different way in order to initiate discussion about the same section of *The Pearl*:

> *Kino seems to think that the pearl is valuable, but the pearl buyers insist that the pearl is practically worthless* [an inquiry frame or expression of common understanding among the readers]. *How can Kino figure out how much value he should place on the pearl?* [the prompt]

We can also imagine that students will offer a variety of observations, some of which require the class to return to the text to verify the evidence that has led them to their conclusions. Several contributors can offer different theories for affirming the pearl's worth: "Pearls are always valuable." "Kino knows from his own experience that it is a good pearl." "Kino knows that the pearl buyers are lying." "Someone else attacked Kino to get the pearl, which shows that it is worth risking getting hurt." Some of the responses might be inaccurate and require testing against rules that we might know about pearls, about valuable possessions, and about human behavior. The inquiry of the group draws from the knowledge of all the members to test assumptions and find evidence. Another possibility is that a student will interpret the question as an invitation to reflect on the relative worth of an object, especially when compared to other values in one's life, and the discussion can venture into another rich field for discourse.

Langer (1993) notes that class discussion serves many purposes beyond the assessment of students' work habits and comprehension. Class discussions that invite many participants to contribute to the exploration of ideas—by hearing a variety of thoughts, by challenging each other's positions, by supporting one's own position, by trying to understand the positions of others, and by assessing and admitting the merit of others' thoughts—involve students in complex thinking processes that nurture understanding and support effective problem solving and decision making. The class discussions that have the features listed above will cultivate habits of thinking that account for multiple perspectives, search for alternative solutions, appreciate the complexity of situations, and show respect for others even when their opinions oppose our own.

At one time, students in junior high were supposed to learn the important lessons and responsibilities of living in a democracy by reading assigned chapters in their civics text. Of course, students would learn other covert lessons when they failed the quiz based on their reading assignment. One would hope, however, that citizens in a democracy would ultimately have opportunities to listen to a variety of opinions about policies and values and contribute their own opinions to the conversation. One would also hope that the conversations would be rational, civil, and polite. Preparation for participation in social and civic conversation comes from practice as a participant, not solely from reading the civics text. Practice is possible when teachers establish classroom environments where open, genuine, and civil discussion is honored and frequently experienced. Such environments are imbued with a democratic spirit, where ideas matter because they move beyond mere prejudice and touch the lives of fellow citizens.

Full participation in lively discussion about topics that students care about occurs through both small- and large-group discussion. Although small-group discussion is likely to accommodate more participation per learner per discussion, large-group discussion still has an important role in the classroom. As Smagorinksy and Fly (1993, 1994) point out, the teacher as facilitator of large-group discussion serves as a powerful model for the students. In other words, when students engage in discussion in small-groups, they are likely to imitate what the teacher does when he or she leads the large-group discussion. If the teacher often paraphrases the responses of others, the students over time are likely to do the same. If the teacher seeks many students to contribute to large-group discussion, the small-group participants are likely to do the same.

The following descriptions provide suggestions for handling large-group discussion. For the veteran teacher, perhaps these are rudimentary ideas, but being an effective facilitator of discussion is a challenging role that requires much practice.

## Framing Questions for Discussion

First reflect on the types of questions that you plan to use. Ideally all the questions are not basic recall of explicitly stated information. Can you pose some questions that ask students to analyze, synthesize, and evaluate? In many situations, it would be especially useful to pose questions that solicit debatable opinions and invite multiple perspectives. Graff (1992) describes the power that conflict and controversy can have in inviting students to examine texts closely and engage in lively debates about values and interpretation. Graff's approach to the discussion of literature includes attention to a body of critical voices that surround the text, because the conflicts among the critical views help each reader to find a position and discover a point of entry into the conversation. Without transforming students into academic literary critics, teachers can make students aware of the competing views that give an issue its significance, and they can influence students to care about how an issue is represented or resolved.

Questions and the problems that they represent are essential for inviting discussion. Christoph and Nystrand (2001) talk about making a "dialogic bid," that is, indicating to the students that the questions under consideration are authentic and do not have predetermined answers. In short, the thinker who described a problem or poses a question can honestly admit to having some doubts about the issues in question.

## Building a Stage for Participation

Of course, it is tough to jump into a discussion without having some time to prepare responses. It makes sense to build a stage into the discussion process that allows students to collect their thoughts through writing or through trying out ideas on a partner. One could structure this preparation stage in several ways, which are described below.

How should one proceed? Every teacher has faced this situation: You pose a particularly thought-provoking question. You select a student at random to answer the question. He responds, "I dunno." You provide encouragement, but the response remains, "I dunno." The temptation is to fill the verbal void and relieve the student of embarrassment. You call on an enthusiastic student who is waving her hand wildly and practically leaping from her desk, fearing the chance that you will possibly select someone else to provide the correct answer that she is certain she has. When you pass up the first student and select the enthusiastic volunteer, the class learns the covert lesson that if you don't want to be bothered, simply say, "I dunno." But what is the teacher supposed to do?

## Offering Answer Choices

One can imagine a teacher's uneasiness when, initially, students volunteer no responses to a question that was supposed to initiate discussion. Here is one possible sequence: First, wait longer than six seconds for the student to respond. If there is no response, rephrase the question. If there is still no response, offer some choices. The exchange might sound like this:

> *Teacher:* Why do George and Lennie want a farm of their own?
>
> *Tom:* I dunno.
>
> *Teacher:* What possible reason would anyone have to own a farm?
>
> *Tom:* I dunno.
>
> *Teacher:* Let me describe some possibilities: They judge that they have an ingenious way to produce larger crops faster than anyone else, and they make a ton of money. Or, they just want some privacy and independence, without anyone bossing them around. Maybe they just hope to take pride in something they own and something they have produced themselves. Which of these choices, if any, make some sense?
>
> *Tom:* They just want to be left alone? I dunno.
>
> *Teacher:* OK, Tom claims that George and Lenny want to be independent, just left alone. What makes you think that, Tom?
>
> *Tom:* Because they always get in trouble when they work for someone else.
>
> *Teacher:* Larry, do you agree with Tom?
>
> *Larry:* Agree with what?
>
> *Teacher:* Tom, could you repeat for Larry what you just said about George and Lenny?

And so it goes. One can imagine the discussion playing out, with the teacher offering some means for the student to be included and building on one student's observations to draw other students into the discussion. One can imagine also that a student still does not respond to the choices that the teacher offers. In a similar way, the teacher could offer what a person might think is a reasonable answer and ask the student if he or she agrees. If the student still does not respond, one can assume that he or she agrees, and it is safe to announce to the class the tacit agreement. Even if the student is in a trance, then, it is possible to have a response. Now it is possible to move on with the discussion. For the benefit of the rest of the class, paraphrase the first student's response. Now call on a second student to explain whether or not she agrees with the response. Other students, then, can contribute to the assessment of the first response.

## Deferring Praise

Another temptation for the teacher is to praise students for their correct responses. The teacher's validation of the correct answer tends to
discourage other participants in the discussion. In other words, the
teacher's assessment of responses as "right," "very good," or "exactly,"
tells the students that the discussion is an assessment, and if they offer
a contribution, the teacher will judge it against the response that he or
she expects to hear. Instead of offering an assessment, however, the
teacher can call on other students to assess a student's answer. This
practice allows for several perspectives and includes several students
in the discussion.

The teacher might also respond in a way that supports students'
efforts without signaling a search for the recitation of a specific, teacher-
endorsed answer. For example, the teacher might offer these affirming
responses: "I hadn't thought of that." "That raises another interesting
point." "That really forces us to think of the issue in another way." Although these responses affirm that students have made valuable contributions to the investigation, they do not tell the students to "keep
guessing until you say the answer that I have in my head."

## Providing Time for Response

Let's imagine one other discussion scenario. The teacher opens a lesson with a large-group discussion of the assigned reading. The teacher
asks, "How do the images from this chapter reveal Hemingway's view
of women, duty, and honor?" Not surprisingly, there are no responses.
Are the students incapable of answering the question? Perhaps. Now,
if the teacher allowed the students some time to think about the question and formulate or retrieve an answer, there might be some hope for
contributions. Pose the question and ask the students to write down their
answers. Here is where journals or "learning logs" prove useful. Another possibility is to allow students some time to discuss the question
with a partner. If you've ever participated in a job interview, you recognize that it is often difficult to respond immediately, even if you are
capable of a thoughtful response. It makes sense to allow students some
time to prepare for discussion.

## Preparing Students to Contribute

As Smagorinsky (1993) notes, it is crucial to *prepare* students to read and
offer a variety of responses. Teachers use a rich variety of prereading

activities to help students to tap prior knowledge, to pose questions, and to develop a language for engagement in analysis of a text. Useful prereading activities range from such simple devices as posing a journal prompt, to the more complex structures of case study analysis and simulations. The uses of such activities are discussed more fully in later chapters of this text. Many sources describe a variety of prereading and prewriting activities that enliven discussion and prepare students for subsequent learning. See, for example, Burke (2003), Wilhelm, Baker, and Dube (2001), Stern (1995), Hillocks (1995), Johannessen (1992), Smagorinsky, McCann, and Kern (1987), and Kahn, Walter, and Johannessen (1984b).

We can recall many class sessions as college undergraduates when discussion was painfully slow and spiritless. Imagine, for example, being assigned to read all the selections from Henry Vaughn that appear in a literature anthology. With no other preparation than the directive *to read*, the student has little clue as to the possible context for the discussion to which she or he will be expected to contribute in the next class meeting. In retrospect, the instructor and the students might have enjoyed a livelier and more enriching discussion if the instructor had prepared the students to think about and question the features and meaning of the text.

Here, then, is a summary of a few general suggestions for handling large-group discussion:

1. Ask meaningful, genuine questions. These would be questions that actually raise doubt, rather than prompt students for a single "correct" answer.

2. Give students half a chance to prepare for discussion: through prereading activities, through writing, or through discussion with partners.

---

**Ten Tips for Facilitating Large-Group Discussions**

1. Ask questions that actually raise doubt, rather than prompt students for a single "correct" answer.

2. Give students half a chance to prepare for discussion: through prereading activities, through writing, or through discussion with partners.

3. Don't automatically accept "I dunno" as an answer.

4. Wait a reasonable amount of time for students to respond.

5. Rephrase questions when necessary.

6. Offer choices to allow for some kind of response.

7. Paraphrase responses frequently and check for clarification.

8. Call on other students to assess the answers of their classmates.

9. Include as many students as possible.

10. Ask appropriate follow-up questions to extend discussion and prompt analysis: Why? So what? Who says?

3. Don't automatically accept "I dunno" as an answer.
4. Wait a reasonable amount of time for students to respond.
5. Rephrase questions when necessary.
6. Offer choices to allow for some kind of response.
7. Paraphrase responses frequently and check for clarification.
8. Call on other students to assess the answers of their classmates.
9. Include as many students as possible.
10. Ask appropriate follow-up questions to extend discussion and prompt analysis: Why? So what? Who says?

These suggestions are extended, expanded, and modeled in later chapters.

Large-group discussion serves as one forum for discourse in the classroom. Among other effects, behavior in large-group discussion serves as a model for behavior in small-group discussion. One would hope that after long practice as participants in discussion, students learn much about reading and writing, and develop habits of reason, sensitivity, and politeness.

# 3 An Activity to Learn How to Facilitate Discussion

Our conversations with the supervisors of preservice teachers suggest that facilitating meaningful discussions is a common and serious difficulty for beginning teachers. How does one learn to be skillful at leading discussion? The problem is a complex one. The ten tips suggested in Chapter 2 are a start, but much more is ultimately involved. A teacher certainly needs knowledge about a particular subject and needs to have in mind some worthwhile purposes for the discussion. As with any skill, one's craft develops over time as a teacher has many experiences that allow him or her to anticipate, draw from previous successes, and avoid past failures. Textbooks and methods classes can offer advice, which will make some sense after attempts, assessment, and refinement. We offer here a beginning model for facilitating classroom discussions. A close look at one activity reveals something about the nature of discussion, and can suggest some additional behaviors that will influence discussion to be active, purposeful, and thought-provoking.

In 1982, Johannessen, Kahn, and Walter offered a scenario activity developed by Hillocks and called "What Is Courageous Action?" as a tool that would engage students in learning defining strategies. The activity presents the learners with a set of specific situations and challenges the learners to decide the extent to which the behavior of the characters conforms to the requisite conditions of a concept. For example, one of the eight "Courageous Action" scenarios poses this situation:

> Corporal Jewkes is lost in the woods near a village that, unknown to him, is in enemy hands. The village is heavily guarded and the surrounding area mined. He makes his way through the mines, of which he is unaware, and into the village. Not knowing what is inside, he enters the first house he comes to. It contains a gun emplacement, but the guards are asleep. Jewkes quickly kills the guards and takes the guns. To this point, should we consider Jewkes' actions courageous? Why or why not? (Johannessen, Kahn, and Walter 1982, 35)

---

An earlier version of this chapter appeared as an article in *English Journal* 92(6). It is reprinted here by permission of the National Council of Teachers of English.

Using a scenario activity of the sort that Johannessen, Kahn, and Walter share can provide the means for training teachers to lead meaningful discussions. The scenario activity was a key element in the work of Hillocks, Kahn, and Johannessen (1983) when they helped students to learn and use strategies for composing extended definition. While a scenario activity can engage students in attempting to define an abstract concept, it can also serve as a *gateway* activity to prepare students for discussing the concept as it applies to situations and characters in the subsequent reading (Hillocks 1995; Smagorinsky, McCann, and Kern 1987; Johannessen, Kahn, and Walter 1982). We propose here that if a teacher can engage students in the discussion of a specific scenario activity, he or she can learn much about the craft of leading any authentic discussion.

## A Brief History of the Scenario Activity

One must acknowledge the importance of the work of Hillocks, Kahn, and Johannessen (1983) and Johannessen, Kahn, and Walter (1982) in their design and sharing of scenario activities, especially represented by one about *courageous action.* Hillocks (1995) reports that the "What Is Courageous Action?" scenarios are based on an examination of courage in Aristotle's *Nicomachean Ethics,* which provides a framework for defining an abstract concept. In the kind of discussion that the "Courageous Action" scenarios invite, a conversation begins by raising doubt in regard to a concept about which participants may have assumed thorough understanding. For example, everyone in a sense "knows" what courageous action is. Another participant challenges that assumed understanding by posing questions or offering certain conditions for testing rules that apply to that concept. As a participant attempts to refine a position, the conversational partner offers additional examples to test any rules that one might assert. Many English teachers would be satisfied with class discussions that include these features. Here is a sample portion of an interchange about the scenario above:

> *Milicent:* Jewkes is being courageous. He's in a war. It's a
> dangerous situation.
>
> *Franklin:* But he didn't know about the dangers. He was lucky
> the guards were asleep.
>
> *Esme:* What if he knew about the mines? Then wouldn't that be
> courageous?

The scenario activity, then, promotes the kind of close examination of concepts that one sees in the work of Aristotle and Plato and encourages participants to think critically.

## A Sample Scenario Activity

Sample scenario activities are available in the work of Johannessen, Kahn, and Walter (1982) and in Smagorinsky, McCann, and Kern (1987). The construction of a scenario activity is relatively simple, yet it requires some careful preparation. Presumably one would choose to explore some concept with which the students have some knowledge and experience rather than an idea that is irrelevant or esoteric. Situations in the literature that students typically study in school will invite them to make judgments about such concepts as justice, romantic love, and friendship. One can be assured that students have knowledge and opinions about such concepts. In contrast, such concepts as *deconstruction, trends, conflicts,* and *transportation* may be abstract, but they are not likely to represent unifying thematic issues in imaginative literature, nor are they likely to be themes about which students are personally invested.

For the scenario activity to support discussion, each scenario must be problematic and raise doubt about some aspect of the concept that is the focus of the current inquiry. For example, a set of six or seven scenarios might help students explore a key concept. The following scenarios provide examples of situations that challenge students to tackle the difficult concept of justice. The activity appears here out of its instructional context. Teachers are not likely to engage students in exploring an abstract concept for its own sake. In a coherent unit of instruction, the discussion of the scenarios might serve as a gateway activity (Hillocks 1995) to help students activate prior knowledge and form concepts so that they have a critical framework on which to rely for subsequent judgments and discussion about a reading that raises questions about the justice of characters' behavior. Examples of conceptual units organized around questions about justice can be found in Smagorinsky (2002) and in Smagorinsky and Gevinson (1989). Although the concept of justice is a tough one, it is also something about which students have often thought: "Are my parents justified in grounding me for coming home after curfew?" "Is a teacher justified in assigning homework over a holiday break?" The situations that are described in the scenarios are familiar to the students. The problematic nature of the scenario and the familiarity of the situation promote wide and active participation in the discussion. The discussion later in this chapter is based on the use of the following scenario activity.

## Justice at Floodrock High?

*Your Group Task:*

The Student Council at Floodrock High School seeks your help in judging the justice of the behavior of the faculty in the following situations. With two or three other students, examine each of the situations and answer the questions that follow. It is important that you explain your decisions. After you have examined all the situations, you should have a list of guidelines that would describe just action.

*The Situations:*

1. In a first-hour Health class, Mr. Phalva, a veteran teacher, discovered Karla Gluko chewing bubblegum. Mr. Phalva had announced at the beginning of the term that he would not tolerate anyone bringing food, drink, or candy into the class. Mr. Phalva did not like the idea that Karla would violate his classroom discipline policy, and he was especially disturbed that Karla would be chewing sugar-sweetened bubblegum after the class had just finished a unit in which they studied the dangers of consuming too much processed, refined sugar. Mr. Phalva insisted that Karla stand up in front of the class while he lectured her about chewing gum in class, noting her lack of thoughtfulness and sensitivity. Furthermore, he predicted that by the time Karla was twenty-one, she would have no teeth. As part of Karla's punishment, Mr. Phalva ordered her to write a ten-page report about the dangers of consuming refined sugar, and he would not allow her to return to class until the report was complete. Were Mr. Phalva's actions just? Explain.

2. During World Geography class, as Mr. Strata lectured, Harlan Fleming noisily wadded a sheet of notebook paper into a ball and sailed it across the room and into the wastebasket next to the teacher's desk. The wad of paper rattled around the metal wastebasket before falling to the bottom. Mr. Strata stopped his lecture and filled out a disciplinary referral form about Harlan. Harlan protested: "You never said we couldn't throw paper away during class." Mr. Strata responded, "You should know by now what kind of behavior is appropriate for class." Harlan went immediately to the dean's office where he was assigned a three-day in-school suspension. After Harlan's departure, Mr. Strata told the class, "From now on, if anyone throws a wad of paper across the room, he or she will

be sent to the dean's office and will probably be suspended." Were the actions of Mr. Strata and the dean just? Explain.

3. At the beginning of the school year, several bathrooms were vandalized: graffiti on the walls, wads of wet tissue paper stuck to the ceiling, broken tissue paper dispensers. Mr. Gristmeyer, an English teacher, identified three students who he thought he saw coming out of a bathroom at the time that it was vandalized. The three students—Frank Roscoe, Bob Bellamy, and Alejandro Mosca—were brought to the dean's office. Mr. Swift, one of the school's deans, decided that Alejandro was the culprit, noting his record of many discipline problems while attending Floodrock High. When Alejandro protested, Mr. Swift said, "I don't want to hear about it. You've done enough already." Mr. Swift then suspended Alejandro for three days and assigned him to a Saturday work detail to help clean the washrooms. Were Mr. Swift's actions just? Explain.

4. As part of the initiation to the varsity football team, new members are expected to perform a challenging task. Seniors design some awkward and sometimes dangerous actions for the juniors to complete. This year, two students—Mario Candida and Salomé Brown—were directed to climb to the roof of the school, take down the U.S. flag, and raise several old football jerseys on the flagpole in its place. The seniors told Mario and Salomé that if they didn't follow orders, they would be ostracized: that is, no one would talk to them, no one would give either of them the ball during a game, and all the seniors would torment them in the locker room. Around three o'clock in the morning, Mario and Salomé climbed to the roof of the high school building to complete their mission. Two police officers who were patrolling the area soon spotted Mario and Salomé and arrested them for trespassing. Later, a judge assigned the two boys to complete one hundred hours of community service by working in a food pantry for the homeless. Did Mario and Salomé receive a just sentence? Explain.

5. When the principal at Floodrock High School learned that students were buying drugs on the school grounds, he solicited the aid of the county sheriff's Drug Enforcement Task Force. The sheriff sent two undercover officers to investigate the problem. The officers dressed in casual street clothes and approached selected students, offering to sell them marijuana. At first they found no one interested.

They focused attention on one student—Albie Cummin—who usually wore a concert T-shirt and torn blue jeans and had very long hair. Three days in a row, the officers approached Albie and asked him if he would like to buy some marijuana. On these three occasions, Albie said that he wasn't interested. On the fourth day, when the officers approached him again, Albie agreed to buy one ounce of marijuana. The officers immediately identified themselves as sheriff's police and brought Albie into the dean's office. During questioning, Albie could not provide any more information about the buying and selling of marijuana on the school grounds or anywhere in the community. Albie was suspended for three days and forced to enter a substance abuse rehabilitation program at Floodrock Community Hospital. Was Albie treated justly? Explain.

6.  Floodrock High School has had a very extensive intramural sports program. Last winter a new basketball that the athletic department purchased for use in the intramural games was discovered missing and presumed stolen. The intramural director and the principal were so disturbed with the theft that they decided to cancel all intramural activities indefinitely. The principal announced to the whole school that there would be no more intramural activities until the missing basketball was returned. Is the principal's action justified? Explain.

It is important to consider the construction of a scenario activity because it says much about the spirit of the discussion that one would want to promote. A few years ago, we shared a scenario activity at a session of a National Council of Teachers of English (NCTE) convention. After the session, one of the participants asked if we could provide the *answer key* for the activity. Obviously there was no answer key because the problems represented in the activity prompt many reasonable responses. A key point in using a scenario activity to promote active discussion is that the conversation cannot be scripted to conform to preconceived answers. This fact is an exciting feature and a significant challenge. The discussion can go in many different directions, as Kahn, Walter, and Johannessen (1984a, 1984b) remind us about discussions of controversial topics. The point of the discussion is not to recite the answers but to promote certain habits of mind that could be labeled critical thinking, analysis, evaluation, and argument.

## Modeling the Process

Obviously, one does not simply distribute a scenario activity and encourage the students to follow the directions and discuss each situation. The teacher needs to connect the discussion to some related outcomes: perhaps the scenarios will lead to the expression of criteria that can be developed into an extended definition; perhaps the criteria will be used as a framework for judging the behavior of characters in literature or film and writing an analysis of the behavior. Students need to know the context for their efforts. Beyond attending to these basic considerations, the teacher also needs to show students *how* to discuss a scenario. The teacher would be wise to use the first scenario as a means for modeling the kind of talk that one would expect in a small group.

The following transcript reveals a teacher leading the discussion of the first scenario in the "Justice at Floodrock High?" activity. After describing a purpose for the discussion and reviewing the procedures, the teacher turns the students' attention to the first scenario, which she reads aloud. In this case, the teacher anticipates that the students will derive a set of criterion statements, such as "The punishment must fit the crime," but she does not have in mind a specific set of criteria to impose on the class. The following dialogue represents only a portion of an extended discussion about one scenario. The teacher sets the context for the activity and starts discussion by asking the students to react to a character's behavior. The teacher might begin by saying something like this: "In the play we will be reading next week, a central character claims that he has been the victim of injustice, although he does not explain his claim. We are invited to judge for ourselves whether or not the punishment that the character suffers results appropriately from his own actions. Our discussion of the scenarios today should help us to develop a framework for judging the character's behavior and for evaluating his claim that he is the victim of gross injustice. So, Juan, what did your group decide in the first scenario?"

> *Juan:* There's no reason to push it that far. She did something pretty minor.
>
> *Teacher:* Okay. Sheila.
>
> *Sheila:* I agree with Juan, but I would also like to say that he didn't hear her side of the story. Maybe it just sort of slipped her mind, because I've done that before, because I can't chew gum in my French class, and it's slipped my mind before because I forget, and then my teacher just gives me a warning, which I think he should have done because there

are possibilities, and I think you should always hear both sides of the story before taking action.

*Teacher:* Okay. So part of it—you mean, in your class, you got a warning because it was like the first instance of this violation, and so you would expect that, and so that would be a more appropriate response, and then in addition, if someone—you're found out, you're found violating the rule, you have a chance to defend yourself.

*Sheila:* Yeah.

*Teacher:* Okay. Nadia.

*Nadia:* I think when he told the class that they can't chew gum that he should have also told the consequences of it, because I'm sure if she would have known how severe the punishment would be, she would have never considered chewing gum.

*Teacher:* It's not enough to know there's a rule, but you have to be aware from the beginning of the consequences for violating the rule. Okay, that seem like another rule there. Bernice.

*Bernice:* It's not like she disrupted the class at all by chewing gum, but he made it so it was a disruption, maybe made a mockery of her, just yelling at her in front of the class. I think that's really wrong. That's overstepping the boundaries as a teacher.

*Teacher:* So to add to what Juan said, he is—it's overkill, especially in the sense that he's publicly humiliating her, and that's—there is no cause for that. Okay. Gunther.

*Gunther:* While I agree with most of what's being said here, I would disagree that you would have to know the exact punishment to go along with the rule, because often there are different circumstances, like, there is a difference between having a little piece of gum shoved in the corner of your mouth and someone sitting in front of the class blowing huge bubbles and stretching it out, whatever. I think there are different circumstances and different things which would determine the punishment after these facts.

*Teacher:* You wouldn't want the system of justice to be so rigid that if you do this, you automatically get this punishment with no possibility for leniency or no flexibility.

*Gunther:* Right, the punishment should match the offense, and creating general umbrella rules like "no chewing gum or this will happen" often doesn't match the intended situation.

*Teacher:* Would you want someone to give a sense of the severity of the punishment, like, how serious I see this kind of an infraction?

*Gunther:* Yes, but I don't think you should be rigid.

Although the teacher may endorse many of the students' observations, she has not imposed on the students a set of rules to define justice. Apparently, the teacher begins with the assumption that the students already know something about justice; and the teacher apparently believes that given the right circumstances, the students would be able to derive reasonable criteria and work with each other to express the precise wording of each rule. Gunther notes that "the punishment should match the offense." Juan notes that the teacher met a due process requirement because "he did tell them not to have candy in class," but Nadia adds that "he should have also told the consequences." Furthermore, Sheila observes that "you should always hear both sides of the story before taking action."

Not only are the students able to offer rules, but they readily invent additional examples, or scenarios of their own, to check the validity or accuracy of a statement. For example, Sheila recalls her own experience to argue against rigidly imposing punishment: "Maybe it just sort of slipped her mind . . . because I can't chew gum in my French class, and it's slipped my mind before because I forget, and then my teacher just gives me a warning." Gunther invents an example to illustrate the idea that one must judge the appropriateness of punishment by knowing the circumstances for the offense. "There is a difference," he says, "between having a little piece of gum shoved in the corner of your mouth and someone sitting in front of the class blowing huge bubbles and stretching it out."

In these few exchanges, the students expressed at least three criteria for determining justice. They have challenged each other and have tested each other's claims. As Smagorinsky and Fly (1993) observe, the teacher's behavior in the large-group discussion provides a powerful model for the students' behavior in small-group discussion. What is the teacher's role in the interchange, and what behaviors are students exhibiting that they can build on in small-group discussion and in subsequent large-group discussions?

Obviously the teacher gets the ball rolling by posing the initial question to prompt a reaction to the scenario. In Christoph and Nystrand's language (2001), a teacher makes a "dialogic bid" to prompt the involvement of other thinkers. In response to a student's contribution, the teacher does not make evaluative statements, like "That's right" or "Very good!" or "That's not quite it." Nor does the teacher pose questions to direct the students to express the criteria that she already has in mind. Instead, she occasionally poses questions to prompt students to substantiate or illustrate the general claims that they make. The teacher paraphrases often and asks the speaker to verify the accuracy of the paraphrase. The teacher's paraphrases apparently do not discourage the students from participation, and although the teacher sometimes acts as conduit, the students also respond directly to each other. Sheila begins her comments by reacting to her classmate's statement: "I agree with Juan, but I would also like to say that he didn't hear her side of the story." The teacher models the same behavior by connecting parts of the discussion: "So to add to what Juan said . . . it's overkill, especially in the sense that the teacher is publicly humiliating her and that's—there is no cause for that." In the next conversational turn, Gunther follows the pattern by acknowledging the contributions of his classmates: "While I agree with most of what's being said here, I would disagree that you would have to know the exact punishment to go along with the rule."

If the question that is the focus of the class's inquiry is an authentic one, then the teacher's role as discussion leader at this point appears to be a relatively simple one and involves the following behaviors:

- The teacher initiates the discussion and manages the order of the contributors.
- The teacher poses appropriate follow-up questions to prompt students to extend their thinking by providing support or illustrations for their general claims. In other words, the teacher asks questions to encourage the students to be reasonable.
- The teacher paraphrases often to check for clarification.

All of these teacher behaviors serve as models for the students who continue the discussion in small groups.

## What Happens in Small-Group Discussion?

After the teacher has modeled the kind of discussion that she hopes students will have in their small groups, she organizes and directs the students into their groups. The small-group discussion allows everyone the opportunity to participate, whereas in the large-group discussion, the more diffident students might hold back from any aggressive and disputatious interchanges. Participation in the small-group activity allows one to try out ideas and refine thought before engaging in the large-group discussion. One would expect to see some of the same behavior that the teacher modeled with the initial scenario as three students tackle another situation. The following dialogue involves three students who are analyzing the second scenario in which a teacher, Mr. Strata, punishes a student for throwing a wadded up piece of paper into a metal wastebasket. The student questions the fairness of Mr. Strata's punishment.

> *Nadia:* Three days? I think, "Excuse me, sir, go out in the hall," would be satisfactory.
>
> *Ned:* Or maybe, like, a simple detention thing. Three days—I mean, I understand he's yelling at him because he's interrupting the—throwing the paper is not the problem. The problem is that he's making noise and interrupting the lecture.
>
> *Leticia:* Well, maybe he had to make an example of him so that this wouldn't happen again, but I don't think that it was outlandish what he did. I mean . . .
>
> *Nadia:* Yeah, but look at what he says, "From now on, if anyone throws a wad of paper across the room . . ." Okay, *now* he tells the rule, you know, that you're going to be sent to the dean's office. Why didn't he say that prior to, you know?
>
> *Leticia:* Because he didn't think he needed to. You don't expect someone to . . .
>
> *Nadia:* Stuff happens though.
>
> *Ned:* He's probably just saying, "No throwing of anything."

The dialogue represents only a small portion of the talk among the three students. They discussed five scenarios in all, and remained on task for the allotted twenty-five minutes. As the group works toward refining a rule, Nadia asks, "Why didn't he say that prior to, you know?" Nadia's implied claim is that a just teacher should inform students about the rules before he holds anyone accountable for breaking the rules. Leticia cautions, however, that some rules are so well known, that no one needs to repeat them: ". . . he didn't think he needed to. You don't expect someone to. . . ." The students in the small-group exhibit some behaviors that are appropriate for the teacher in the large-group discussion: they let everyone participate; they ask appropriate questions to challenge each other; they invent examples to test claims and extend thinking; and they work toward closure by searching for rules that would represent their thinking about the central concept.

## What Happens in the Large-Group Discussion?

The whole-class discussion represented in the dialogue below followed the small-group work with the justice scenarios. One would expect that the students have used the small-group experience to collect their thoughts, to test their claims under public scrutiny, to defend their positions, and to refine the articulation of concepts. The teacher's role in the subsequent discussion would be to manage the turns in the conversation and provide the forum for the expression of the ideas that the students have recalled or formed. The following discussion focuses again on the second scenario. The teacher does little more than pose the initial question and paraphrase the responses. Note the length of the students' turns, especially compared to the exchanges in the small-group discussion.

*Teacher:* You're claiming that the boy should be punished?

*Leonard:* Like, he threw the paper across the room, like, he should probably just assume that there would be a rule not to do that.

*Teacher:* Okay.

*Leonard:* Like, kill someone or something.

*Teacher:* All right. So certain rules we don't have to be told; we should know. Okay. Sheila.

*Sheila:* He should have been told, because even if some people may know the rules, other people don't really think of it. It may be common knowledge, common sense, but other people, maybe they just didn't think about it because some people don't think about it. I don't think he should have been punished. He should have been warned that if he did it again he would get punished for it.

*Teacher:* All right. So since this is—it might have been disruptive, the teacher should have, because it's the first time, presumably, just given a warning and then moved on. Okay. Violet, what were you going to say?

*Violet:* Well, I was going to say what Sheila said, but, like, also, I mean, I think it's hard because, I mean, yeah, the teacher should have maybe said something, but it's kind of common sense. I mean . . . you're supposed to know what you can or can't do in the classroom. You know you're not supposed to, like, disturb the class. I think a lot of teachers say that, and they don't say, you know, exactly what, they just say, "Don't make any classroom disturbances," and, obviously, you know, throwing a wad of paper across the room into the garbage can is going to make a lot of noise and is going to be a disturbance . . . . . but I think the punishment is too harsh.

*Teacher:* So . . . we had an earlier rule that before someone is punished that person should be informed about what the rules are and possible consequences. You're saying in this case that you don't have to spell out every rule and every consequence because there might be a general rule—like you don't disrupt the class—and [Harlan's] violated that. Okay. Gunther.

*Gunther:* I basically agree with what has been said.

*Teacher:* So it would be reasonable to expect a student to know not to do that?

*Gunther:* Students have a right to learn, and teachers have a right to teach, and you shouldn't disturb that. I think it was fairly obvious that . . .

*Teacher:* Okay. So if this person has had nine or ten years of experience in school, he should know something about the appropriate decorum in class and would know that's a rule that he was violating. Okay. Sean.

*Sean:* I can't remember what I was going to say.

*Teacher:* All right. Maybe it will come to you; we'll come back to you. Sheila, then Violet.

*Sheila:* I think—I mean, I can hear what Gunther is saying, but I think throwing away a piece of paper isn't always necessarily always a distraction, because, I mean, I've done it before, and I've never disrupted the whole class. I mean, maybe . . .

*Teacher:* Okay.

*Sheila:* I mean, I've done it before and disrupted the class.

*Teacher:* Okay. Sheila's making a confession here today. There might be a case where someone gets up to sharpen a pencil and that sawing away at the pencil causes a disruption, but it's not such a big deal. Some teachers would just say, "Could you just save that for later?" and wouldn't [feel it deserves] any punishment. Okay. Violet.

*Violet:* You wad up a ball of, like, paper, he threw it all the way across the room, causing a distraction, you know, I mean. It's going to be a distraction throwing it across the room.

*Teacher:* It would cause everybody's attention to be focused on that rather than something else that's going on. We might laugh about it. It might fall short, hit Gunther, Gunther would get angry and go after Paul and. . . . Okay. Jeannie.

*Jeannie:* I think that it is common sense that you shouldn't do it, but, like, the person—the person does have a point that, you know, he never said that he couldn't do that. So, I mean, even though it says, "oh, you can't, like, disrupt the class," I think that he should have just gotten a warning, like, if you were talking or something, some classes when you sharpen your pencils—I mean, I don't think you suspend someone for that. So you would just say, you know, "Would you

please not do that while I'm talking?" I mean, that's the
same thing the teacher could have said. He could have said,
just, like, "Don't throw away"—like, "Don't throw anything
across the room while I'm talking"—and so I think the
punishment was too harsh, but he still needs to just give a
warning first and then, like, they do it again, like, right after
he said don't do, suspend them or do whatever.

In this second large-group discussion, the teacher selects a student to initiate the discussion and then does little more than manage
the turns in the conversation. The teacher does not have a long list of
questions to drive discussion. The teacher is not probing students to
recite the predetermined "correct" answers. The teacher makes no evaluative comments and makes no substantive contributions of her own.
Instead, the teacher paraphrases frequently and asks questions to determine if she accurately represented the speakers' contributions.

The teacher merely paraphrases in this exchange. But paraphrasing is an important and developed skill. It requires, first of all, that the
discussion leader listen actively and carefully. The leader's function is
not to judge the correctness of the responses and search for accurate
answers. Instead the discussion leader in the whole-class discussion is
trying to understand what the contributors are saying and is attempting to represent the responses as accurately as possible, and to the
speaker's satisfaction, before other contributors respond.

One has to wonder, however, if the students actually say anything
of substance without the teacher providing corrective feedback or guiding students to correct answers. What do the students do in the large-
group discussion when the teacher does little more than paraphrase?
In the discussion above, Leonard provides an explanation of his group's
analysis of the scenario. He suggests that while a person should be informed of rules, there are certain rules that should be common knowledge and do not need to be reiterated. Sheila and Violet explore
Leonard's idea further by noting that there may be exceptions. They
work from Leonard's initial observation to note that there is some difficulty in determining when one can assume knowledge of rules and laws
and when one must report the rules and laws explicitly. One speaker
builds upon the other. Leonard speaks; then Sheila restates what
Leonard says but notes an exception; then Violet begins by saying "Well,
I was going to say what Sheila said, but. . . . " As the discussion continues, the students offer contexts for their own contributions. Before
Gunther offers his own contribution, he notes, "I basically agree with
what has been said." When Sheila has her next turn, she begins, "I mean,
I can hear what Gunther is saying, but. . . . "

By the time Jeannie comments, she attempts to put several considerations together in one extended contribution: "I think that it is common sense that you shouldn't do it, but, like, the person—the person does have a point that, you know, he never said that he couldn't do that, so, I mean, even though it says, oh, you can't, like, disrupt the class, but I think that he should have just gotten a warning . . . He could have said . . . don't throw anything across the room while I'm talking . . . I think the punishment was too harsh but he still needs to just give a warning first . . . . " It appears that the exploration of ideas in the discussion has allowed Jeannie to determine that achieving justice necessitates adhering to several rules: The punishment must fit the crime. One should be held accountable only for the rules or laws about which one has been informed, although there are times when one has to judge whether or not the rules or laws are common knowledge and do not have to be explicitly reiterated. It appears that the discussion has supported Jeannie in reaching these reasonable conclusions about justice, even though the teacher did not pose the series of questions that would guide her down a path to reach teacher-sponsored correct answers. Because Jeannie's contribution is lengthy and developed, it is uncharacteristic of typical classroom discussions. She is not reciting. Instead, she has measured the observations of others, incorporated the ideas with which she agrees, refined the expression of her ideas, and generally synthesized her own responses and the statements that other students have made throughout the large-group discussion.

The scenario activity described above could engage a class for several days. In some classes, and with some scenarios, it appears that the discussion could go on endlessly. How would anyone know how to bring the discussion to closure after a reasonable period of time? If class discussion is actually no more than recitation, determining closure is easy: the discussion ends when one has heard all the "correct" answers. In a more open-ended discussion, however, several factors guide closure. One would want to judge whether the discussion has become tedious, with students saying more or less the same thing over and over. The discussion leader listens to note signs that the students are demonstrating certain thinking skills. For example, are the students defining a concept by noting reasonable criteria and illustrating or testing the criteria with examples that they are able to interpret? The discussion leader also needs to have in mind some long-range goals. The discussion of justice might be useful in itself. Exploration of the concept might help students to be more articulate, more reasonable, or even more responsible; but the discussion also prepares students for subsequent reading and writing. Closure might be determined by judging whether students have accessed relevant declarative knowledge and demonstrated appropriate procedural skills to be able to complete subsequent tasks successfully.

## Conclusion

We began with the claim that if teachers use a scenario activity as a basis for initiating and developing class discussion, they can learn much about discussion in general. How does the scenario activity help a teacher to develop some skills at leading discussion? Inherent in an activity like "Justice at Floodrock High?" is an assumption that a genuine discussion will begin with the *doubt* raised by an authentic question. The goal is not to repeat the correct answers but to deliberate in a civil and reasonable way about tangible problems. The teacher's role as discussion leader is not that of a quizmaster; rather, he or she is a manager of the conversation that goes on among the students. The teacher initiates the discussion, keeps track of turns in order to include as many people as possible, poses some follow-up questions to extend the thinking, and occasionally contributes examples to test claims. A key behavior for the teacher is to paraphrase what the students say. Paraphrasing forces one to listen carefully and to avoid making evaluative comments that might stifle contributions. The teacher works toward closure by making judgments about the development of thought and about the progress toward subsequent learning. Apparently simple behaviors, like paraphrasing, take practice; and it is always useful to seek the aid of an observer to help one reflect on the refinement of skills.

One would expect English classes to involve active discussion almost every day as teachers and students examine literature and language and explore significant concepts and themes. The talk should support discovery, promote diversity, and engage students in thinking processes, such as defining, analyzing, and arguing, that transfer to students' writing and to their interpretation of literature. Few English teachers enter the profession with an easy facility for engaging groups in meaningful discussion. It would be useful for the preservice or beginning teacher to use a scenario activity as the basis for discussion, reflect on the structure and behaviors that promote active involvement in the discussion, and attempt to apply regularly the same structures and behaviors to fashion a classroom environment in which student talk is more than mere recitation.

Although we have focused here on *techniques* for initiating and sustaining discussion through the use of a scenario activity, the power of discussion accrues over time when the conversation leads students to new and broader understandings. The *substance* and *process* of the discussion are important. It is relatively easy to introduce a topic that many adolescents will want to talk about, but most teachers hope that the conversation is substantive, linking knowledge, transferring to new learning, and creating pathways to new fields of inquiry. The process of frequently conferring with others to tangle with thorny issues and difficult questions exposes students to the benefits of thinking with others and gaining insight from the collisions with alternative and sometimes competing perspectives.

# 4 Strategies for Organizing and Managing Small-Group Discussions

When our colleague Steve Kern was in the early stages of his teaching career, he enthusiastically relied on small-group discussions in his classroom. Steve believed that he saw students working constructively in small groups to investigate critical questions about the texts that they were reading and to prepare for the writing they were expected to do. In his youthful exuberance, Steve eagerly reported to his colleagues that small-group discussion had a powerful, positive impact on his students' reading, writing, and critical thinking. One of Steve's supervisors, whom we will refer to here as Dr. Glokspurtz, grudgingly attempted to use small-group discussion in his literature class, after which he contemptuously shared with Steve that the discussions were unproductive and concluded that small groups "just don't work."

Curious to account for the "failure" of the small-group discussion, Steve pressed his supervisor for some details about the lesson. "What were the students supposed to do in small groups?" Steve asked. The supervisor described the following small-group task: "Get into groups and discuss how the plant imagery in the novel *Green Mansions* contributes to the author's Jungian world view." When we heard this story of a failed small-group discussion, we smugly laughed because it seemed apparent that the task and the directions would discourage any group of adolescents from engaging in purposeful discussion. The experience that Dr. Glokspurtz's students faced does not convince us that small groups "just don't work" but, rather, illustrates that for small groups to be useful, a teacher must do some careful planning and attentive managing.

While research indicates that purposeful small-group discussion rarely occurs in schools, the use of small-group discussions as an integral part of learning in the English classroom is nothing new. Hillocks, McCabe, and McCampbell (1971) note the importance of using small groups as an opportunity to involve all students in the discussion: "Even in a classroom characterized by the discovery method and indirect patterns of influence, a teacher is lucky if more than 50 percent of the students respond. But in small-group discussion (limited to four or five students), when the problem is appropriate, nearly every student participates, and few, if any, remain uninvolved" (312). In their influential methods text, Hillocks, McCabe, and McCampbell cite a study by Flanders (1965), who concludes that students learn best when they are involved and can contribute to the lesson; the authors also note the influence of Bruner (1960), who encourages teachers to engage students in purposeful and appropriate problem-solving situations.

We offer here a few suggestions for basic practices in planning and managing small-group discussions. One can find book-length guides to small-group discussions (e.g., Book and Galvin 1975; Hawkins 1976), and we do not mean to repeat their efforts or claim to be exhaustive. We describe procedures here and illustrate in later chapters some specific small-group discussion activities and examples of students' responses.

We do not want our vision of small-group discussion to be confused with cooperative learning. We recognize that not all small-group discussion is cooperative learning and not all cooperative learning involves small-group discussion. The reader can rely on experts like Kagan (1992) and Slavin (1991) for guidance in structuring and managing cooperative learning experiences.

Some reflection on Dr. Glokspurtz's failed attempt at small-group discussion offers us a starting point by illustrating what one should *not* do. The short list of bad judgments would include the failure to define group membership, the possible inappropriateness and uncertainty of the task, the lack of specific procedures, and the doubtfulness of the endeavor's relevancy. Discussing these missed steps, or "things not to do," brings us into a discussion of what *to do* and, specifically, several steps that Dr. Glokspurtz could have taken to give his students a reasonable chance for purposeful conversation in their small groups.

> **Planning and Managing Small-Group Discussion**
>
> - Create a safe environment.
> - Establish group membership.
> - Direct the formation, location, and proximity of the groups.
> - Set the small-group task.
> - Outline the group procedures.
> - Monitor group behavior.
> - Evaluate the groups' dynamics and individual performances.
> - Bring the conversations to closure.

## Creating a Safe Environment

A central purpose to engaging students in small-group discussion is to allow all students to have an opportunity to contribute to the classroom discourse. One can imagine the student who is too reserved to offer responses in a large-group format but has much to say in the comfort of a small group. At the same time, one can imagine a student's reluctance to participate in a small group if the members are rude or excessively judgmental. It is crucial, then, that the teacher is influential in creating a classroom environment that encourages the participation of everyone and provides a reasonable guarantee that contributors will be treated with respect, even when they disagree with one another.

How is such an environment possible? Since the teacher's behavior in facilitating large-group discussion serves as an influential model for the way that students will conduct themselves in small-group discussion, one starting point is for the teacher to model the kind of behavior that one would hope to see in the small groups. As discussed in earlier chapters, the teacher can signal in both overt and subtle ways that everyone is invited to contribute: through the kinds of questions that one asks, through the inclusion of many class members, through the withholding of initial judgments about contributions, and through the use of the students' responses as a means to extend and widen discussion.

Just as participants might do in beginning important work as part of a committee, the students can openly discuss their expectations for how they want groups to function. Before embarking on any small-group activity, a teacher might ask the whole class, "What rules would you like to see apply to the way that you work as a team in your small groups?" Typically, students respond with considerations like these: "Don't disrespect anybody's ideas." "Let everybody have a chance to speak." "Everyone has to contribute something." "Don't make one person do all the work." Of course, the teacher can impose rules for group behavior; but it is best for group work to be governed by the rules that the students frame themselves.

Ultimately the standards upon which the group agrees can be posted somewhere in the room, and class members can refer to them as the obligations that will guide their behavior. It is dangerous to assume that everyone has a common understanding about how to operate in small groups, so it is crucial to discuss concerns openly so that everyone is encouraged to be part of the action.

## Establishing Group Membership

How should the groups form? Dr. Glokspurtz assumed that groups would develop naturally, with everyone finding others to join them. Laws of probability would allow for the possibility that productive groups could form in roughly even numbers. If small groups had met often in Dr. Glokspurtz's class, then it would be safe to assume that students knew the routine and could quickly join their groups and set to work. However, if the routines have not been established and one does not wish to leave matters to chance, establishing some grouping procedures can be a tremendous help.

Some teachers like to rely on random processes to form groups:

1. Count off by six (or five, or seven, depending on class size and the desired size for each group) and have all students with the same number meet.

2. Line up from tallest to shortest and then, working from each end, have the students from each end of the line match as a pair and join another pair to form groups of four. (One could follow a similar procedure by lining up from oldest to youngest.)

3. The teacher puts students' names into a hat and draw names in sets of three, four, or five to establish the groups.

Random means of grouping will ensure some variety of perspectives, abilities, and personalities in each group. And while these techniques provide a useful way to begin the group formation, as the teacher gets to know the students, she might want to try other means to define group membership.

When matters are left to chance, the possibility remains for some less-productive groups to form. Perhaps, for example, you inadvertently group two members of the Insane Devil Zombies street gang with two members of their rivals, the Satan Nocturnal Hardheads. In another instance, it is possible that one group consists of painfully shy persons who never speak, while another group has only vociferous extroverts who compete to be heard by shouting louder and louder. Or, it is possible that four chauvinist male athletes form one group, and four members of the pom-pom squad form another. The potential for trouble is obvious: In some cases, groups will have only one point of view; in other cases, a group's extreme difference in points of view could be volatile; in still other cases, one may never know if anyone *has* a point of view.

The teacher might choose to stack the deck by insuring that each group has both variety and a reasonable chance to draw everyone into the conversation. Group formation can be a bit of a puzzle. Here are some considerations to promote some heterogeneity:

- Are both genders represented?
- Are the groups ethnically diverse?
- Have all the athletes or all the musicians or all the skateboarders been grouped together? Does each group have some talkers?
- Is anyone in the group task oriented?
- Is there a second-language learner in the group, and, if so, does the group also include a bilingual student who can provide some support?

In short, one might go about group formation the way one might go about forming a committee to complete a formidable task: blend together a mix of talents, perspectives, and personalities.

Once the teacher has taken pains to form groups, should the students remain in the same groups for weeks? There is no right answer here. Some teachers like the students to develop a capacity for working with a variety of people, and they reconstitute the groups frequently, with the expectation that any student must develop an ability to work with any other person. Other teachers want the groups to form their own identities so that the members know each other and have formed positive long-term working relationships. In such cases, a teacher may even arrange classroom seating so that the members of each group can be close to one another, accommodating quick movement into groups. Either view has merit.

The students, however, will not likely want to stay with the same group for a whole grading period. Perhaps the teacher can achieve a balance between the two possibilities by having the students work in a long-term group for some discussions and reforming into other temporary groups for other discussions. In other words, the nature of the small-group task might suggest which groups should form.

## Directing the Formation, Location, and Proximity of the Groups

Initially, it will be helpful to suggest to students how and where to arrange themselves to begin small-group discussion. It may seem too controlling and unnecessary to tell students where to sit and how to sit, but a little attention to these details can help focus the discussion by creating a smaller and somewhat distinct environment for each group.

First, if a teacher refers to each group by number (e.g., all the number ones, etc.) or by name (one teacher assigns the names of fish or exotic birds to her classroom's groups), he or she can assign a specific classroom location for each group to meet. This information can be noted on a diagram that then is posted on the board, on the overhead projector or on a video screen. Imagine the teacher saying something like this: "Group number one will meet over by the door, group two will meet under the poster of Willa Cather, and group three will meet by the windows. . . ." This step is simple but helpful.

The point in assigning a meeting area is twofold. First, the students need to know a place to be. You don't want students carrying their desks around the room and competing for a prime location. Everyone wants to know where he or she is supposed to be. Second, the conversations among the groups should not be competing with each other. Of course, one is bound to hear the general muttering of the many voices from the several groups, but when groups are right on top of each other, the conversations from competing groups become intrusive and distracting.

Students also benefit from having directions about how to position themselves within the group. Here are some common directions: "Position your desks toward the center of the group so that you can see everyone else face to face" Some teachers have a diagram displayed on a poster that remains on the classroom wall all year. Small discussion groups should not be L-shapes or conga lines; as much as it is possible for rectangular desks to do, they should resemble a circle when they meet together, or small squares, with students facing in.

## Setting the Small-Group Task

A question that students often ask, even if only to themselves, is, "What am I supposed to do?" It is reasonable for students to want to know what is expected of them. The nature of the task and how it is expressed are both important instructional considerations.

First, students need to have something of substance to discuss. Kahn, Walter, and Johannessen (1984a) advise us that "controversy is the key." This does not mean that small-group discussion will "work" only if students explore some emotionally charged and sensational current issue. The point is that if students are going to engage actively in discussion with their peers, they need to tackle a question or problem that has no obvious or clear-cut solution. In other words, the task must introduce doubt that challenges a group of thinkers to sort through various perspectives and arrive at an enriched, although probably tentative, position.

Students need to know the context for grappling with the problem:

- How does this question relate to anything else we've done in this class?
- How will our discussion deepen our understanding of important concepts?
- How will our discussion prepare us to read a text or to reflect or write on what we have already read?

Consider the following contrasting tasks:

NOT GOOD: Identify five uses of personification in the story.

NOT GOOD: Get in your groups and discuss what you thought about last night's reading.

NOT GOOD: Discuss the use of figurative language in the poem.

BETTER: We've been discussing the conditions under which someone might be justified in breaking a law, and we listed some "rules" that could guide a person's behavior. Using those rules, make a case showing that the character did or did not act ethically.

Minimally, students need to know that there is something tangible to be accomplished during the course of group meetings. If the small-group discussion is a step in a longer sequence of activities, the students will need to know how, as a result of discussion, they will be equipped to participate in the next phase of the lesson or series of lessons.

## Outlining the Group Procedures

First of all, it is best to explain all instructions to a whole class of students *before* the students move into small groups. Once the students move into groups and begin conversations, it will be more difficult to capture their attention in order to explain procedures.

Set a time limit for the discussion. Many teachers find it useful to set a rather conservative time limit. If the students need more time, the teacher can generously extend the time in five-minute increments.

Students will want to know if they are being graded on any aspect of their small-group discussion. It is only fair to announce if you expect that a written product or some other performance will result from the discussion. Students will also want to know if each person in the group is required to write or if a representative can serve as note taker.

Some teachers prefer to assign roles or have students select roles. For example, one person could be the discussion leader, another is the recorder, and yet another is the reporter. Some teachers include a role for an "encourager," who promotes participation among all members of the group. A teacher might have a random system for determining and varying roles. Other teachers prefer to allow the students to select roles. The point is that if you expect the students to perform specific roles within their groups, it is appropriate to state this expectation explicitly.

## Monitoring Group Behavior

If the teacher has set a specific task and has provided the class with clear instructions and reasonable procedures, there is a very good chance that the students will function quite well on their own. However, we discourage teachers from retreating behind their desks with the daily newspaper or a stack of papers to grade while students are discussing in groups. Obviously, an awareness of the teacher's immediate presence in class encourages on-task behavior. But, beyond the effect of controlling the students' behavior, the teacher's monitoring of the small-group activity provides him or her with the information that will guide further instructional decisions. So, the main point here is that the teacher needs to move among the groups to see what is going on.

What, then, should the teacher do as he or she is strolling around the room and eavesdropping on the discussions? First, the teacher will want to know if the students understand the task. The teacher can answer questions or ask questions to see if the students comprehend the task. Sometimes the teacher might model for the students how to respond to a problem or a question in order to provide a little momentum to get the group started. It is appropriate for the teacher to sit briefly with a group to contribute to the discussion and to judge the nature of the discussion without taking up permanent residence and ignoring the rest of the class.

The constant monitoring of the small-group activities will help the teacher to make instructional judgments. She can gauge, for instance, whether students understand the basic task and the procedures. (It might be necessary on occasion to call the attention of the whole class to review the procedures.) She also can see if students need more time than originally planned, and, if so, announce the time-limit extension. Finally, by staying in close proximity to the class, the teacher also can determine when the students have finished their task and it is time to reconstitute the large group to share the many observations. But one will never know any of this if he or she remains behind the teacher's desk, oblivious to all behavior.

## Evaluating the Groups

Some teachers devise elaborate means for assessing the work of each small group. One can design checklists and tally sheets and embed an "evaluator" within each group. The checklist might support a tally of each student's contribution to the discussion under various categories: initiated discussion, asked a substantive question, asked a procedural question, offered an extended response, made a cursory response, and so on. Some of us have been lucky to remember to take attendance; never mind keeping track of tally sheets for each small-group discussion.

Perhaps more important than the teacher's evaluation of the small group's productiveness or functionality is the opportunity for each group to reflect on themselves and how they work as a group. This would be especially important when the teacher has established long-term groups. Each group can return to the stated norms for group discussion and judge whether any norms have been violated. The group can then propose means to correct violations and improve the group dynamics. The teacher will also want to know if some groups are struggling to work together so that he or she can intervene to help a particular group or, if necessary, reorganize some or all of the groups.

## Bringing the Conversation to Closure

Some small-group discussions seem to be able to go on forever. All of us can recall conversations about perennial questions (e.g., What is justice? Must we obey authority?) when students were unable to come to consensus in their groups and instead continued the conversations as they returned to their lockers or headed for the cafeteria. The time limits for class periods and the limits we artificially impose for small-group work, however, will require some form of closure. Although the teacher may have played a small part in the conversations themselves, he or she can perform the important function of summarizing and synthesizing what has been done and what has been said. The teacher also reminds students of the discussion's place in the larger scheme of things by expressing the links between the current discussion and the previous and subsequent lessons. Langer (2001a) reports that students benefit from the teacher's explicit discussion of the links among the various activities in their course of study.

Ultimately, closure of the discussion does *not* mean that the teacher validates a correct answer that someone expressed. If the topics and the discussions are rich ones, it will be impossible to come to complete closure anyway. There is always room for the doubt that extends the thinking across weeks and months to come. The important consideration about the function of discussion and how that function guides closure is that the students have been engaged in thinking processes as they talked to each other.

# 5 Strategies for Initiating Authentic Discussion

James Barton (1995) points out that "leading an effective discussion can be one of the most difficult tasks of teaching" (346). Christoph and Nystrand (2001) compare the process to starting a campfire, with a spark exposed to easily combustible conditions, managed carefully by gradually supplying additional fuel to build to larger effect. Many of us failed outdoorsmen find it difficult to start a campfire, especially under unfavorable conditions. For many teachers, it is equally difficult to initiate a meaningful discussion, with broad, active participation. The two activities described below model ways to begin discussion and nurture the resulting skills until the discussion becomes an extended discourse that informs reading, writing, and critical thinking.

## Lost at Sea: What Would You Do?

The activity that we call "Lost at Sea: What Would You Do?" is adapted from Kahn, Walter, and Johannessen (1984b). It can serve as a prereading activity for works such as William Golding's *Lord of the Flies,* Richard Connell's "The Most Dangerous Game," Jack London's "To Build a Fire" and *The Call of the Wild,* or any work or group of works that involve the theme of "survival: values under stress." The discussion that the activity generates helps students to activate relevant prior knowledge that supports the processing of new material and guides them in making judgments about themes and characters. The immersion into a situation that is similar to the stressful conditions that the characters in the literature face fosters an empathic response when the reader judges the behavior of characters. The activity is intended to put students in a "survival mode"—to make them think about what it takes to survive in a given environment. In addition, this activity also gives students practice in the skills and thinking strategies involved in argumentation. In fact it might be used for that instructional purpose alone, in a unit on writing argument. Like the scenario activity described in Chapter 3, one of this activity's key features is that it involves a challenging problem with built-in controversy. There is no one simple answer. In addition to preparing students for reading about characters who find themselves in challenging situations in the natural environment, the activity helps students practice rhetorical strategies such as generating evidence to support a claim, challenging others' viewpoints, clarifying reasoning, answering objections from an audience, giving evidence and explaining how it supports a claim, and criticizing faulty logic.

---

**Lost at Sea: What Would You Do?**

A ship is sinking, and you have managed to board a lifeboat with twelve other people. Most of the people were not able to reach the cabins to get warm clothing, so they are in street clothes. One woman is in a bathing suit. The ship is in the North Atlantic, where the air/water temperature is about 32 degrees Fahrenheit, and strong winds and high waves pummel the lifeboat. The lifeboat has no motor, so it must be rowed. You may have to spend several days at sea, depending on when the boat is spotted. The ocean is foggy with low, heavy clouds. The boat is dangerously overloaded so you **must** dump sixty pounds of weight. You must decide which items you will remove. For safety reasons, you may not suspend any items from the lifeboat. You may not remove any of the people. These are the items from which you must choose:

    5 raincoats with hoods—2 lbs. each
    30 cans of tuna fish (flip tops)—1 lb. each
    a 2-gallon container full of water—10 lbs.
    a battery-operated signal light—8 lbs.
    3 skin diving wet suits—5 lbs. each
    2 buckets for bailing—3 lbs. each
    4 wool blankets—2 lbs. each
    a large S.O.S. flag—3 lbs.
    a first-aid kit—10 lbs.
    8 oars—5 lbs. each
    Total—140 lbs.

---

For this activity, students initially work in small groups to propose their solutions. After fifteen or twenty minutes (or longer if the teacher judges it to be necessary), the class reforms for a large-group discussion. In the large-group format, the students present their solutions and discuss differences. Usually this activity generates such a lively discussion that the teacher needs to ask only one question and the debate begins. But here is a set of guide questions that might prove useful in keeping the discussion moving and the students focused on the task:

- What is one thing your group decided you could definitely get rid of? Why?
- What is one thing you should definitely keep? Why?
- What item on the list hasn't been mentioned? What would you do with it? Why?
- How does your list give the group the best chance for survival? Why?

Following is a sample of the kind of discussion that this activity ignites. Here, in a whole-class discussion, a group of ninth-grade students considers the necessity of keeping some or all of the emergency food.

*Student 1:* [Our small group] decided to get rid of eighteen cans of tuna fish.

*Student 2:* But what are you going to do for food?

*Student 1:* You don't, like, die of starvation because you don't have food for a couple of days.

*Student 3:* Yeah, but it says here you could be at sea for several days before someone spots you. We thought it would be a good idea to keep most of the food.

*Student 4:* That's exactly why we decided to keep the water and get rid of most of the food. It's more important to have water than to have food. The water was more important.

*Student 1:* We didn't think of that.

*Student 5:* But it says the weather's really bad. We thought it'd be important to keep the food, so that we could keep up our strength until somebody finds us. You know, we could be out in the ocean for quite awhile.

One important point is that giving students a concrete situation results in emotional involvement in the problem. Also important is the fact that a number of possible solutions exist. Had the list of items included a number of clearly nonessential items such as benches, food storage boxes, and an anchor, the solution could be too clear-cut to be arguable. In this discussion, students consider what it will take to survive given the harsh weather conditions of the North Atlantic, and this situation parallels the situation the unnamed protagonist must contend with as he faces a winter storm in the Yukon wilderness in Jack London's "To Build a Fire." Even though the activity primarily focuses on the physical necessities for survival, often the activity reveals values inherent in the problem, and the discussion then focuses on the social dimensions that parallel situations in the literature. For example, some of the students seem not to be concerned about the dangers posed by harsh weather conditions much like the brash young protagonist in Jack London's story who fails to heed the wisdom of the advice he receives from the old-timer about how to survive in the frigid temperatures of the Yukon wilderness.

Once all of the students have had a chance to express their views, we often have students discuss arguments that seemed particularly strong and what made them strong, what kinds of arguments seemed weak and why, and why certain arguments could be refuted. As a follow-up, students write to convince others that certain choices (of what to keep and what to throw away) will give the group the best chance for survival.

The activity creates controversy because it doesn't offer an easy solution, and the problem connects to students' lives. Students become emotionally engaged in arguing their viewpoints, so much so that sometimes one student will say to another, "Hey, calm down. This isn't real."

## The Soldier's Dilemma

Another activity that teachers have used with considerable success to engage students in authentic discussion is "The Soldier's Dilemma," which has been adapted from Kroll (1992), who reports that it is based on a real problem that the U.S. Army uses to train prospective officers for leadership. The activity serves a number of purposes, but it might be most useful as a prereading activity for modern combat narratives such as Ernest Hemingway's *A Farewell to Arms* or Tim O'Brien's *The Things They Carried.* The activity is set up to prepare students for what soldiers have to deal with in modern warfare, as well as some of the themes, issues, and especially moral dilemmas that students will encounter in their reading. It helps them to understand the characters, their motivations, and their actions.

---

**The Soldier's Dilemma**

During the Vietnam War, an infantry squad was patrolling deep in enemy-controlled territory near the Cambodian border. At one point in this operation, the squad leader, Sergeant Johnson, decided to scout along a trail that ran through a valley, leading toward a village a short distance away. Johnson told one of his rifleman, a private named Dillon, to stay on a small hilltop as a lookout, while the

---

rest of the squad followed along the trail in the valley below. Johnson expressed concern about a possible ambush on the trail and reminded Dillon that their platoon had been ambushed in this same area and suffered a number of casualties some weeks prior to the present operation. "Don't take any chances," Johnson warned. "Better to kill a few of those murdering villagers than to let any more Americans die."

As Dillon watched the squad make its way along the trail, he saw a Vietnamese woman suddenly appear on the trail just ahead of the squad, but around a bend so that the squad could not see her. From Dillon's vantage point, the woman appeared to lean over the edge of the trail and then quickly move back into the underbrush—out of sight of the squad, but still visible to Dillon.

Dillon was immediately suspicious. This was enemy-controlled territory, and the woman could easily be part of the local guerrilla forces. On the other hand, many innocent peasants lived in and around the villages. Was the woman a guerrilla soldier who might set off a mine or spring an ambush when the squad came around the bend in the trail? Or was the woman simply a peasant who had perhaps dropped something on the trail in her haste to hide from the advancing American soldiers? Also, what about the things Johnson had told him? As a soldier, he was taught to obey all orders of his superiors. To disobey is a crime.

As these thoughts went through Dillon's mind, the squad kept moving and now was almost at the spot where the woman was hiding. The squad was too far away for Dillon to call out to them. Even a warning shot would probably not stop them from proceeding around the bend. Dillon raised his rifle and lined up his sights on the woman in the brush. But as his finger tightened on the trigger, he hesitated.

If he shot the woman and there turned out not to be a mine or booby trap on the trail, he would have murdered an innocent person. But if he didn't shoot her, a number of his friends might be blown to bits if the woman detonated a mine.

*Questions*

What should Dillon do: Hold his fire or shoot the woman? Why is that the right thing for him to do? Do you agree with what Sergeant Johnson told Dillon? Why or why not?

Students read the case, and then they write a short composition answering the questions posed at the end. The next step is to have students meet in small groups, read their papers aloud in their groups, and try to reach a consensus on what they think Dillon should do and why. After fifteen or twenty minutes, the class comes back together for a large-group discussion. Depending on the class, the groups might start by reading the paper that best represents their viewpoint, or if there is disagreement among them, several students present their solutions and discuss the differences. In either case, the result is usually a lively discussion. Here is a set of discussion guide questions on which one might rely to keep the discussion moving and to keep students on task:

- If Dillon holds his fire, why does the fact that the people in his squad are his "friends" make a difference? (Or does that make a difference?)

- If Dillon decides to shoot the woman, and it turns out that she was just an innocent peasant woman caught in bad circumstances, and she is dead, do you think he has done anything wrong? Why or why not?

- If Dillon killed an innocent civilian under such circumstances, would you be willing to call him a murderer? Why or why not? If yes, what should his punishment be? Why?

- If Dillon decides not to shoot the woman, and it turns out that she is a guerrilla soldier who sets off a mine or booby trap, and some of his fellow soldiers are killed and wounded, do you think he has done anything wrong? Why or why not?

- If Dillon fails to shoot the woman and some of his fellow soldiers are killed and wounded as a result of his failure to shoot, would you be willing to say that he has committed a crime? Why or why not? What crime has he committed, and what should his punishment be? Why?

- What do you think the morals of war are? What guidelines or criteria can someone use to live by in war?

In the small-group and whole-class discussions, students wrestle with the same sort of problems and questions with which the characters must contend in the literature. In addition, as in "Lost at Sea," students are verbally practicing the critical thinking skills involved in analytical and argumentative writing. Students discuss and debate whether Dillon, as a soldier, should follow the orders Sergeant Johnson gave him or whether there is a higher order, or morality, that he must follow. They wrestle with the question of what is the right thing for him to do. Students discuss and debate the extent to which the orders Johnson gave him are lawful and legitimate. Ultimately, students consider a possible set of guidelines for right action in war, and they generate a list of those guidelines. Later they use the guidelines to evaluate the actions of the characters in the literature. As part of the discussion, the students also examine the actions of real soldiers. One possible extension of the discussion of the case of Private Dillon would be a comparison to the case of former Senator Bob Kerrey and his actions as a Navy SEAL team commander during the highly controversial Thanh Phong incident on February 25, 1969, during the Vietnam War.

What is particularly striking about the nature of the discussion, and what makes it stand out as authentic discussion, is that students are actively engaged in an inquiry into the problem posed and issues raised. One of the strengths of the activity is that the problem is posed in real terms and connects to their lives.

Students rarely, if ever, agree on what Dillon should do. As a result, one natural follow-up writing activity is to have students return to the case, and, in light of their discussion and having developed a set of criteria for deciding right action in war, have them determine what Dillon should do in this situation. Should he hold his fire or shoot the woman? More important, why is that action the right thing for him to do based on the criteria a soldier can use to live by in war? In writing their viewpoint, students consider the orders that Sergeant Johnson gave Dillon.

In one sense, students are revising their original compositions, but most students do not see this follow-up assignment in this way; most of them write substantially different essays than they originally wrote. This time, their arguments are much more developed and complex as a result of the small-group and whole-class discussions, and unlike many of their first attempts, the written responses of most students now consider the full implications of Dillon's situation. Here is an excerpt from a longer paper written by one of Larry's undergraduate university students. Notice how this twenty-year-old student considers the implications of her decision that Dillon should shoot the woman, and how this part of her paper is clearly derived from the class discussion of the case.

> You see, I put myself in Dillon's shoes and it all came down to
> what I could live with once I got home. Now I don't know if I
> could live with shooting the woman if she turned out to be inno-
> cent. I really don't. Maybe I could have; maybe it would have
> destroyed me. Even if the woman wasn't innocent, I probably
> still would have regretted what I had done for the rest of my life.
> I don't know. However, what I *do* know is that if men died be-
> cause I didn't shoot her, I *never* could have lived with that. I know

that I could not live with the fact that I could have prevented them from going home in body bags. Now, I know that killing another person is wrong, ethically and morally wrong, no matter what the circumstances. But, if I had to compromise some of my beliefs in order to assure that my fellow soldiers, my friends, spent one more day alive, I'd do it. I probably would hate myself for it the rest of my life, and so would Dillon maybe, but that's not really the point. The point is those men spent another moment on this earth.

This excerpt suggests a number of things about the nature of the discussion that preceded it and what students are learning through the discussion. This student wrestles with the anguish of either killing the woman and having to live with that or not killing her and possibly having to live with the deaths of her fellow soldiers, her friends. As a result of the discussion fostered by this activity, students are prepared to read about this issue in the literature. The excerpt also shows the high level of critical thinking in which the students are engaged as they wrestle with the moral and ethical issues involved in the problem. This kind of thinking is essential when they must interpret and write about literature.

## Strategies for Initiating Authentic Discussion

These two activities utilize the following seven strategies that we have found to be helpful in initiating authentic discussion:

**1. Create controversy.**
The instruction needs to present a puzzling event, question, or problem. It needs to engage students in exploring problems that are intrinsically interesting to them, that have no quick or easy solutions but are open to a variety of solutions and/or interpretations, and that are complex but not too complex or abstract for their particular level (Kahn, Walter, and Johannessen 1984a). An important dimension of instruction is that the teacher provides a set of data such as the items on the boat or the specifics of Dillon's situation (or devises a means for students to collect data) that they can bring to bear in attacking the problem.

**2. Use small-group collaboration.**
This element is important because it helps students gain a greater understanding of other perspectives. As students' ideas or hypotheses are challenged by others, they revise and refine their thinking. Small-group collaboration also provides scaffolding for students while they are learning new strategies so that ultimately they internalize procedures and

are able to tackle new tasks effectively on their own (Hillocks 1995; Johannessen 2001; Johannessen and Kahn 1997; McCann 1996; Smagorinsky 1989, 1993; Smagorinsky, McCann, and Kern 1987).

**3. Pose questions or problems that do not have easy answers or obvious solutions.**
If the solution to a problem is one that can be arrived at easily or quickly, then the question or problem should be redesigned. Another way to think of this is to design problem-based activities that encourage multiple perspectives.

**4. Connect the questions or problems to students' lives.**
It is vitally important that we design our questions and problems so that they connect to the lives of our students if we hope to engage them in meaningful classroom discussion. As Michael Smith warns in *Authorizing Readers: Resistance and Respect in the Teaching of Literature* (Rabinowitz and Smith 1998), the real danger is that when we focus on what we think is important, we might very well end up "torturing" our students with questions or problems that are important only to us as he did when he had his students read *The Scarlet Letter*, and asked them to discuss the hat motif and other symbols and motifs in the novel (103). His students hated it, and as he indicates, they were interested in a whole set of other questions, like, "Why the hell didn't she just leave if they treated her that way?" (103)

**5. Connect students' knowledge to the literature they study.**
Smagorinsky (1993) and Smagorinsky, McCann, and Kern (1987) remind us that when designing questions or problems, we need to make sure that we are tapping into our students' prior knowledge or connecting what they are learning in the activity to the literature under consideration. One of the points that the two activities presented above illustrate, is related to this issue. Students have difficulty connecting with Jack London's story "To Build a Fire," in part because most students have never had to face a life-threatening situation from severe weather conditions. The "Lost at Sea" activity puts students in a survival mode and forces them to have to consider their actions. Once students have done this, it is easier for them to connect to the situation in the literature.

**6. Explore questions or problems that require students to think critically.**
It isn't enough for teachers to design interesting and challenging questions or problems that are important to students; these questions or

problems must also encourage or require our students to engage in critical thinking. In other words, they must ask our students to use the kinds of procedural knowledge that will help them develop analytical and critical thinking skills important in solving problems, analyzing literature, and writing thoughtful papers. Langer (2001a) and Hillocks (2002) report that instructional practices that promote frequent, meaningful discussion among students, discussion that requires critical thinking, will make a significant difference in learning and achievement.

### 7. Give students adequate time to respond to complex questions.

We suggest in Chapter 2 how important it is to give students time to prepare for discussion. Research indicates that one of the mistakes many teachers make is that they do not allow students enough time to answer complex questions (Rowe 1974). Indeed, many teachers, particularly new ones, seem to be deathly afraid of silence in the classroom. However, it is important that we recognize that when we ask complex questions, we cannot expect students to be immediately ready with an answer. Rowe (1974) found that many teachers are impatient with students when asking questions. Her research indicates that the wait time between asking a question and either answering it for the student or calling on another student was found to be only a few fractions of a second. We need to recognize that complex questions require more time for students to think and formulate a response and that all classroom silence is not bad, particularly when you are asking a question in a discussion. Some research even shows that failing to provide adequate wait-time with higher-level questions can lead to low-level student responses (Riley 1986).

> **Strategies for Initiating Authentic Discussion**
>
> 1. Create controversy.
> 2. Use small-group collaboration.
> 3. Pose questions or problems that do not have easy answers or obvious solutions.
> 4. Connect the questions or problems to students' lives.
> 5. Connect students' knowledge to the literature they study.
> 6. Explore questions or problems that require students to think critically.
> 7. Give students adequate time to respond to complex questions.

## The Discussion-Based Classroom

The strategies discussed here are only a place to begin to promote authentic classroom discussion. The practices suggested here promote the idea that we need to create a new kind of classroom, a classroom that is inquiry driven and is not dominated by teacher talk. In *Pedagogy of the Oppressed*, Paulo Freire (1970) writes about the change that occurs in a discussion-based classroom: "The teacher is no longer merely the one-who-teaches, but one who is himself taught in a dialogue with students, who in turn while being taught also teach. They become jointly responsible for a process in which all grow" (67). For many teachers, the most exciting part of teaching is the classroom dialogues that engage students and teachers together. In a conversational environment, the teacher finds that everyone functions in a mode of discovery, and the teacher learns along with the students.

# 6 Discussion as Preparation for the Reading and Analysis of Literature

How can we get students actively involved in discussions that prepare them for reading and analyzing literature? In some situations, it is a simple matter of posing particularly thought-provoking questions or asking students to share the reflections that they have written in their journals. When these means for prompting prereading discussions have failed us, we have turned to more structured introductory activities as part of students' preparation for the critical study of literature.

Introductory activities are preparatory experiences that bridge the gap between the world of literature and students' life experiences; they attempt to connect students' prior knowledge to themes and issues important in particular literary works; they provide a context—a place to start—for understanding and interpreting literature; they prepare students for what they will encounter in a work they are about to read; they provide a clear purpose for reading, which enables students to use their prior knowledge when they read; they often motivate students to read by engaging them in issues, problems, and ideas they will encounter in their reading; and they provide what Smagorinsky (2002) describes as the "scaffolding" that is necessary for students to process what they read and to make critical judgments about the texts they study. Of course, as we note in earlier chapters, the heart of these kinds of activities is engaging and challenging discussion that presents a problem, a puzzling event, or a situation that demands or encourages thoughtful exploration (Johannessen, Kahn, and Walter 1984; Kahn, Walter, and Johannessen 1984b; McCann and Flanagan 2002; Smagorinsky 1993, 2002; Smagorinsky, McCann, and Kern 1987).

The rest of this chapter offers a set of introductory activities designed to engage students in discussions that draw on knowledge they already have as a way of preparing them for problems they will encounter in a work of literature or literature unit. We limit ourselves here to examining four kinds of activities: opinionnaire/survey, case study/scenarios, role playing/simulation, and personal experience/writing about related problems.

## Opinionnaire/Survey

An opinionnaire or survey is a set of controversial statements designed to get students thinking about issues they will later encounter in the literature. Sometimes statements might come directly from the literature itself. For instance, for a unit titled Politics, Patriotism, and Protest Literature, an opinionnaire might include one statement quoted directly from *Julius Caesar:* "Cowards die many times before their deaths; the valiant taste of death but once." If the literature provides no such provocative statements, then the teacher needs to develop them based on the issues that students will eventually think through while reading.

A successful opinionnaire typically contains ten to twenty statements, depending upon the length and difficulty of the literature, the focus of instruction, and the age and ability level of students. The statements are keyed to specific interpretive problems and ask students to respond, answering agree or disagree, true or false, or yes or no for each statement. A teacher needs to understand two important factors prior to designing an effective opinionnaire: (1) the concepts in the text that are the focus of the study, and (2) the concerns and experiences of the students. With these two components in mind, the teacher then designs controversial statements that will spark a lively discussion related to the problems students will encounter in their reading.

The key to writing an effective opinionnaire is to use statements that will encourage disagreement among students. This disagreement should lead to discussions of issues central to the problems that will arise in the literature. In constructing items for an opinionnaire, it is advisable to compose statements that will help students think through what they already know about the themes and issues included in an opinionnaire. In addition, the shared responses to the statements should get students to wrestle with and refine their ideas about the themes and issues in light of the contrasting opinions expressed by their classmates as they discuss and debate the various statements on the opinionnaire.

A teacher can use opinionnaires in a variety of ways. He might pass them out and go over the statements in order, having a discussion of each, or he might have students complete the opinionnaire individually, and then meet in small groups to discuss their answers and finish with a whole-class discussion. And after the class has discussed all of the items in the opinionnaire, a teacher also might ask students to write a composition about the theme or concept based on the class discussion they have just experienced.

Here is a sampling of a few statements from an opinionnaire containing eighteen statements about "true love." Students are asked to agree or disagree with each:

1. Physical attraction must precede true love.
2. You have to work hard to have a successful love relationship.
3. Teenagers cannot experience "true" love.
4. Love at first sight is possible.
5. You are never too young to fall in love.

Opinionnaires and surveys are obviously similar. As with the opinionnaire, the survey also draws on student opinions to create interest in the literature. However, the survey format we use requires students to gather and compile the views of others besides their classmates. In addition to having each classmate fill out the survey independently, the data set expands when students interview, for example, an adult, a ninth-grade student, and an eleventh-grade student in order to reveal a variety of opinions about true love. After allowing students a few days to gather their data, they bring their completed surveys to class and tabulate the results, using a three-step process. First, students add their totals of agreement and disagreement for each statement. Then, the class organizes into small groups, and one person in each group compiles the group totals. Next, one student writes all of the statements on the board, and after reading each statement, a spokesperson for each group reports the group's totals for each item. Meanwhile, other students work on adding the group totals for the entire class. When the totals are compiled, the students analyze the results. A lively discussion typically follows these questions: Are you surprised by any of the results? Can you identify any clear trends? Do different age groups respond differently to the statements?

By compiling the survey results in class, students generally feel comfortable contributing to class discussion, because the focus on the current data makes for a nonthreatening situation. The amount of participation is likely to be quite high at this point as students spot trends, and as they either agree with or take exception to the results. As Kahn, Walter, and Johannessen (1984b) explain, although most teenagers think they have a pretty good idea about what love is, throwing out the discussion question, "What is love?" is a sure conversation stopper for most teenagers—as well as most adults. The use of a survey about true love, then, circumvents this problem by asking students to respond to specific statements about love and to survey others outside the class as well. Through the survey and the discussion of the results, the students examine their own viewpoints about love as well as the viewpoints of others. Coming at the topic in this way, students end up challenging many of the clichés about love—clichés that they otherwise might have accepted without question.

One of the obvious benefits to using the survey format is that it introduces a framework for examining love from different points of view, and, as a result, it helps to make students' reading more purposeful. As students start reading, the teacher can encourage them to ask themselves how the characters in the literature would answer the survey and how the author would answer the survey.

For example, a teacher might ask students to respond to a "True Love Opinionnaire" prior to reading Shakespeare's *Romeo and Julie*, and then have them return to it later as they read the play. Ultimately students conjecture about what Shakespeare wants his readers to understand about love. At different points during their reading, students, in small groups and then individually, can complete the opinionnaire as they think a particular character would respond: Romeo, Juliet, Capulet, Lady Capulet, Friar Laurence, and the Nurse. After students complete the opinionnaire for a character, a class discussion explores their responses, this time supported by evidence from the play.

When students think about key issues prior to reading, they gain confidence in discussing them in class. The statements on the opinionnaire provide students with specific and concrete ways to talk about the actions and motives of characters. As a result, these discussions usually involve wide participation and extended responses. For example, one can imagine considerable debate over how Juliet would respond to the statement from the opinionnaire that "Children have a duty to love and obey their parents." Some students argue that Juliet would agree with this statement. They point to Juliet's response to her father's request that she consider Paris for marriage. Students point directly to the line in which Juliet dutifully tells Capulet, "I'll look to like if looking liking move." Other students argue that while Juliet would have gone along with her father's wishes early in the play, she changes and becomes more independent as the play develops. She loves her parents but doesn't believe they should choose whom she marries. They point to the balcony scene where Juliet says that if Romeo would refuse his name, she "would no longer be a Capulet." Other students offer differing viewpoints and evidence to support their interpretations, often challenging previous interpretations.

After students finish reading *Romeo and Juliet*, it is worthwhile to have them fill out the opinionnaire again. This time, however, they should complete it as they think Shakespeare would respond to the statements. In discussing their responses, inevitably students begin to formulate important conclusions about Shakespeare's message regarding love. In discussing various statements from the opinionnaire in light of the play, many students conclude that the suicides are immature and impulsive acts, and many judge that the real tragedy involves the destruction of love in a world filled with hate. As one of our students concluded, "Shakespeare wants us to see that you shouldn't hate because hate can destroy love." The "True Love Opinionnaire" activities helped this student establish a framework for understanding. Once again, the teacher's role is to facilitate the discussion, to help students inquire, problem solve, and synthesize ideas brought forth.

As a final step, students can complete the opinionnaire one last time for themselves in order to compare their current responses to their earlier responses before they read the play. In many cases, their opinions change. In looking back at how they marked the eighteen statements on the opinionnaire prior to reading the play, most students usually change their opinion on at least one statement as a result of their study. Class discussion invites students to explain how and why their opinions changed. This discussion is important because it helps students to see the impact that the play has had on them. As one student said, "I always thought that when two people fell in love, nothing bad could happen. It was like love could conquer anything. But now I think it's a lot more complicated than that."

## From Discussion to Writing

The opinionnaire activity or series of activities establishes a powerful framework to help students do some additional thinking and writing. Consider what students do in a series of opinionnaire activities that prepares them for analytic writing. In the initial prereading opinionnaire activity, students argue their viewpoints to an audience of peers regarding the statements in the opinionnaire, and they present evidence and reasoning to support their views and refute opposing viewpoints. In addition, if the teacher uses the opinionnaire to have students examine characters' and an author's viewpoint, then they are orally practicing the skills necessary to turn their viewpoints and interpretations into effective literary analysis compositions.

The idea then is to get students to use what they have learned through the opinionnaire activities. For example, with the support of the discussions about the "True Love Opinionnaire," students can readily compare and contrast their own views on love (two of the statements from the opinionnaire) to the views of a character (either Romeo or Juliet) and provide reasoning for their own views and reasoning and textual evidence to support their interpretations of a character's view.

The point is that the discussions allow the students to rehearse their ideas before they transform their talk into their writing.

Opinionnaire introductory activities are relatively easy to write and quite versatile for gateway discussions about a wide variety of literary works, whole units, and courses. The activities lead to authentic discussion that helps engage students in literature.

## Case Studies/Scenarios

Scenarios and case studies describe problematic examples of people who find themselves in thorny situations that parallel the circumstances of the literary characters or involve one of the key concepts found in the literature to be studied. Scenarios are brief vignettes. A useful set of scenarios typically contains five to ten different situations that represent a range of possibilities. In designing a set of scenarios a teacher needs to identify a central concept or compelling question represented in the literature. The facets or nuances of the concept, question, or problem form the basis for a series of scenarios, which relate to the concerns and experiences of students in a way that the students easily recognize. Chapter 3 contains an example of a scenario-based activity, "Justice at Floodrock High?" which is designed to focus on the concept of justice. The "Heroism: What Is a Heroic Act?" scenarios (adapted from Johannessen 1992) prompt students to think carefully about the qualities or characteristics of a heroic act and to confront viewpoints that may differ from their own before reading a work of literature dealing with this concept. The activity is best done just before students start reading a work in which the concept of heroism is critical for understanding the text.

---

**Heroism: What Is a Heroic Act?**

**Part I Directions.**
Rank the following actions from the one you think is the MOST (1) heroic to the one you think is the LEAST heroic (10). Be prepared to explain your reasons for ranking each action the way you did.

| 1 | 2 | 3 | 4 | 5 | 6 | 7 | 8 | 9 | 10 |
|---|---|---|---|---|---|---|---|---|----|

---

A. An accident leaves a gymnast paralyzed. For more than five years, she spends twelve to fourteen hours a day in therapy to try to regain the use of her legs. Her hard work results in a miraculous recovery, and she wins a gold medal in the Olympics.

B. A school teacher, invited to be a part of the seven-person crew on the Space Shuttle, dies as the rocket explodes shortly after takeoff.

C. An eleven-year-old boy who sees two men sexually assaulting a thirteen-year-old girl, threatening to stab her if she resists, rides off on his bicycle and gets the police. The officers rush to the scene but arrive too late to prevent the rape; however, the boy's actions probably saved her from being killed.

D. A lifeguard rescues a six-year-old boy from drowning in a public pool by dragging him out with a hook.

E. A scientist works for more than ten years and finally makes a discovery that will help cure thousands of people with heart disease.

F. A woman is swimming in the ocean. Sharks are spotted near her, so her husband runs into the water to save her. Part of his leg is severed by sharks, but he manages to pull his wife and himself to safety.

G. A man runs into a burning building that is about to collapse to rescue a child trapped inside. As he is running out with the child, a portion of the building falls, killing them both.

H. When a boat capsizes in a storm, four people are clinging to a small raft that will hold only three. An old man with a fatal disease knows he will die in a few months, so he gives up the raft for the others. He drowns in the waves.

I. A bystander saves a woman from drowning after her plane crashes in a river. The water is very cold, and only a few minutes of exposure could result in death. The bystander is able to save the woman but freezes and drowns in the process.

J. A man finds that the company he works for has been cheating customers. He reports his finding on a television news program. Shortly thereafter, he is fired from his job.

**Part II Directions.**

In the space below, write your definition of a heroic act. Your definition should identify at least two key characteristics or rules that could be used to judge whether or not someone's action is a heroic act.

*continued on next page*

_____

_____

_____

_____

_____

_____

_____

_____

_____

_____

_____

Adapted from Larry R. Johannessen, *Illumination Rounds: Teaching the Literature of the Vietnam War* (Urbana, IL: NCTE, 1992), 149–50.

Students complete Part I on their own: that is, they rank the scenarios from least to most heroic. Then, after students finish the scenarios, they work in small groups to attempt to reach a consensus on their rankings and to complete Part II of the activity by writing out their definitions of a heroic act. However, reaching a consensus is no easy task. As students try to convince others that they are "right," they must argue the reasons for their choices. For instance, in deciding why Example A in the scenarios is more or less heroic than Example B, students discover characteristics that they think an action must have to be heroic and the qualities that can be used to judge whether one action is more or less heroic than another.

After the small groups complete their discussion, a whole-class discussion about their findings follows. At this point, the debate begins all over again as the groups defend their rankings and their definitions. As the debate continues, students express the qualities or criteria for deciding whether an action is heroic. As students generate ideas, it is useful to list them on a chalkboard or overhead projector and have students copy them down for the next step in the activity. Students typically generate ideas such as the following: For an action to be heroic, there must be real danger; the action must involve serious consequences or possible consequences; and the potential hero must express a willingness to sacrifice for others.

But students rarely agree on their rankings. As a result, a natural follow-up writing activity is to have students pick one of the incidents that the class was unable to agree on and argue why the person's action in the incident is or is not heroic according to the criteria the class has generated. The students could also explain in their written compositions why the person's action is more or less heroic than that of one or two other characters in other scenarios. Most students find the writing challenging yet approach it confidently because they have already rehearsed their ideas through the preceding discussions.

This activity serves as an excellent introduction to works that deal with heroism, including the mythic, epic, and modern hero. As students read the literature after doing the activity, they apply the qualities they generated and determine where within their rankings a particular character would fall. By examining these scenarios before they begin reading, students derive a complex understanding of heroes.

## Creating Case Studies

The basic structure and design process of scenarios and case studies are similar. Once again, a teacher needs to write a case study keeping in mind what the literature provides and what the students have experienced. Chapter 5 contains two examples of case studies: "Lost at Sea: What Would You Do?" and "The Soldier's Dilemma." A third case study is included here, "Does She Deserve Honor?" If students are going to read Nathaniel Hawthorne's *The Scarlet Letter* or study literature that involves a conflict with authority or society's norms, then this activity would provide an excellent introduction.

---

### Does She Deserve Honor?

Jennifer Dinesen, a high school senior, was denied induction to the National Honor Society (NHS) because she is an unmarried mother. A faculty selection committee at Streamridge High School invited Jennifer to join the school's National Honor Society but then revoked the offer when it discovered that the eighteen-year-old had a daughter. Students are selected for the National Honor Society based on four criteria: character, leadership, service, and scholastic achievement. Dinesen met the academic requirements, but the committee felt that because she is an unwed mother her character is in question and she is not a good role model (leader) for other students.

The rules of the National Honor Society state that "pregnancy cannot be the basis for automatic rejection," but each school is allowed to set its own standards as long as they are applied consistently. The superintendent explained that Jennifer Dinesen is not the

---

first student at Streamridge to be denied membership in the school's honor society because of sexual activity.

As a senior, Jennifer has a 3.8 grade-point average. She has been a member of the Spanish Club since freshman year and served as secretary of the club her sophomore year. She was a starting player on the junior varsity girls' basketball team her freshman and sophomore years. During her junior year, she was in charge of decorations for the school's homecoming dance, and she also worked as a volunteer four hours a week at a local day care center for disabled children. All of her out-of-school time during her senior year has been spent caring for her baby daughter. She has not received any discipline referrals for four years.

Jennifer says, "I'm deeply hurt by the school's decision because I have worked so hard for four years."

*Questions*

What is at issue are two qualities the honor society demands: leadership and character. As an unwed mother, has Jennifer lost her character? Will she lead others in the wrong direction? Do you agree with the faculty committee's decision not to induct Jennifer Dinesen into the National Honor Society? Why or why not?

Adapted from Larry R. Johannessen, "Teaching Thinking and Writing for a New Century," *English Journal* 90 (6) (July 2001): 38–46.

"Does She Deserve Honor?" puts students in a problematic situation that will make them think about and ultimately decide if an unwed teenage mother who has an excellent academic record should be admitted to the National Honor Society after she was denied admission by a faculty committee because they claim she lacks character and leadership. The case is a fictional version of an actual situation, one that may be repeated in one form or another in many communities. After the students read the case, they join in small groups to discuss the case and answer the questions posed at the end of it. In other words, the groups attempt to reach a consensus on whether Jennifer Dinesen should be admitted to the National Honor Society. After sufficient time for small-group work, the class reforms for a large-group discussion. Students present their responses to the questions and the groups' decision, and then discuss differences. The discussion begins with one group presenting their responses and decision and listening to responses and decisions from the rest of the class. At this point, the class discussion usually becomes quite lively as students argue their positions and refute others. This discussion requires students to explore with a larger audience why, for example, an unwed mother would or would not "lead" others in the wrong direction. Here is an example of an exchange that took place in one tenth-grade class after students had discussed the questions in small groups:

> *Student 1:* We thought Jennifer exhibited strong leadership because after she had her baby, she devoted all of her out of school time to her most important responsibility—"caring for her baby daughter." She is showing others that she is taking responsibility for her actions.
>
> *Student 2:* We said exactly the opposite. She lives at home with her parents. Her parents are supporting her, and, as it says right here on the paper, "they take care of the baby" when she is at school. If she was really a leader, she would get a job and support herself and her baby instead of letting her parents support them.
>
> *Student 1:* You're wrong. When most high school girls get pregnant, they usually hide it so that nobody knows. Jennifer is just the opposite. She is taking a lot of stuff from other kids in school. It shows a lot of courage to stay in school, keep her daughter, and face all the stuff from other kids. She is showing other kids that you can make a mistake and live with that mistake.
>
> *Student 3:* You just said it: "Mistake"! By getting pregnant, she made a mistake that shows she lacks leadership. A true leader would not go crying to everyone about how "deeply hurt" she is by the faculty selection committee's decision because she has "worked so hard for four years."

This exchange continued in a similar manner for several minutes. This brief example illustrates how the activity engages students in discussing the problem presented in the case. What is most interesting is that their discussion requires complex thought as the students present arguments and counterarguments and present evidence for their differing positions. For example, each of the students presents a claim with evidence from the case for his or her position. Student 1 argues that Jennifer showed strong leadership because she took responsibility for caring for her daughter. Student 2 raises a counterargument—that Jennifer is not taking responsibility; her parents are. At the end of this exchange, Student 3 counters with the point that Jennifer made a mistake in having a child in the first place and therefore lacks leadership.

It is important to note that there is no prespecified answer for this case study problem. This openness inevitably leads to lively small group and whole-class discussions in which students are actively debating; they are engaging in a rich, lively discussion of issues that are key to understanding the literature they are about to study.

There is rarely complete agreement as to what should be done in Jennifer's case. The series of discussions prepare students for a follow-up writing situation. An obvious assignment is to have students write a composition explaining why Jennifer should or should not be admitted to the National Honor Society, encouraging the students to provide evidence from the case to support their views. As students study the related literature, they often come back to this case and discuss how they think various characters in the literature would respond to the problem presented in Jennifer's case. Another related writing assignment would have students write about how one of the authors the students have studied would respond to Jennifer's case and why. In this way, the introductory activity provides a framework for the critical reading of literature and supports subsequent discussions about the literature.

## Role Playing/Simulation

Perhaps the most dramatic method of sparking authentic discussion and preparing students for what they will encounter in the literature is a simulation activity. Such an activity works by placing students in a situation similar to one that a major character or characters face in the work that the students are about to read.

As with other types of introductory activities, in order to design an effective simulation activity, the teacher needs to do the following things: (1) identify important literary issues that students will need to confront in order to understand the material; (2) mentally enter the students' world to create circumstances into which the students can easily project themselves; (3) and develop circumstances and roles for students to play. The key element of this kind of activity is that, in a simulated way, students will have the same kind of experience that the literature's character (or characters) experience.

Elsewhere we report the usefulness of a simulation called "The Factory" to introduce Jack London's short story "The Apostate" (Johannessen, Kahn, and Walter 1984). The story involves child labor in factories. Students who are far removed from the days when child labor was more pervasive often have difficulty relating to the problems faced by the main character, who works on an assembly line.

Here's how the simulation works. Begin by explaining to the class that they will be divided into two or three equal groups. Each group must choose a supervisor; the rest of the students in each group are assembly-line workers. One student from the class serves as the quality control inspector. Then, the teacher shows the class a piece of paper with several simple drawings on it. Each student receives a copy of the model. Each group receives about twenty-five blank sheets of paper on which they will have to reproduce the drawings of the original model. The directions specify that each group, drawing in nonerasable pen, must reproduce twenty good copies of this model. The goal is to find out which of the two or three assembly lines can produce the twenty good replicas in the shortest amount of time. The quality-control inspector can reject products that do not meet his or her standards.

After the groups select a supervisor, that person organizes the workers and sets up the assembly line. The quality-control inspector is free to inspect the work at any point and should examine all completed replicas. Any replica that does not meet his or her standards is thrown into the trash.

As the factory begins operation, the students acting as supervisors are transformed from friendly classmates into unrelenting bosses; the student acting as the quality-control inspector becomes the hated top boss, as he or she ruthlessly rips up poor reproductions and throws them into the trash.

After the simulation has been completed (perhaps twenty or thirty minutes), a class discussion focuses on the following questions:

- How did you feel while working on the assembly line? Why?
- Did you find the work monotonous and boring? Why or why not?
- What problems did you encounter on your assembly line? Why was this a problem?
- What was your attitude toward your supervisor? Why?
- What was your attitude toward the quality control inspector? Why?
- What was your attitude toward your fellow workers? Why?
- What would it be like to have to do this kind of work for ten or twelve hours a day, day in and day out? Why?
- Have you ever had a job that is like this kind of work? What was it? How was it like this kind of work?

The discussion is extremely important in helping students put the experience they have just had into a context that will help them empathize with the main character. In other words, it prepares them for reading the story and promotes empathy with the main character because they have gained insight into the problems he faces working on an assembly line.

Like simulations, role playing activities ask students to imagine themselves in situations similar to those experienced by characters in a work of literature. However, while simulations attempt to recreate an experience in the classroom or make it as close to an actual experience as possible, role-playing activities are somewhat more removed from the reality of an experience. As with the simulation activity described above, the actual role playing itself is only the first step. The discussion that follows a role-playing activity is just as important as the experience of playing a role. For instance, Smagorinsky (1993) suggests a role-playing activity for students who are reading about cultural conflicts (i.e., Chinua Achebe's "A Man of the People," Pearl S. Buck's "The Frill," Christopher Isherwood's *The Berlin Stories*, Joseph Conrad's *Heart of Darkness*, and E. M. Forester's *Passage to India*). Smagorinsky indicates that students might role play situations in which characters from different cultures come into contact with each other. In the classroom, a teacher would assign students to pairs or small groups and give them different situations in which two or more people from different cultures come into contact, and their task is to role play the situation in front of the class. It would be helpful to provide students with some additional information about the cultures that they will have to deal with as they role play characters in their assigned situations. Once students have had a chance to role play at least one situation, the next step is to lead a discussion that focuses on what happened in the role play and how they felt in the situation. This discussion gives students insights into the issues that the main characters will face in the literature.

## Writing about Personal Experiences and Related Problems

Students can write informally—perhaps in journals, reading logs, or "quick writes"—about experiences that are similar to those of the characters they will encounter in the literature. These writing tasks prepare the students for discussion. In addition, Smagorinsky (2002) maintains that the act of writing can promote reflection about important experiences that will help students make connections to the problems confronted by the characters. A focused writing prompt will help students think about personal experiences that may contribute to their understanding of these concepts and problems and prepare them for discussion. For example, if students were going to read literature dealing with the theme of friendship, they might be given a choice of writing prompts that cover a range of suggestions:

1. Describe an experience you have had in which another person you thought was your friend turned out not to be. What did this person do to reveal that he or she was not a true friend?

2. Describe an experience you have had in which a good friendship nearly fell apart but managed to survive. What caused the friendship to nearly fall apart? How was it saved?

3. Describe an experience in which your best friend asked you to do something wrong and told you that if you are his/her best friend you will do this wrong thing. What did you do and why? Did your friendship survive? Why or why not?

An alternative activity involving personal experience writing would ask students to interview a significant person in their lives about friendship and then prepare a narrative about that other person's experience. As a follow-up activity, students gather in small groups, read their narratives aloud, and then pick one that they think is the most interesting to share with the whole class. In this way, students see a variety of examples of possible behaviors to prepare them for feeling and thinking about the problems experienced by the literary characters.

Walter (adapted from Johannessen, Kahn, and Walter 1984) offers an example of an activity that can serve as an introduction to John Steinbeck's *The Pearl*. A common challenge for many adolescent readers is relating to some of the problems faced by the main character, Kino. To prepare for discussion, each student draws one of the following prompts:

1. What if this happened to you? Your father has just won the millionaire's drawing of the state lottery. How do you think this will affect your family? What kinds of things will your family do with the money? What would you like your father to do with the money? Would you like anything specifically for yourself? If so, what, and why do you want it? If not, why not?

2. What if this happened to you? You have had the same best friend since grade school. You feel that you really understand your friend and have a close relationship. After being elected to the student council, your friend seems to develop a new set of interests. You believe that your

friend has changed; you do not understand him or her anymore. How do you feel about this? What do you do? Why?

3. What if this happened to you? You are very good in art. You have spent a long time on a painting that everyone says is very good. Your art teacher urges you to sell it to an art dealer and suggests $85 is a reasonable price to expect. You try selling your painting to the three art dealers in your area. Each of them offers you only $35. You have the feeling that they are making this low offer because you are "just a teenager. "How do you feel about this? What do you do? Why?

Each of these situations has its parallel to a problem Kino faces in *The Pearl*. Kino, too, faces discrimination, the desertion of friends, and the decision of what to do with sudden wealth.

Each student independently writes a response to one prompt. After students have written their paragraphs, they share their writing and enter a class discussion about the different problems and various solutions and feelings students wrote about in their paragraphs. At the end of the discussion, if the teacher alerts the students that Kino faces similar problems in the novel, they are likely to be motivated to find out how the main character handles the situations that they wrote about and discussed.

## A Pathway to Authentic Discussions of Literature

Many times it is difficult to engage students in authentic discussion because they struggle to make meaningful connections to the literature we ask them to read in school. Introductory activities are a powerful tool for engaging students in purposeful discussions that prepare them for the reading and analysis of literature. What stands out is that when students engage in these activities, they make rich connections to literature.

It is important to recognize that introductory activities are not going to solve all of our problems with teaching literature. However, the kinds of discussions that result from introductory activities can enliven literary study, help students learn how to read and interpret literature, and help them become more independent learners. Introductory activities help to focus the classroom on the students and their own inquiry, giving them a more active voice and lessening their reliance on the teacher.

# 7 Discussion That Extends Our Experience with Literature

The previous chapter models ways to prepare students to engage in a meaningful way in discussions about the literature that they study in common. The preparation taps students' prior knowledge, constructs critical frameworks, and equips students with language and procedures for negotiating the meaning they derive from texts. Even with the preparation for reading and discussion, however, we find ourselves working consciously at keeping discussions from lapsing into recitation. The following examples reveal the potential for decline, and we suggest some strategies for involving students in working with each other to explore the meanings they can derive from the literature. Examine the following excerpts from two different classes focusing on the poem "Fame is a bee" by Emily Dickinson. The four-line poem is an extended metaphor comparing fame to a bee because of its "song," "sting," and "wing."

**Class A**

*Teacher:* What is a metaphor?

*Student 1:* It's when you say "like" or "as."

*Teacher:* Well . . . that's a simile. What about a metaphor?

*Student 2:* It's a comparison without using *like* or *as*.

*Teacher:* Yes, "the world's a stage." As opposed to, "The world is *like* a stage." What's the metaphor in this poem by Emily Dickinson?

*Student 3:* It says, "Fame is a bee."

*Teacher:* Good. How is fame a bee? Why does the poet compare fame to a bee?

*Student 3:* It has a song, a sting, and a wing.

*Teacher:* Yes, great! Do you know what the term is for a metaphor, like this, that is developed over several lines or, as in this case, the entire poem?
[*Silence.*]
It's called an *extended* metaphor. So what is the meaning of this extended metaphor?

[*Silence.*]

Okay, why does the poet say that fame has song? What does that mean?

*Student 4:* I'm not sure. Does fame mean, like famous?

*Teacher:* Yes. What does it mean to have song?

*Student 4:* Maybe that when you're famous you're happy and singing all the time.

*Teacher:* Good. What about a sting. What would that mean?

*Student 2:* Isn't that that fame can be bad, like a sting?

*Teacher:* Good. So, fame has its positive side, song, and its negative side, a sting. Isn't that so true! Fame can bring a lot of attention, favors, and adoring fans. But don't you think that might get old? Famous people have no privacy; their every move can be plastered all over the tabloids. That might not be so pleasant after awhile. What aspect of fame is shown by saying it has a wing?

*Student 5:* It can fly away.

*Teacher:* Yes, good. You can have fame one day and lose it the next. You can be a beautiful young star, but that won't last forever.

**Class B**

*Teacher:* What do you think this poem is about?

*Students:* [*Several students answer at once.*] Fame.

*Teacher:* What about fame?

*Student 1:* I don't know. Is fame, like famous?

*Teacher: Fame* is the noun form of *famous*. Someone who **has** fame **is** famous. What do you think the poem is saying about fame?

*Student 1:* It says it's a bee.

*Teacher:* A bee?

*Student 1:* Yeah, I'm not sure what that means. It's a bee.

*Students:* [*Several answer together.*] It doesn't make sense. Yeah, it's dumb. Is this for real? It only has four lines.

*Teacher:* Okay, those are some points we'll need to come back to. Any ideas? What is the poem saying about fame?

*Student 2:* It's a bee because it has a song, a sting, and a wing. That doesn't make sense. What does that mean?

*Teacher:* Can anyone address that? What does "It has song" mean?

*Student 3:* Maybe, it's like it is happy, like you feel if you're famous.

*Teacher:* Happy?

*Student 3:* Yeah, you feel good; people admire you, look up to you.

*Teacher:* What about "a sting"?

*Student 4:* It hurts you. Fame can hurt you.

*Teacher:* Hurt you; how can that be?

*Student 4:* Maybe you lose all your money, and you're no longer rich.

*Teacher:* So you're saying fame could make you lose all your money?

*Student 4:* Well, yeah, maybe not fame, but you could not have fame any more and lose all your money. I don't know . . .

*Teacher:* Okay. Any other ideas? Fame has a sting—[Student 4] said it could hurt you.

*Student 5:* You could be followed around by reporters all the time, trying to spy on you.

*Student 1:* People might rob you because they know you have a lot of money.

*Student 6:* And jealousy.

*Teacher:* Jealousy?

*Student 6:* People could be jealous of you and hate you, like, because they aren't famous.

In each of the two classes, about the same number of students participate in this segment of the discussion of the poem. The teacher asks questions or participates about the same number of times in each class. Also, the students seem to be operating at a similar level of sophistication in terms of their understanding of literature and this poem in particular.

Yet the nature of the student responses differs in the two classes. Class A is engaged in a question-and-answer session following the traditional initiate-respond-evaluate (IRE) pattern. In the IRE pattern, conversation proceeds with the teacher *initiating* a question that has a predetermined answer, the student providing a *response*, and the teacher *evaluating* the adequacy of the response. Notice that in Class A, student responses tend to be unelaborated. The teacher tends to elaborate on student answers in such a way as to take over the role of making the higher-order interpretations rather than encouraging students to articulate the interpretations (i.e., "So, fame has its positive side, song, and its negative side, a sting. Isn't that so true! Fame can bring a lot of attention, favors, and adoring fans. But don't you think that might get old? Famous people have no privacy; their every move can be plastered all over the tabloids. That might not be so pleasant after awhile.").

Class B is engaged in a more authentic discussion of the poem—the teacher engages the students in a collaborative process of interpreting the poem. The teacher begins with an open-ended question: "What do you think this poem is about?" After that, the teacher allows students' comments to set the agenda for the discussion. When a student says that the poem is about fame, the teacher then asks, "What about fame?" When a student asks what it means that fame has song, the teacher asks the class if anyone can help in explaining this.

In contrast to Class A, the teacher in Class B prompts students to elaborate rather than elaborating for them. The teacher does not suggest that there is a predetermined answer. For example, she says, "Hurt you: how can that be?" A student replies, "Maybe you lose all your money, and you're no longer rich." The teacher continues to follow up by asking for further clarification: "So you're saying fame could make you lose all your money?" The teacher appears to see an inconsistency with the student's interpretation that a harm caused by fame could be "losing all your money." By asking the student to elaborate, she encourages the student to reflect further on her own statement ("Well, yeah, maybe not fame, but you could not have fame any more and lose all your money. I don't know . . .").

At one point, when students in Class B begin to show frustration with the poem ("It doesn't make sense," "It's dumb," etc.), the teacher accepts their ideas ("Okay, those are some points we'll need to come back to.") but brings the conversation back to the point that was previously being addressed ("What is the poem saying about fame?"). In this way, the teacher keeps the conversation focused but continues to let student responses guide the direction of the discussion. In Class A, however, it is the teacher's questions that determine the direction of the "discussion." As a result, it becomes an IRE session rather than an authentic discussion.

As discussed in Chapter 1, recent research has demonstrated a strong connection between discussion-based approaches—those in which students frequently engage in authentic discussion—and student achievement in English language arts (Applebee, Langer, Nystrand, and Gamoran 2003; Langer 2001a, 2001b; Nystrand 1997). Unfortunately, the studies of classrooms reported in Chapter 1 reveal that most classroom "discussion" is actually the IRE question-answer format.

## Generating Authentic Discussion of Literature

So why is authentic discussion so rare, and most important, what can we do to generate more authentic literature discussions in our classrooms? How, also, does participation in authentic discussion deepen students' understanding of the literature that they read?

First, unless teachers understand what authentic discussion is, value authentic discussion, make a deliberate effort to engage students in it, and can accurately evaluate the extent to which it has and has not occurred in their classrooms, it is unlikely that it will happen consistently. We've each had experiences observing a class in which a teacher led an IRE recitation and concluded, "That was a really great discussion today." We've found that many teachers who have not been directly involved in analysis of the differences between authentic discussion and IRE recitation believe they have had a good discussion when (1) students are prepared for class, having read the material, etc., (2) many students are volunteering answers, and (3) students are generally attentive and on task, even if the nature of the interaction has actually been an IRE recitation.

In addition, given the pervasiveness of the IRE pattern, after many years of schooling, secondary students may have come to expect the teacher to do most of the significant talking in the classroom. They may have experienced the IRE pattern so frequently that it is firmly engrained. Marshall, Smagorinsky, and Smith (1995) see the traditional pattern of classroom conversation as what Bakhtin refers to as a "speech genre" that becomes "'privileged,' or widely and perhaps dogmatically accepted as the 'right' way of communicating in particular settings" (1986, 7). Therefore, students may believe that classroom conversation is supposed to follow this pattern with the teacher asking questions to test them on their knowledge, students giving brief answers, and then the teacher commenting or elaborating—often at length—on the accuracy and sufficiency of their answers (Johannessen and Kahn 2005). We've experienced situations where some students have felt shortchanged when their peers, instead of the teacher, were doing most of the talking because they felt the teacher's knowledge and comments would be more "educational" than their peers'.

Student personalities can have a significant influence on the frequency and level of authentic discussion. Over many years of teaching, we have sometimes had classes in which the students are unusually quiet and very hesitant to talk. They sometimes have overwhelming concerns about how others will perceive them. Other classes are so talk-ative that it is a challenge to get them to take turns talking, to listen to each other, and not to talk over each other.

Another significant impediment to authentic discussion is students who have not read the literature that is the focus of that day's discussion. It is particularly difficult when only a portion of the class has read a text in preparation for class and another portion has not. Finally, participating in a discussion—especially within a large group of twenty-five to thirty people—takes a certain amount of effort and energy on the part of the students as well as the teacher. At times there just doesn't seem to be any momentum (Johannessen and Kahn 2005).

On occasion, authentic discussion occurs serendipitously. For example, Christoph and Nystrand (2001) describe one class in which IRE recitation tended to dominate. However, in one discussion of *A Midsummer Night's Dream,* the teacher asked students who they thought was the most important person in the play. Immediately, four students offered markedly different responses, leading to a debate in which over half of the class contributed vocally and those who did not participate vocally were unusually attentive and engaged. As the teacher encouraged students to present and defend their different viewpoints, the exchange among students turned into an instance of authentic discussion. Although this discussion ran only 2:41 minutes long, Christoph and Nystrand (2001) report that it had a disproportionately large effect on students for the rest of the semester. For weeks after the discussion, several students continued to mention it to each other in passing between classes. This incident illustrates the power of authentic discussion on students. It has a strong and lasting impact on students' engagement and understanding.

But what can we as teachers do rather than just wait for the serendipitous?

## Approaching the Classroom as a Forum for Collaborative Inquiry

In the above classroom interchange on "Fame is a bee," the teacher of Class A appears to see his role as the "pathfinder" who leads students toward a predetermined understanding of the poem (Marshall, Smagorinsky, and Smith 1995; see also Chapter 9). He doesn't appear to see discussion as an opportunity to involve students in an exploration of different interpretations and to engage them as participants in critical conversation about the poem (Graff 1992).

Unless the teacher's goal is to have students grapple with a text and engage in a process of inquiry, then the environment is not going to be conducive to authentic discussion. But what about questions that have a definite answer? Are we suggesting that there are never misreadings of a text? How can a teacher take an inquiry approach without suggesting that "anything goes" in reading a text?

Consider the widely anthologized short story "The Most Dangerous Game" by Richard Connell. Many of the ninth-grade students that we teach are confused about the ending of the story, which requires them to make several inferences. The ending states:

> Rainsford did not smile. "I am still a beast at bay," he said, in a low, hoarse voice. "Get ready, General Zaroff."
>
> The general made one of his deepest bows. "I see," he said. "Splendid! One of us is to furnish a repast for the hounds. The other will sleep in this very excellent bed. On guard, Rainsford . . . ."
>
> He had never slept in a better bed, Rainsford decided. (*Elements of Literature* 2005, 22)

After reading the story, our students almost always enter the classroom saying, "What happened at the end?" "Does Zaroff die?" Before discussing the story, we ask students to write a summary of what they think happens at the end (after Rainsford jumps out into the sea). Responses usually vary. Some students conclude that Rainsford hides in Zaroff's room and shoots him. Some decide that Zaroff lets Rainsford live because he won the game. Some conclude that the two men have a sword fight. Some argue that the text doesn't indicate what happens to the two men. A number believe that Rainsford kills Zaroff, but most do not say anything about Rainsford tossing Zaroff's remains to the dogs (even though most of the textbook versions provide a footnote defining *repast*).

We read aloud or list the different possibilities that students come up with on the board (without identifying students' names). We then invite a discussion, letting students explain what they think happened, what didn't happen, and what evidence supports their views. We work hard to avoid evaluating answers and instead leave it to the students to address a comment such as, "It doesn't tell what happens to Zaroff." We have always had students finally arrive at a consensus about what happens at the end after they have listened to all the evidence that emerges in the discussion. The discussion of the ending also typically leads to another question: Whether Rainsford will take over General Zaroff's place or whether he will reject Zaroff's theory that "the weak of the world were put here to give the strong pleasure" (14). This question easily lends itself to authentic discussion as students provide evidence to support their views.

One strategy that teachers can use to encourage authentic discussion—one that works even at the level of figuring out "what happens" in a work—is "polling the class," asking students to write their responses to a specific question or questions and turn them in. The teacher can then quickly sort through the responses, compile the results, and display them for the class. Of course, no names are identified. Students are then asked in discussion to evaluate the various responses and to provide supporting evidence from the text. Usually, simply asking students to state their responses orally in class does not produce the variation that occurs when students each write their ideas individually and turn them in and, therefore, does not illicit as much discussion.

## Showing Students That There Are Different Levels of Questions

Sometimes it is difficult to engage secondary students in authentic discussion of literature because, depending on the type of instruction that they are used to, they may think that there really isn't anything to discuss. Their reasoning is that there are right answers and wrong answers, and it is the teacher's job to see who knows the right answers and to make sure that those who don't are corrected. Or they think that questions have no right or wrong answers, it's whatever the reader thinks. So, therefore, what's the point of giving or listening to answers when all of them are right?

We have found that in these cases it is helpful to show students that there are different types of questions one could ask based on relationships among reader, author, and text. There are a number of different question hierarchies or taxonomies that work effectively with secondary students (see, for example, Chapter 9). One we have used that is fairly simple and works well, especially with younger students, is Raphael's (1982) "Question-Answer Relationships (QAR)" (Figure 7.1). One purpose of showing students the QARs is to illustrate that while there are some questions with definite right or wrong answers clearly present in the text, there are also questions that involve inferences and interpretation.

To illustrate the QARs, we have used the poem "Base Details" by Siegfried Sassoon (1918).

### Base Details

If I were fierce, and bald, and short of breath,
    I'd live with scarlet Majors at the Base,
And speed glum heroes up the line to death.
    You'd see me with my puffy petulant face,

Guzzling and gulping in the best hotel,
    Reading the Roll of Honour. "Poor young chap,"
I'd say—"I used to know his father well;
    Yes, we've lost heavily in this last scrap."
And when the war is done and youth stone dead,
I'd toddle safely home and die—in bed.

                —Siegfried Sassoon

We ask students to read the poem and respond to six questions and determine where each falls on the QAR matrix:

1. What do the "scarlet Majors at the Base" do?

2. What does *base* mean? What does *petulant* mean?

3. What is the "Roll of Honour?"

4. What is the meaning of the title?

5. Is the speaker of the poem praising the majors or criticizing them? Provide supporting evidence from the poem for your viewpoint.

6. What comment is Sassoon making about war? Provide supporting evidence from the poem for your viewpoint.

We then ask students to share their responses. Students usually point out that the answer to the first question (What do the "scarlet Majors at the Base" do?) is "Right There" in the text. They say that the majors "send soldiers to war," "send men to die in battle," and "drink beer in hotels." They point out that Question 2 (What does *base* mean? What does *petulant* mean?) is "On My Own" and not in the text, particularly if one asks students to give meanings of *base* in addition to a military

| IN THE BOOK QARs | IN MY HEAD QARs |
| --- | --- |
| **Right There**<br>The answer is in the text, usually easy to find. The words used in the question and the words used to answer the question are **Right There**, close together in the text. | **Author and You**<br>The answer is *not* in the text. You need to think about what you already know, what the author tells you in the text, and how it fits together. |
| **Think and Search** (Putting It Together)<br>The answer is in the story, but you need to put together different story parts to find it. Words for the question and words for the answer come from different parts of the text. | **On My Own**<br>The answer is *not* in the text. You can answer the question without reading the text. You need to use your own experience and prior knowledge. |

**Figure 7.1.** Question-answer relationships (QAR). Taken from T. E. Raphael, "Question-Answering Strategies for Children," *The Reading Teacher* 36 (1982): 186–90.

base. For Question 3 (What is the "Roll of Honour"?), students tend to either see it as "Right There" or "Think and Search" or "On My Own," usually depending on how easily they were able to figure it out. Questions 4 and 5 (What is the meaning of the title? Is the speaker of the poem praising the majors or criticizing them? Provide supporting evidence from the poem for your viewpoint.) illustrate "Think and Search." The final question (What comment is Sassoon making about war? Provide supporting evidence from the poem for your viewpoint.) illustrates an "Author and You" question because it asks students to infer a generalization from the fabric of the poem as a whole.

Of course, it is not important whether students identify a "right" QAR; some are, of course, arguable. What is important is that students explain their thinking and try to describe processes they used in searching for answers to the questions.

Our purpose in conducting this kind of discussion is to illustrate for students that the answers to questions about texts aren't always "right there." Some are, but some of the most important questions and those that are most worth discussing aren't; they involve interpretation. Also we hope to illustrate that for some questions there isn't just one answer, but that some interpretations may not hold up well upon critical examination and debate. For example, some students will begin by arguing that the poem is praising the majors because they are fighting a war, which is a heroic and courageous thing for anyone to do. However, other students challenge this interpretation by pointing out that the majors send the young soldiers to die while they have an easy, comfortable life. As students explore these two possible interpretations, they usually all come to realize ultimately that the latter is more defensible based on the evidence in the poem. Our purpose is to help students see how discussion can be a process of collaboratively "figuring out" or constructing meaning (Johannessen and Kahn 2005).

## Using the Uptake Technique

*Uptake* comes from the work of Marshall, Smagorinsky, and Smith (1995) and Nystrand (1997). It has been shown to be an effective way to generate and sustain authentic discussion. Uptake provides an alternative to the IRE pattern. Uptake involves turning a student response into a statement or a question in order to encourage further elaboration.

To illustrate this strategy, we will use a discussion of the poem "Base Details." The teacher begins a discussion of the poem by asking students to think about who's described in the poem and what we learn about them.

> *Mona:* The majors are described.
>
> *Teacher:* Okay, the majors are described. In what way?
>
> *Mona:* Fierce, bald, and short of breath.
>
> *Teacher:* Okay, fierce, bald, short of breath.
>
> *Jen:* Scarlet
>
> *Mike:* But wait, that's not . . . it's "I."
>
> *Teacher:* It's I?
>
> *Mike:* "If *I* were fierce, and bald, and short of breath." It's not the majors.
>
> *Teacher:* So someone . . . the speaker of the poem . . . I? So what do you make of that?
>
> *Mike:* I'm not sure.
>
> *Teacher:* Any ideas?
>
> *Mary Kay:* The "I," I guess the author, says that if he were fierce and bald then he'd be like the majors because that's what they are. He's saying, "I'd be like them."
>
> *Teacher:* So the majors *are* fierce and bald and short of breath?
>
> *Mary Kay:* Yes, and they send young heroes to die.
>
> *Teacher:* So, they send young heroes to die. So you're saying the speaker would want to be like the majors.
>
> *Mary Kay:* Yeah. Well, not to send people to die. Well, sort of . . . he doesn't want to be like the ones who die.
>
> *Teacher:* So the speaker would want to be like the majors and not like the "glum heroes." What else did you come up with about the majors?
>
> *Sammy:* They sit in hotels and drink a lot.
>
> *Teacher:* They drink. How is that described?
>
> *Marta:* Guzzling and gulping.
>
> *Teacher:* Guzzling and gulping, sort of sounds like . . .
>
> *Marta:* [*Others join in as well.*] Gross. Disgusting. Drunk.

Notice that in this exchange, the teacher sometimes restates the student's comment as a way to encourage further elaboration. For example, Mary Kay says that the majors "send young heroes to die." The teacher responds, "So, they send young heroes to die. So you're saying the speaker would want to be like the majors." This leads Mary Kay to further elaborate: "Yeah. Well, not to send people to die. Well, sort of . . . he doesn't want to be like the ones who die." Or sometimes the teacher restates the student response as a question: "So the majors *are* fierce and bald and short of breath?" The teacher also uses uptake by letting the student responses guide the direction of the conversation. When a student makes the point that the poem has a speaker who is speculating about what he would do, the teacher then pursues this idea by saying, "So someone . . . the speaker of the poem . . . I? So what do you make of that?"

In brief, uptake involves responding to students in ways that are neutral and nonevaluative and that therefore promote further elaboration by students. One important aspect of uptake involves deferring praise, which is discussed in Chapter 2, since praise tends to imply closure and discourage further student responses. As suggested in Chapter 2, in following up a student response, the teacher can either say nothing, while conveying a look that says "That's interesting," or make a neutral comment, such as "Interesting observation," "That's another viewpoint," "I hadn't thought of that," "That's a point we need to consider," and so forth. Or the teacher can restate the student response either as a statement or as a question. This strategy can be used with individual students or with the whole class.

If we as teachers accept all responses without evaluating them, what about ideas or interpretations that are problematic? For example, as discussed above, what if a student says that the majors are courageous because they are fighting a war? The teacher can use uptake in this situation, too, by accepting the response: "Okay, we have some who are saying the majors are courageous, and others who are seeing them more as cowards." This invites further discussion. Concentrating on using uptake consistently is one way that we have found to help avoid slipping into an IRE pattern during discussions.

## Asking Broader, More Open-Ended Questions That Focus on a Key Issue or Interpretive Problem

Uptake works best when used with the strategy of asking broader, more open-ended questions that focus on a key issue or interpretive problem. Let's return to the discussion of "Fame is a bee." The teacher in Class A began the discussion with the following questions: What is a metaphor? What's the metaphor used in this poem by Emily Dickinson? How is fame a bee? Why does the poet compare fame to a bee? These questions tend to promote an IRE pattern of response.

The teacher could begin a discussion of "Base Details" by asking, "What are the meanings of *base*? Who is the speaker of the poem? How does the poem use irony?" But these kinds of questions are likely to lead to IRE.

An alternative approach is to pose a broad, open-ended question that focuses on a significant issue or interpretive problem, give students some time to think about their responses, and perhaps have students work with others briefly in collaborative pairs or small groups before attempting to run a class discussion (see also Holden and Schmit 2002). For "Base Details," one might ask students, "Who is described in this poem, and what do we learn about them?" With this approach, students have an opportunity to prepare responses. It is also likely that students will have different ideas to contribute, as the excerpts above illustrate.

In selecting texts and developing focusing questions for discussion, teachers need to have a good understanding of their students. Elizabeth knew from using "Base Details" in the past that a key interpretive problem for students is understanding the relationship between the speaker of the poem and the majors described. The students have difficulty interpreting the irony. She knew that a question such as "How does the poem use irony to make a point?" would not be effective in generating an authentic discussion. Most students would have little to say. They might say, "I can't remember what irony is." But most likely, even given a definition, they would not generate many ideas. One student might give a response explaining the irony and the others would probably just say, "That sounds good." Also, a question like this that is frequently found in textbooks cues the students that the poem is ironic and takes away the opportunity for the students to make this realization themselves.

Elizabeth felt that asking students who is described and what they learn about them would generate a number of different ideas and would lead students eventually to interpret the irony in the poem, as they examined the details. In order for a discussion to work, the teacher has to design key questions for the particular students and context—keeping in mind the students' age level, sophistication, interests, reading skills, social relationships, and so forth (Johannessen and Kahn 2005).

## Designing Student-Run Discussions

Another strategy for encouraging more authentic discussion of literature is to help students learn to run and participate in discussions on their own without the teacher leading. Holden and Schmit (2002) provide detailed descriptions of how to create successful Socratic seminars.

A variation on this approach is the fishbowl. Elizabeth uses this strategy with her ninth-grade classes, which tend to be large (around thirty students). She divides the class into four groups of seven to eight students each. Each group is given an open-ended question on which to focus.

At the end of a unit on heroes in Greek mythology and *The Odyssey*, she has used the following questions:

- Who is the greatest of the Greek mythic heroes? Provide supporting evidence for your viewpoint. Why is the hero you have chosen superior to each other possible candidate?

- Which of the Greek heroes makes the most significant mistake(s)? Provide supporting evidence for your viewpoint. Why is the mistake(s) you have chosen worse or more significant than other mistakes by Greek heroes?

- Who is the most heroic woman of Greek mythology? Provide supporting evidence for your viewpoint. Why is the woman you have chosen superior to each other possible candidate?

- Which of the Greek heroes is the cleverest and most intelligent? Provide supporting evidence for your viewpoint. Why is the hero you have chosen superior to each of the others in terms of cleverness and intelligence?

Each student is responsible for examining the question given to his or her group and then preparing a response and notes or highlighting for the discussion. We explain to the class that the group discussion should proceed without the teacher doing any direction or giving any input. We suggest that the groups each select a moderator to make sure that everyone gets a chance to speak, to ask questions of the other group members in order to clarify points, or to bring someone into the discussion who has not participated, etc. We also suggest that they may want to start the discussion by having each group member briefly present his or her viewpoint and then open up the discussion for response.

Another activity that works well at this point is to have the class collaboratively develop a rubric for evaluating the fishbowl discussions. Students can begin by answering a question such as "What will we observe happening in the best discussions?" We list ideas on the board or on the overhead, developing them into specific criteria for a good discussion. These criteria can then be used by the teacher and students in evaluating the strengths and weaknesses of each discussion.

The groups are given about five to ten minutes to organize. Then, one of the groups sits in a circle in the middle of the room. The rest of the class forms a circle around them. Students in the outer circle are responsible for writing down comments or ideas that they want to respond to after the group concludes their discussion. The first group then begins. It usually seems to work best, especially when students are novices at this type of discussion, when each group member briefly presents his or her viewpoint. After that, students begin to challenge ideas presented by others and debate tends to ensue. For example, in her opening statement, one student argued that Theseus was the greatest hero because he had less help from the gods than did Perseus, who received a number of tools from the gods, such as a cap of invisibility, winged sandals, and so forth. Later, another student challenged this point, responding that even though Theseus killed the Minotaur without any direct instruments from the gods, he was responsible for the death of his father, which made him less heroic. Many times, the group discussions become quite lively, and students in the outer circle have difficulty waiting to join in. After the group discussion seems to be waning, we then provide a chance for the outside circle to comment on the discussion.

Each group has its turn to be the inner group, to be inside the fishbowl. Usually this activity works best if the teacher chooses a group to start that he or she suspects will provide a strong model for everyone. Then subsequent groups tend to strive to participate at the same level.

The fishbowl activity tends to elicit different viewpoints and arguments. Students can then be asked to think about all the arguments and evidence presented and to write their viewpoint on one of the questions, recognizing counterarguments and counterevidence that were presented in the discussions, and defending their interpretation in light of the challenges to it. At this point, students can also reflect on what they have learned from the discussion about what the Greeks consider heroic and to what extent they agree or disagree.

## Authentic Discussion of Literature

At the heart of what we have argued is the need to find ways of engaging students in collaborative inquiry as they discuss literature. The strategies we have presented have helped us to move away from IRE recitation in order to promote authentic classroom discussion that helps our students construct meaning, achieve deeper understanding, and make connections to literature.

# 8 Joining a Big Conversation: Discussion and Interpretations of Literature

M any English teachers would appreciate classes in which their students vigorously debate each other about the ways in which they have interpreted the literature that they have been asked to read. In the preceding chapters, we suggest ways to support students in interpreting texts and debating their interpretations. Here we provide ways to engage students further by enlarging their perspectives to include issues debated among literary scholars and critics.

Too often, students appear to care very little about how someone else has read a text. If students even recognize that another reading is possible, they seem reluctant to challenge each other. Perhaps they fear being challenged themselves, or perhaps they conceive of arguments about interpretation as rude and disagreeable affairs. If students are willing to entertain someone else's alternative reading of a text, the dominant attitude seems to be this: "You have your interpretation, and I'll have mine; let's not argue about it." In the long run, active discussions, imbued as they often are with argument, help readers to figure out what sense they make of a text and how they judge its merits. It is hard to imagine a serious literary scholar who analyzes a text without regard to what past and contemporary readers have had to say about the same text. Discussion about interpretations, which necessarily involves argument, is crucial to understanding a text and to recognizing where one's interpretations and opinions about a text fit into a broad conversation that has likely been sustained for years.

In many instances, students are hesitant to participate in the broader conversation about interpretations of literature. Furthermore,

An earlier version of this chapter appeared as an article in the *Illinois English Bulletin* 87(3). It is reprinted here by permission of the Illinois Association of Teachers of English.

Johannessen (1998) reports that many teachers operate from a cultural transmission paradigm and seem reluctant to open up dialogue to include multiple perspectives. How can teachers assure students that it is all right to argue, especially when the discussion focuses on the interpretation and judgment about texts? How can teachers foster an environment in which students recognize that there are several reasonable and legitimate ways to read the same text, and where it matters how one has interpreted that text?

## Simple Texts; Complex Thought

Experience suggests to us that the use of some relatively simple texts, especially selected children's picture books, even in high school and college, can introduce students to the world of intellectual academic discourse, where the participants debate and negotiate the meaning they gather from texts and the value they place on them. The following discussion describes the use of two picture books: Dr. Seuss's *And to Think That I Saw It on Mulberry Street* (1937) and Shel Silverstein's *The Giving Tree* (1964). These texts are useful because they are problematic and controversial. Students are likely to read them in a variety of ways and are willing to argue energetically about their interpretations of the texts and the value they place on them. Every reader is bound to read a text in a way that is at least slightly different from the way others have read the same text. All readers' prior knowledge and past experiences will influence how they recall a text and how they value characters, actions, and themes.

The work of Chiesi, Spilich, and Voss (1979) illustrates that readers' prior knowledge will influence how they recall and make sense of a text. In their experiments, when a researcher read to subjects a description of an inning of baseball, those subjects who had substantive baseball knowledge recalled much about the game situation and strategy; those who knew little about baseball recalled mostly the details surrounding the game: the weather, the clothing of the fans, the vendors in the stands. In other words, the subjects used domain-specific knowledge about the rules and strategies of the game to order their recall. Furthermore, Pichert and Anderson (1977) demonstrate that the directions that one provides for reading a text influence how one experiences and recalls the reading. Specifically, two groups of subjects read the same text, which described the location and features of a house. One group of subjects received directions to read the text as if they were in the market to buy a house; the other group was directed to read the text as if they were burglars. The researchers report that the subjects who received the home buyer instructions recalled such details as the leaky roof, the fireplace, the mildew smell in the basement, and the number of bathrooms. The group with the burglar instructions recalled the presence and location of the furs, the coin collection, the stereo, and the ten-speed bicycles. The prompts clearly influenced how the subjects read the text. The results offer good news and bad news for teachers who provide focus questions for reading, but the experiment demonstrates that the teacher can influence and exaggerate the variety of ways that students read a text, thus producing circumstances ripe for discussion and debate.

Using popular children's picture books to model academic discourse holds three attractions: (1) The text can be read quickly so that everyone in a class can assume mastery of the reading before discussion. (2) Many students are familiar with other works by the same author, which enables the reader to make connections to other texts and conjecture about the author's intent. (3) If students fondly remember the author from their childhood reading experience, they are sensitive to attacks against him or her and can easily be provoked into debate.

The first example involves the use of Dr. Seuss's *And to Think I Saw It on Mulberry Street*. Here are the procedures:

1. Each student receives a one-paragraph prompt. (The four prompts follow below.) The teacher instructs the students to read the prompts silently. The teacher cautions the students not to share the "secret" prompt with anyone. After reading the prompt, the student writes a brief response: Do you agree with the ideas expressed in the paragraph? Why? Do you disagree with the ideas? Why? The students then submit their written responses to the teacher.

2. The teacher then reads aloud Dr. Seuss's *And to Think That I Saw It on Mulberry Street*. As the teacher reads, he or she pauses occasionally to display the illustrations.

3. After reading the story aloud, the teacher distributes a copy of the story to all the students (A text only version is available on the internet). The teacher directs the students to read the story again silently.

4. After the students have read the story, the teacher instructs them to write an explanation of the meaning of the story: "It is customary for

the writers of children's stories to use the narrative and the accompanying illustrations to teach children a lesson. In this case, what lesson or message do you get from reading the story?"

5. After the students have produced their written responses, they arrange their desks into a large circle.

6. The teacher selects someone at random to begin the discussion: "What do you think is the meaning of the story? What message did you get from your reading?"

7. Each subsequent speaker can continue only after he or she has paraphrased the response of the previous speaker.

8. After the discussion, the students will return to their initial written response to the story and reconsider: Would you change anything? Do any of the other interpretations that you heard have any merit? Why, or why not? Have you been influenced by the discussion?

Before the students actually hear or read the Dr. Seuss text, they respond to the prompts listed on page 90, which are intended to exaggerate the differences in interpretation. The initial conversation about the story reveals the influence of the prompts, with some readers seeing a positive message that celebrates imagination, while others see a warning that cautions readers not to exaggerate. Initially, students are willing to offer contrasting interpretations but are not yet invested in the significance of trying to negotiate with others some limits as to how one reads the story.

There is certainly an artificiality to using the prereading prompts as a device to encourage discussion; but when students are not inclined to explore with others the various possibilities for the interpretation of a text, the structured means for prompting discussion influences students to extend their thinking and to care about how they and their classmates read a text. In using the prompts, the teacher helps to establish the environment that demands that students engage with others in the negotiation about how to read the story. Along with the prompt, the students receive these instructions: "Please answer the following questions: Do you agree with the ideas expressed in the paragraph? Why? Do you disagree with the ideas? Why?"

### *Mulberry Street* **Prompts**

1.  Delusions are dangerous. Each person must guard against imagining things that do not *really* exist. Of course we all have dreams and fantasies, but we need to separate fantasy from reality. A person should not live in a dream world. Someone would clearly jeopardize his or her physical and emotional well being by imagining and acting upon things that were not really there. It is likely that an habitual dreamer would alienate (i.e., turn away) other persons, who are bound to think the dreamer is crazy.

2.  Children have vivid imaginations that support their creativity and mental health. When children are very young, they can imagine unusual places, people, and circumstances. Look at a child's drawings some time. They are very comfortable in drawing an orange sky and a purple cow. This does not mean that they have vision problems or that they are crazy. As each person grows older, he or she loses some of that ability to imagine, until we reach the point of focusing only on practical, dull, everyday concerns.

3.  An important function for parents is to keep their children firmly grounded in reality. For example, when a child sees a cartoon character fall from a cliff and get up to walk away, the child must realize that this cannot really happen. It would be dangerous for children to think that persons could *really* fly like Superman. A parent has a responsibility to help a child to make the distinction between fantasy and reality. A *limited* amount of dreaming might be harmless, but when the dreaming becomes exaggerated, a parent *must* intervene to make the child realize the reality of a situation.

4.  Parents are often at fault for suppressing their children's imaginations. It is healthy for young children to engage in dreaming and imagining. Their fantasies provide a means for them to make sense of the world. Children use fantasies to express their hopes and their fears. Parents often lack sensitivity to those needs. Adults often discourage a child's imaginings because the adult must focus on the drudgery of everyday concerns. It is neither fair nor healthy for adults to judge children by adult standards.

Of course, students are able to express a series of slightly different interpretations, and they are able to paraphrase the observations of other readers, but so what? At first there is nothing at stake, and it doesn't seem to matter to the students how anyone reads the story. Missing from the discussion is the idea that some readings might be more fully supported by the text than other readings. However, why should we care? As Graff (1992) aptly points out, the controversies surrounding the text, or the notion that some critic might attack the text or its author, provokes students to care about interpretation, to reexamine their own interpretation, and to engage in serious discussion with others. In the case of *Mulberry Street*, critics have challenged the text on the grounds that it contains racist and sexist images. The publisher has apparently been sensitive to these challenges, because there are several changes from the earlier editions to the later "anniversary edition." Notably, in the later edition, the "Chinaman" has now become a "Chineseman," his braided hair has shortened considerably, and his complexion has faded from yellow to white. One can easily find fault with Seuss's ethnic stereotypes. In addition, the reader might wonder why, in the world of *Mulberry Street*, there are no female characters in positions of leadership or responsibility. Not satisfied with his initial imaginative vision, the character Marco notes, "Even *Jane* could think of that." The teacher might introduce the challenges, debate them before the class with another teacher, or present them in the form of a letter of complaint to the publisher. Faced with the challenges, students are introduced to the world of literary criticism and intellectual academic discourse. Students are typically eager to come to Seuss's defense. It is hard for them to accept their beloved Seuss as a racist or sexist. A few students, however, find some merit in the attacks. The energy level, the attention, the eagerness to respond, the willingness to engage in argument, all increase when the students contend with the challenges. In a Vygotskian sense, the reader's "thought bumps into the wall of its own inadequacy" (Vygotsky 1986), and the student strives to reconcile inconsistencies between his or her reading of a text and the contrasting or alternative interpretations of others.

In a similar way, one could use Shel Silverstein's *The Giving Tree* as a subject for introducing a level of academic discourse in students' oral and written discussion. Again, as an initial stage, the teacher prompts each student to read the text from a particular perspective. The following four prompts do influence different readings, exaggerating the contrasts in interpretations to provide the conditions for discussion.

---

### *Giving Tree* Prompts

1. If you consistently do favors and give gifts to other persons, eventually those other persons will begin to take you for granted and expect *you* always to be the one to pay, to give in, and to sacrifice. Although someone might consider your behavior generous, it is actually destructive because you hurt yourself and make others dependent.

2. The world is a better place because some kind persons are *very generous.* Of course, being generous means giving up something that you would value. If you give up things that are really of no value to you, you can hardly be considered generous. Although this kind of sacrifice might be difficult, generosity is a very important trait to develop as you grow older; and children need to learn the importance of generosity when they are young.

3. Some *selfish* persons expect others to give them whatever they want. Selfish persons think so highly of themselves that they cannot imagine someone *not* wanting to give them things. These selfish persons find it impossible to recognize the pain and difficulty of another person's sacrifice. The selfish person cannot put himself or herself in the place of the one making the sacrifice. Everyone will be at least a little selfish at times, but you should learn to reduce your selfishness as you grow older.

4. The worst possible relationship occurs when one person is always giving and sacrificing and the other person is always wanting and taking. At first you would think these two persons are compatible, but actually the relationship is destructive for both. The person who constantly gives will lose self-esteem and feel that only the other person is worthy of comfort, satisfaction, and pleasure. The selfish person will come to expect the sacrifice of the other person and will take him or her for granted.

---

Again, in each case, the prompt asks the students to respond in this way: "Do you agree with the ideas expressed in the paragraph above? Why? Do you disagree with the ideas? Why?"

## Complicating the Problem of Interpretation

The prompts do influence the students' reading, and the variety of views does help to generate discussion. Typically, students read *The Giving Tree* as a story about greed or generosity. Some students read the book as the portrayal of a positive romantic or even parent-child relationship. Others see the story as an illustration of the inevitable separation that occurs as one person changes and the other remains stagnant. But how does one account for the following interpretation?

### Giving Too Much
By I. M. Green

Readers who attempt to make sense of Shel Silverstein's *The Giving Tree* must consider the historical context in which it was produced. Silverstein published the book in 1964. This was a time of heightened sensitivity about the damage that modern industrialized countries were causing to the environment. In this deceptively simple book, Silverstein warns the child and the adult reader that insatiable use of our limited natural resources will leave everyone tired and unsatisfied amidst a barren landscape.

The tree represents Nature itself. It provides beauty, comfort, recreation, sustenance, and commercial resources. The child represents human beings as consumers, entrepreneurs, and industrialists. At first, the relationship between human and Nature is a positive and idealistic one. The boy and the tree appear to cherish each other's company. The tree has much to offer the boy. Its leaves provide shade and comfort. The tree's limb allows the boy to swing, which provides him with recreation. The relationship is so intense and positive that the boy proclaims love for the tree by carving their initials with a heart cut into the tree's bark. Although the relationship appears to be romantic, in the sense of a close harmonious relationship between the individual and his environment, the closeness results in the scarring and defilement of the tree.

As time passes and the boy turns his attention to other interests, he appears to forget and neglect the tree. He abandons the tree until he realizes that the tree can supply a perceived need. When the boy thinks he needs money, the tree provides apples that the boy can sell. Of course, the situation reminds the reader of the human reliance on Nature for sustenance and for the production of food for profit. Seldom does the supplier reflect on the impact that wasteful food production has on the environment. For example, through the persistent growing of only those crops that have the highest cash value, food producers will deplete the minerals and nutrients in the land until the land can produce no more.

Later the boy needs building material, and the tree surrenders her branches to allow the boy to build a home. The image is startling. The once beautiful tree is stripped of its limbs and foliage. Of course, humans strip Nature of any number of resources: timber, coal, minerals, oil, ore. Lumber, oil, and mineral interests care little for the condition of the land and water after they have extracted what they want.

Silverstein suggests that humans are their own worst enemies. They continue to take from Nature until nothing is left. When the boy wants to travel far from the tree, he cuts down the trunk of the tree in order to fashion a boat. All that remains is a stump. The tree does not resist any request, and the boy takes all. Silverstein could hardly anticipate more recent developments, but the deterioration of the ozone layer, especially in the face of many warnings, validates the implied claim that humans neglect and destroy the environment that would sustain them.

It makes sense to read *The Giving Tree* as a warning against ravenous use of natural resources. Like the tree, Nature selflessly supports us. Unlike the boy, humans can become conscious of the danger and heed Silverstein's warning.

Green's interpretation forces the reader to entertain another possibility. Students experience the idea that they can find something of merit in another view, because the critic expresses the view through reasonable arguments; yet, some students may find the new interpretation lacking or unsatisfying. The student incorporates this extension of thought into his or her own analysis.

To complicate matters further, how would students contend with a demand to remove *The Giving Tree* from the shelf of the school library? Students are eager to respond to the critic in Figure 8.1.

While the students might have been complacent initially, they find the charges against Silverstein outrageous and are eager to defend a more positive interpretation. Now the business of reading a simple picture book becomes much more complicated and significant. When there is a threat to take the book out of circulation, how one interprets its message becomes very important. As the following example reveals, the analysis of the text begins by alerting the readers to the need to think about one's interpretation:

> Some readers believe that Shel Silverstein's *The Giving Tree* is about how men have always oppressed women and how women give everything until they have nothing else to give. Some others believe this is a story about a child depending on "mother" and about children growing and drifting away from the parent but always coming back to get something they believe they need. These interpretations of the book are in a way correct, but more generally, the story shows that every day we give ourselves to others.

Dear Teacher:

I urge you to stop reading Shel Silverstein's *The Giving Tree* with your classes, and I recommend that you remove the book from the Learning Center's collection. This book does nothing but promote bad behavior and highlights negative role models whom school age children should avoid.

First, the tree character is female. The book conveys to impressionable young girls that if you want to have friends and have people care for you, you must give away everything of value. What a horrible idea, and what a hideous image of the tree reduced to a stump!

Second, the book promotes greed. The boy never tires of expecting and taking gifts from the tree. But the narrator tells us that "The tree was happy"! The image supports the idea that it is valid for a person to take everything from someone else and leave almost nothing behind.

Finally, I am appalled by the book's portrayal of a relationship between two individuals. The situation in which the tree is "happy" and the boy is satisfied is the essence of a dysfunctional relationship, whether the relationship is boy-girl, man-wife, or parent-child. The book's implication is that happy relationships involve one partner who gives all and another partner who expects and takes all. This dynamic is actually the essence of a destructive relationship, where one person is the victim and the other is the beneficiary. I wouldn't want any child to close the book and retain the impression that Silverstein's story offers a representation of a good relationship.

Children already have a difficult time in forming friendships and establishing positive relationships. I dread to think of the lessons that children are likely to learn from this book. I implore you to stop using it and take it off the shelf.

Respectfully yours,
B. Laver

**Figure 8.1.** A critic of Shel Silverstein's *The Giving Tree* writes a letter to a teacher to condemn it.

The discussion about interpretations of the text reveals that there is a genuine critical problem, and the competing critical perspectives are explicit. Anyone who has attempted to teach young writers to write an introduction by framing an authentic problem recognizes the difficulty. The composing of an effective introduction is no easy task. In his text, *Clueless in Academe,* Graff (2003) discusses what linguist Joseph Williams refers to as the "problem problem." Here is Graff's commentary:

> One reason why students often resist the academic fixation with problems is suggested by Wayne Booth, Gregory Colomb, and Joseph Williams in their valuable primer on academic writing,

*The Craft of Research.* Booth, Colomb, and Williams discuss the difficulties inexperienced students have with the conventions used to set up the problems that form the starting point of most expository essays. Yet the difficulties students have in constructing the kind of problem that launches an essay stem not only from their unfamiliarity with the conventions of problem-posing but from deeper uncertainties about the "problematizing" role itself.

Booth, Colomb, and Williams do not mention these uncertainties, but they provide a clue to them when they distinguish between problems that are recognized to be such and those that are not. Problems of the first kind, like earning a living, finding a mate, curing diseases, preventing air pollution, or eliminating poverty and homelessness come to us with an apparently *pregiven* quality. These problems are already so widely acknowledged that writers can usually take them up without having to make an argument for seeing them as problems, though there are situations in which they might have to (for example, talking about poverty with an audience of Social Darwinists). Many of the problems with which academics deal, however, lack this pregiven quality, as when they concern the meanings of words, abstract concepts, and texts, or the actions of people long dead. In such cases, where we can't assume that others will see the problem we are taking up *as* a problem, we have to work to sell them on its reality and importance. Academics not only cultivate problems that are unrecognized as such, they like to *invent* problems that most people are unaware of, or look for new ways to describe already recognized problems.

In short, students who are inexperienced in the ways of academic writing are likely to blurt out a thesis or general claim, without identifying the context that would suggest the significance of what the writer has to say. The reader would see an introductory claim (e.g., "Silverstein's book is about generosity.") and wonder, "So what?" The reader might rightfully ask, "Wouldn't everyone arrive at the same conclusion?" or "Who cares?" By framing a problem (e.g., "Some readers believe that Shel Silverstein's *The Giving Tree* is about how men have always oppressed women, and how women give everything until they have nothing else to give. Some others believe this is a story about a child depending on 'mother' and about children growing and drifting away from the parent but always coming back to get something they believe they need."), the writer suggests the gravity of the discussion and the need to read on to see how the writer has corrected the observations of others or has extended the thinking of other writers.

## Writing in a Critical Context

In responding to *The Giving Tree*, the student quoted below has not ignored other critics. The writer grounds her claims about the book's meaning within the context of the existing critical debate about its messages and its worth. She supports her reading of the text and notes two alternative perspectives:

> We give a little of ourselves to those we meet and know every day. But the moral of *The Giving Tree* is that we do not achieve true happiness by making others happy. That happiness is a false one and only lasts for a little while. We lose a bit of ourselves as we give to others without gaining anything back. We must learn that to be truly happy we must give and *receive* love from those around us. The tree throughout the entire book gives the boy everything it can, starting with its leaves and shade, and ending with its whole self; and the tree does this without complaining or even thinking twice about fulfilling any of the boy's wishes. This teaches us that without giving anything back for what we have taken, we will have nothing left when we are old.
>
> The claim that this story tells us about how women have been oppressed by men and how the man takes everything, leaving the woman nothing, has one major flaw. In some cases, the role is reversed and the only reason the author called the tree a female is because most of the time we all consider anything that has to do with nature a female (as in "Mother Nature"). Another critic reads the text as a story about a small child coming to its mother and how it drifts from its mother slowly and comes back to get what it needs. The critic seems to have forgotten that a small child gives his/her mother love and affection throughout life. The position that every day we give a little of ourselves to those around us and that we die slowly when we do not receive a little bit back from others is the most valid and reasonable. During the story, the small child at the start gave love to the tree, and the tree was happy. At the end, when the tree had given everything to the man, she was no longer happy because she did not feel the love from the man to her. So the moral of this story is that one should give back to another what was once given to you.

This writer does more than acknowledge other perspectives; she rationally assesses the merits of their views. As she matures as a reader, critic, and thinker, she relates her ideas to the ideas of others, drawing from their thoughts when appropriate, assessing the accuracy and validity of their claims, and using the context of the ongoing conversation as impetus for sharing her own interpretation. Although the students might not recognize labels for the various critical views they hear in the discussion, they do contend with a number of lenses through which they must reassess their own judgments about meaning and value. Appleman (2000) makes a case for teaching high school students about literary theory. She points out that the practice of working with various critical views benefits students beyond helping them to read texts: "Perhaps even more important, these multiple ways of seeing have become vital skills in our increasingly diverse classrooms as we explore differences between and among us, what separates us and what binds us together" (3).

Although the materials recommended here might appear very simple, the process of negotiating an interpretation is complex. With the appropriate prompts and provocations, students eagerly engage in discussion to discover and refine meaning. They see that the way one reads a text *does* matter, even though there could be many reasonable but varied interpretations. The analysis of interpretation goes beyond unsupported opinion. Students provide a context for discussion, assess alternative and opposing perspectives, and share the reasoning process that led them to their own conclusions. Through discussions that offer a variety of distinct and competing perspectives, students examine recurring critical questions and prepare to join broader conversations that include the voices represented by the critical tradition that surrounds the literature that they study in school.

# 9 Metaphors, the Questions We Ask, and How We Ask Them

In previous chapters, we emphasized the positive impact that participation in discussion has on learning, and we offered practitioners advice and models to guide them in refining their skills as discussion facilitators. This chapter broadens the examination of discussion by inviting the reader to think about their conceptions of communication in general and to reflect on the ways that those conceptions influence their practices in the classroom.

## Metaphors as Communication Frames

As part of their research of adolescents and talent development, Csikszentmihalyi, Rathunde, and Whalen (1993) equipped high school students with pagers and trained them to use a response form to report what they were thinking about at the time that they were paged. Csikszentmihalyi and colleagues provide this description of students' responses to a lecture in history class:

> In a typical history classroom where the teacher was lecturing about Genghis Khan's invasion of China and conquest of Beijing in 1215, only 2 out of 27 students were thinking about China when they were signaled. One of the 2 was remembering the meal he had when he last ate out with his family at a Chinese restaurant, and the other was wondering why Chinese men wore their hair in a ponytail. (196)

Let's imagine sharing the data with the teacher who conducted the lecture, and asking the teacher for a reflection on how the lesson went. The teacher might offer a number of observations, but experience with such conversations suggests that the teacher would likely offer these kinds of assessments:

- These kids just don't *get it*.
- Maybe I have to think of other ways to *package this* for them.
- I might have to slow the pace so it is easier for them to *pick it up*.

When a teacher uses terms similar to those listed above to account for the students' apparent failure to process what he or she was trying to communicate, it becomes apparent that a *conduit metaphor* influences the way that the teacher explains how humans learn and how teachers guide learning. Reddy (1979) describes the *conduit metaphor* in this way: "In the framework of the conduit metaphor, the listener's task must be one of extraction. He must find meaning 'in the words' and take it out of them so that it gets 'into his head.'" (288) Reddy goes on to note four implications of the conduit metaphor:

1. language functions like a conduit, transferring thoughts bodily from one person to another
2. in writing and speaking, people insert their thoughts or feelings in the words
3. words accomplish the transfer by containing the thoughts or feelings and conveying them to others
4. in listening or reading, people extract the thoughts and feelings once again from the words. (290)

A teacher who is guided by a conduit metaphor thinks of the instructional task as *packaging* information in order to *deliver* it to students who may or may not be *receptive*. For this teacher, the important elements of instruction include (1) selecting important information, (2) conveying the information to an audience, and (3) relying on the learners to be open to receiving information. The teacher might account for any failure to learn as the students' failure to receive the information. Reddy discusses the limits of using the conduit metaphor as a frame for communication, and by extension, as a frame to guide instructional efforts: "That is, the major framework sees ideas as existing either within human heads or, at least, within words uttered by humans. The 'minor' framework overlooks words as containers and allows ideas and feelings to flow, unfettered and completely disembodied, into a kind of ambient space between human heads" (291). The implication, if one is governed by the conduit metaphor, is that there is a kind of clean packaging and transferring of thoughts from speaker to listener, from writer to reader. The conduit metaphor does not allow for a vision of communication as a messy process of speakers and writers attempting expression, and listeners and readers making efforts to construct some meaning from what they hear and see.

The conduit metaphor as a pedagogical frame has obvious limitations, but what are the alternatives? Reddy notes that another possibility is a *toolmaker metaphor*. He tells a complicated story to explain the toolmaker metaphor, but the supposition is basically this: People from different environments and with different experiences send crude blue-prints to each other to share their knowledge about the construction of tools that they have found useful in their own environments. Of course, the tools that people make by attempting to interpret the blueprints, based on their own needs and the features of their own environment, are all different from what the originator of the blueprint had in mind, yet the new tools might be more useful and appropriate to the new environments.

The two metaphors that Reddy describes provide a way to recognize the communication frames that can guide our behavior as speakers and listeners and as readers and writers. The two metaphors are also useful for thinking about the frames that guide teachers in their decisions about whether or not to engage students in discussion and in the decisions about how to proceed with discussion, including what questions to ask, and the order in which to ask them.

Of course, the kind of questions one entertains will influence how classroom discussions proceed: e.g., whether the questions solicit basic recall only, whether the questions are open-ended, whether questions are student-generated. However, the question types in themselves will not guarantee a lively and authentic discussion. Also important is the way that the discussion facilitator proceeds with discussion, which will be guided by the conception that he or she has about the way that humans communicate.

The following discussion provides a brief review of taxonomies of objectives and the question types that they would imply, a description of three classrooms where two different communications frames seem to govern, and suggestions for teachers to move away from the confining limits of a conduit metaphor to expand into a discussion environment that is closer to the toolmaker paradigm. Reddy's descriptions of a conduit metaphor and of a toolmaker metaphor will serve as a framework for analyzing what teachers do and how they appear to think as they facilitate classroom discussion. In addition, the insights of Hillocks (1999) also provide help in explaining why teachers do what they do.

## Taxonomies of Objectives and Question Types

Several taxonomies of objectives have influenced teachers in expressing instructional goals and have guided teachers in designing questions to focus reading and to prompt discussion (Bloom 1956; Pearson and

Johnson 1978; Hillocks, McCabe, and McCampbell 1971; Hillocks 1980; Hillocks and Ludlow 1984). A taxonomy of objectives provides important guidelines for the teacher. It helps the teacher develop discussion and assessment questions from all levels of the taxonomy. A taxonomy can help a teacher become aware of the types of questions that she or he habitually asks. A taxonomy can guide a teacher to find a way out of a narrow pattern of questioning that limits the students' engagement with a text. When a taxonomy is used as a guide in preparing a reading inventory, the teacher is made aware of the type of questions with which his or her students are having difficulty, and the responses to the inventory can suggest starting points for initiating discussion about the literature that the students read. For example, if the results of a reading inventory reveal that, by and large, students can readily answer literal level questions about characters and plot, then there would be no need to open discussions habitually by having students verify that they can recall the literal details. The taxonomies in Table 9.1 offer different labels and different emphases but share several similarities.

Similar to Raphael's question-answer relationships (QAR) presented in Chapter 7, the Pearson and Johnson (1978) taxonomy identifies three general areas: textually explicit, textually implicit, and scriptally implicit. Textually explicit questions require the reader to find information that is "right there" in the text; in other words, one should be able to point to the explicit detail from the reading. Textually implicit questions require the reader to make connections from the details of the text and form conclusions. Scriptally implicit questions require the reader to go outside the text to bring world knowledge (e.g., about other books, about language, about human behavior) to the interpretation of the text.

Christenbury and Kelly (1983) offer a similar model to describe a hierarchy of comprehension skills and question types. They see reading as an interactive process involving the following areas: the subject matter; the individual's experiences, values, and ideas; and the experiences, values, and ideas of other peoples and cultures. Christenbury and Kelly describe these three areas as interlocking circles ("the Questioning Circle"). The complexity of the question type is defined by where the circles overlap.

No matter how one conceives of the levels of difficulty in comprehension and different levels of question types, it is important for teachers to recognize that the different levels exist. At the same time, although the taxonomies suggest hierarchies, it is not necessary to operate in the classroom from the lowest level to the highest; that is, from

**Table 9.1.** Taxonomies for Learning Objectives

| Hillocks and Ludlow (1984) | Bloom (1956) | Pearson and Johnson (1978) |
|---|---|---|
| **BASIC STATED INFORMATION:** Identifying frequently stated information that represents some condition crucial to the story. | **KNOWLEDGE:** Bringing to mind specifics, methods, patterns, structures, or settings. | **TEXTUALLY EXPLICIT:** Dealing with obvious answers that are "right there in the text." |
| **KEY DETAIL:** Identifying a detail that appears at some key juncture of the plot and that bears a causal relationship to what happens in a narrative. | | |
| **STATED RELATIONSHIP** Identifying a statement that explains the relationship between at least two pieces of information in the text. | **COMPREHENSION:** Summarizing, paraphrasing, interpreting facts, as opposed to just recalling them. | |
| **SIMPLE IMPLIED RELATIONSHIP:** Inferring the relationship between two pieces of information usually closely juxtaposed in the text. | **APPLICATION:** Using abstractions (such as rules of procedure, generalized ideas or methods) in particular and concrete situations. | **TEXTUALLY IMPLICIT:** Dealing with a level of comprehension in that there is at least one step of logical or pragmatic inferring necessary to get from the question to the response and both the question and the response are derived from the text. |
| **COMPLEX IMPLIED RELATIONSHIP:** Inferring the relationship among many pieces of information spread throughout large parts of the text. | **ANALYSIS:** Clarifying the basis for an arrangement of a communication. | |
| **STRUCTURAL GENERALIZATION:** Generalizing about how parts of the work operate together to achieve certain effects. | **SYNTHESIS:** Putting together, arranging, and combining pieces of data in such a way as to have a structure or pattern not clearly there before. | **"SCRIPTALLY" IMPLICIT:** Dealing with a level of comprehension in which the database for the inference is in the reader's mind, not just on the page. |
| **AUTHOR'S GENERALIZATION:** Inferring a generalization about the world outside the work from the fabric of the work as a whole. | **EVALUATION:** Judging the value of materials and methods for a given purpose or purposes. | |

the easiest to the most difficult. Sometimes one can begin with higher order questioning, knowing that a particular class has command of the literal details of the text. At other times, one might want to start at the lowest level and gradually build toward the higher order skills. At still other times, it is necessary to move back and forth in the taxonomy. How one proceeds will depend in large measure on what the students already know. How one proceeds also reveals how one conceives of communication and of the way that students learn.

## Metaphors as Frames for Classroom Discussion

The following excerpt is a fictionalized version of a class discussion about Ray Bradbury's *Fahrenheit 451*. The discussion follows a familiar pattern. The teacher anticipates that the students have had some difficulty with comprehending the assigned reading from the novel. He hopes to build on the details that the students recall from their reading, having students express their recall of the "facts" of the narrative so that all the students can synthesize the literal details in a way that will allow them to infer some common understanding of the themes of the book. Using the terms from Hillocks (1984), we have labeled in brackets the kinds of questions the teacher is asking.

> *Mr. Haus:* What has Montag done? [basic stated information]
>
> *Marty:* Hidden the book under his pillow.
>
> *Mr. Haus:* What has he done, then? [simple implied relationship]
>
> *Alice:* Committed a crime.
>
> *Mr. Haus:* You can see that the marriage between Montag and his wife has deteriorated. They argue a lot. She doesn't seem to understand him. What has caused them to grow farther apart? [simple implied relationship]
>
> *Marty:* She is just one of society. She is one of them.
>
> *Alice:* They think for her.
>
> *Mr. Haus:* How is the book affecting him physically? [simple implied relationship]
>
> *Ben:* He gets sick. He throws up.
>
> *Alice:* He doesn't want to go to work.
>
> *Mr. Haus:* What does Mildred notice about him? [basic stated information]
>
> *Felice:* She notes that he has never been sick before.

*Mr. Haus:* That whole car thing—what do you think that's about? [simple implied relationship]

*Marty:* They just want people to go as fast as they can.

*Mr. Haus:* Is Mildred happy with her life? [simple implied relationship]

*Marty:* No.

In this exchange, the teacher asks the students to make some simple inferences. When it is necessary to provide an extended summary in order to make a transition in the pattern of thought, the teacher provides this elaboration. When the teacher provides a question that might invite speculation from several students and the citation of details to support any observations, the teacher accepts a one-sentence response from one student and quickly poses another question that seems to shift the focus of the discussion. Although the teacher does ask some inferential questions, he seems satisfied with a one-sentence or one-word answer and does not feel compelled to bring other students into the conversation to probe any individual question further. The questions, then, that seem to require the making of inferences might actually be cues that prompt students to recall what the teacher judges to be obvious to all readers. For example, the teacher asks, "That whole car thing—what do you think that's about?" The question has the potential for opening up a line of inquiry about the kind of society that encourages citizens to race around their cities at breakneck speeds. Exploring questions in this direction would require some complex inferences, requiring comprehension on a "scriptally implicit" level. Instead, a student reports, "They just want people to go as fast as they can," which the teacher seems to accept as a "correct" answer before moving on to the next question.

The next exchange represents a discussion that would come a little later in the same lesson, with the students still reviewing their assigned reading from *Fahrenheit 451*. It seems rather obvious that the students are participating in recitation, with the questions sequenced in a way that the teacher hopes will help the students to arrive at what he deems the necessary understanding.

*Mr. Haus:* He talks about other people in the room. . . . So what's going on here? What's so confusing?

*Frank:* You're not telling us what it means; *that's* what's so confusing.

*Mr. Haus:* What's real and what's not?

*Alice:* Dreams are not real.

*Marty:* The TV thing was real.

*Felice:* Have you ever had a dream and then it happened?

*Mr. Haus:* What are the big things in his life right now?

*Ben:* The book.

*Marty:* His job.

*Mr. Haus:* So he is thinking about his book and his job. What did he just witness?

*Alice:* The lady burned to death.

*Mr. Haus:* He basically witnessed a woman burning herself alive. What happened on the way back from the fire?

*Felice:* They didn't smoke.

*Marty:* They missed the turn.

In the second exchange, one student's reaction reveals that it is rather obvious that the students recognize that the teacher knows the answers to the questions he poses, and that he is more or less quizzing the students to recite what he already knows. Frank says, "You're not telling us what it means; that's what's so confusing." The teacher poses a series of questions that ask the students *what* happened in the story. The discussion suggests that the teacher sees his role as "pathfinder," to use Marshall, Smagorinsky, and Smith's (1995) language. In this notion of the role of discussion leader, the teacher poses the questions that will lead the students down the path to arrive at the same understanding that the teacher already has about the story. The teacher appears to operate under the assumption that if everyone in the class recognizes the commonly understood set of "facts" of the story, then everyone will arrive at the same broader conclusion about a meaning or effect of the story. When a student offers a response that could divert the discussion, even when the diversion could conceivably be related and potentially enriching, the teacher simply ignores it and forges on: "Have you ever had a dream and then it happened?" As the teacher continues, he asks the students again to recall the events of the story.

The pathfinder metaphor and the conduit metaphor have much in common in that the teacher seems to be guided by a belief that there can be an objective understanding about the events, speech, images, and structures of a text that can be transmitted from one person to another. In commenting on one teacher's predominant mode of instruction, Hillocks (1999) describes the epistemological view in this way:

> If one tells or gives students appropriate information, their learning will indicate that they have received the information and made use of it. Through much of the 18th, 19th, and even 20th centu-

> ries, teachers of English, as well as of other subjects, believed that
> with proper grammar, people could, in Lindley Murray's 1795
> phrase, "transfuse . . . sentiments into the minds of one another"
> (1849, 5). That is, knowledge could be conveyed directly through
> words and could be apprehended directly by anyone having ad-
> equate facility in the language. Such a model has epistemological
> implications, namely that knowledge is objective and may be ac-
> quired directly through words and the senses. This telling may
> take place through a textbook, a lecture, recitation, or visual dem-
> onstrations. Although this model is often referred to as teaching
> by transmissions, I will refer to it as *objectivist* to emphasize epis-
> temological implications. (18–19)

Hillocks's description of an *objectivist* frame sounds very much like
Reddy's description of the conduit metaphor. It is apparently very difficult to break away from the conduit metaphor in order for teachers to
conceive of other possibilities for communication, for learning, and for
discussion behaviors that will support both communication and learning in a rich, meaningful way.

   In another instance, the teacher appears initially to open up an
authentic discussion that will allow students to explore a problem and
arrive at their own well-reasoned conclusions. As the discussion
progresses, however, the teacher begins to attempt to redirect the students' thinking when some positions do not seem to him to be correct.

   The teacher, Mr. Reed, sequences a discussion of a hypothetical
case as a way to introduce some issues that he anticipates the students
will encounter in their reading of *Flowers for Algernon*. He introduces
discussion by describing to the students an affirmative action case: students from two different communities compete for admission to a university. The teacher asks, "Who is most deserving?" The scenario and
the teacher's question about who deserves admission invite higher-order thinking and encourage wide participation among the students. As
the discussion progresses, one would anticipate that the students would
engage in analysis, synthesis, and evaluation. Participation in the discussion is not an assessment of mastery of a body of information, so
many students are inclined to express their judgment and offer supporting ideas. Here is a portion of the discussion:

> *Nan:* I would look at the ACTs and GPAs, which is an equal
>    standard.
>
> *Judy:* You can compensate for your background. You can have
>    the will to overcome your condition.
>
> *Mr. Reed:* But Marcus works several hours a week. Shouldn't
>    some compensation be made because he has this additional
>    burden?

*Joe:* Yeah. You gotta give him a chance because he is working so
   hard.

*Mr. Reed:* So you're saying that Marcus has the potential to
   perform just as well in school, but he has been systematically inhibited from advancing.

*Joe:* It is hard for Marcus to walk down the street. It will be hard
   to go to the library.

*Mr. Reed:* Marcus has had to overcome many challenging
   obstacles to achieve anything that he has achieved. That is
   an issue, *absolutely*.

*Judy:* I don't think Marcus is prepared for college, so Cornelius
   deserves it.

*Mr. Reed:* What do you mean by *preparation*? Cornelius does not
   exert himself. How is he *preparing* himself?

*Nan:* I think they should have an affirmative action school for
   people like Marcus. Life is not fair.

*Janice:* My sister went to Northwest [a regional state university].
   They let *anyone* in there. It's a zoo. Middle Border [a large,
   competitive state university] has certain standards.

*Alfonso:* The college can't see this, but we can. Cornelius has his
   friends do his homework while Marcus does his own work.

*Dave:* Cornelius has potential, too, so he can go to another
   college.

In this case, the teacher merely paraphrases those responses that
he agrees with. For example, he responds to one student with this paraphrase: "So you're saying that Marcus has the potential to perform just
as well in school, but he has been systematically inhibited from advancing." The paraphrasing in itself is affirming, but the teacher affirms only
one side of the issue. He asks challenging questions of those students
whose position he disagrees with: "What do you mean by *preparation*?
Cornelius does not exert himself. How is he *preparing* himself?" While
the discussion is in part authentic, the teacher seems to be attempting
to lead students to take a position that he would endorse himself. He
tells Joe, "Marcus has had to overcome many challenging obstacles to
achieve anything that he has achieved. That is an issue, *absolutely*." He
reveals through patterns of speech what his agenda is, and students are
astute and experienced enough to recognize the patterns and realize
which position will gain them dividends with the teacher who assigns
the students their grades.

In one last example, the teacher engages a class in a large-group
discussion after the students had talked in small groups about a set of

scenarios that introduced problems related to a citizen's obligation to obey laws and rules. The activities serve as a gateway to the study of *To Kill a Mockingbird*. The segment here focuses attention on the following scenario:

> Ashley Wilkins and Melanie Melatti thought that they would pass a Saturday afternoon at a movie at the local theater. The local theater has four screens. Ashley and Melanie had already seen the movies that were being shown on three of the screens. The one remaining screen was showing an R-rated movie called *A Whirl of Romance*. A week earlier, Ashley and Melanie had seen the trailers for this movie. It looked very appealing. They had also seen the ads for the movie in the local paper and had read a couple of movie reviews online. They were convinced that *A Whirl of Romance* was the movie they wanted very much to see. The problem was that Ashley and Melanie were only fourteen years old, and the film rating and the theater policy required that the viewers be at least sixteen. Although they were two years below the age limit, Ashley and Melanie looked to everyone to be at least sixteen. They could easily fool the movie attendants and gain access to the film they wanted to see. Should Ashley and Melanie go in to watch the R-rated film?

The teacher, Ms. Dub, opens discussion by asking a group to report what they have concluded in their small-group conversation.

> *Rocio:* We said they shouldn't watch the movie, because the reviews would not reveal the objectionable material. They could break the law if they had the parents' permission.
>
> *Bob:* If they get in, it is the theater's fault.
>
> *Jason:* They should see it, because eventually, it will come out on video, and they'll see it anyway. If they see it now, at least the theater will make some money.
>
> *Bob:* It's not breaking the law if the theater lets you into the theater.
>
> *Tatiana:* If they get parents' consent, they would be breaking the theater's law but not their parents' law.
>
> *Bob:* It's not a big deal, because you could buy the movie later on DVD.
>
> *Ms. Dub:* Does anyone want to express a rule that would cover our decision in the second case?
>
> *Lara:* If the movie is educational, you should be able to see it. We watch R-rated movies in school. We just have to get parents' permission.
>
> *Peter:* Something as small as seeing an R-rated movie wouldn't make a difference.

This short exchange would be part of a longer discussion, which could actually extend across several class meetings, and reveals students' active efforts to grapple with a difficult problem: When might a person be justified in breaking a law or rule? Although the students are struggling to a certain extent, that effort represents progress toward refining and deepening their understanding of the problem. The students struggle, but their struggles are not blind, ill-informed gropings to make sense of a question.

Consider the pattern of thought in the exchange represented in the transcript above. First, Rocio anticipates that someone might judge from reviews that the movie has important artistic and entertainment merits; but she notes that without this information, the moviegoer has no basis for saying that the rating policy inappropriately excludes her from a potentially enriching experience, so the moviegoer must obey the ban. Bob insists on two occasions that it is the theater's responsibility to keep underage viewers out, not the underage viewer's responsibility to avoid entry. Jason claims that the prohibition is futile, and cites an economic reason for admitting the young customers. Tatiana notes a new condition: parents might give their permission for the girls to view the film. In her judgment, Tatiana determines that when two possibilities must be weighed—the permission of parents and the restriction of the theater—it is better to follow the parents' inclinations. Bob claims that the restriction is futile because the potentially objectionable material would be available to the young viewers at a later date. To sum up, Lara offers a general rule that if a film has educational value, even if the rating would otherwise restrict young people, they should be able to see the film. Peter concludes that the experience of a young person seeing an R-rated film is so inconsequential that the restriction does not protect anyone from danger and should be ignored. All together, considering all the contributions of the students during the discussion in Ms. Dub's class, the class explored a tough perennial question in some complexity.

During the exchange, the teacher made one contribution: "Does anyone want to express a rule that would cover our decision in the second case?" Her question is a procedural one. She does not offer her analysis or impose her conclusions. Ms. Dub, however, does remain involved in the discussion. She establishes the context for inquiry and creates the environment for encouraging participation. As the discussion progresses, she manages the participation to include as many voices as possible. She attends carefully to all the contributions so that she can serve as recorder for the class's general conclusions. She is also prepared to ask questions to press students to clarify, test their claims, and extend their thinking.

It appears that Ms. Dub's conception of communication and discussion is more consistent with the toolmaker metaphor than with the conduit metaphor. One might characterize her approach to instruction as *constructivist*; that is, according to Hillocks (1999), "that what is learned may only be learned in terms of what we already know and that learners must construct what is to be learned for themselves" (19). Unlike Mr. Haus and Mr. Reed, she is not compelled to direct students down a path to recite what she has embraced herself as factual, correct, or worthwhile. Like Mr. Haus and Mr. Reed, Ms. Dub has definite instructional goals, but her goals seem to emphasize the development of procedural knowledge rather than the mastery of particular content. She seems to operate with the belief that students need to interact frequently in a purposeful way.

## Shifting Metaphors

How does a teacher become more like Ms. Dub? How does one change communication frames or make an epistemological shift? Hillocks (1999) suggests some directions for teacher change, offering models for procedures that could be part of teacher education. For the current practicing teacher, perhaps the first step is taking a close look at the amount, direction, source, and quality of talk in the classroom.

It is possible for any teacher to collect data to allow for an examination of what happens when a teacher attempts to engage students in discussion. A constructivist teacher might introduce a group of students to a problem and plan the means for students to examine the data that would allow them to investigate the problem through a rational process. In a similar way, the teacher who wants to investigate the problem of promoting authentic discussion in the classroom will want to collect and study relevant data. It is common practice for athletes to videotape their performances in order to examine the data that reveal what happens during performance, rather than relying solely on the impressions one has in recalling the performance. In a similar way, teachers can find strategic approaches to examine their work in the classroom. Hillocks (1999) observes that teachers are likely to make a shift in the way they conceive of knowledge and learning and how this conception guides their instructional practices only if they are able to reflect on their own practices and recognize a need to change: "Change in thinking and reflective practice will almost necessarily entail that teachers reconstruct their knowledge, especially if teachers hold nonoptimistic beliefs about students and if they have adopted an objectivist epistemological stance" (135). The recommendations that follow suggest ways to collect data about discussions in one's own class and describe frames for analyzing the data that one collects.

An obvious way to capture what happens during a discussion is to videotape it. Digital recordings can be especially useful for allowing one to pinpoint moments in the discussion and reviewing them repeatedly. Researchers often rely on audiotapes of discussions. The audiotapes allow one to produce the transcripts to be able to examine the language and sequence, conversational turn by conversational turn. It is also useful to invite a colleague or supervisor to come into the classroom to take notes. In a simple form of note taking, the viewer would attempt to write down everything that he or she hears. Although the note taking of this sort may not be as accurate as the audiotaping, it may be less intrusive, with students less concerned about being recorded. Some classroom observers use various ways to tally and track the participation in a class. Flanders (1970), for example, suggests a method for noting the direction and frequency of contributions. Such a method would reveal who is doing most of the talking and where the participants direct their comments. (See Chapter 13 for an explanation of the Flanders Interaction Analysis.)

After collecting the data, what does one do with the information? It is a good idea to share the data with another teacher, and together discuss what the data reveal. Here are some questions that can guide reflection on what happens in the classroom:

1. Who is doing all of the talking? Hillocks (1999) reminds us that a constructivist teacher is not likely to be someone who is doing all of the talking. The teacher can ask, "How do I turn over most of the talk to the students?" The data might reveal that two or three students consistently bear the burden of answering the teacher's questions, working with the teacher to convey information to the rest of the students. The teacher might ask also, "How can I get most of the students to contribute regularly to purposeful discussion?"

2. What kind of questions does the teacher ask? If the questions never depart from literal recall, the teacher implies that learning involves the transmission of selected information from one person to the other. The conduit metaphor is at work. The teacher can at least become sensitive to the goal of asking higher-order questions, especially if those ques-

tions link with broad themes or concepts that might unify a sequence of lessons.

3. How does the teacher navigate a taxonomy of question types? Authentic discussion is not simply a matter of asking the right questions. Do the data reveal the teacher as pathfinder? Is it possible to begin asking higher-order questions and move to literal level questions in the course of connecting details of a text and interpreting them by applying the knowledge that readers have about language, other books, and human behavior?

4. How does the teacher respond to students' contributions? Does the teacher consistently validate one side of an issue? Does the teacher challenge the speakers who disagree with his or her view? These may be signs of the conduit metaphor creeping into the classroom, influencing the teacher to direct thought down a particular route.

5. Do transcripts or other data reveal that students are grappling together in a purposeful way to deepen their understanding of problems and concepts? Does the grappling represent the misinformed leading the misinformed, or does it represent a process of extension and refinement of thought?

It will be enlightening for most teachers to look at the evidence of their practices in the classroom. It is not wise to go it alone in analyzing the data. If it is worthwhile for students to join their peers in a deliberate attempt at solving problems and investigating questions, then it also makes sense for teachers to join colleagues in examining what they do in the classroom and in finding ways of making shifts that are likely to encourage more frequent and meaningful student talk. Reddy (1979) and Hillocks (1999) make strong cases that the way that we conceive of communication, knowledge, and learning influences our practices. The tough task is to make an epistemological shift that will lead to a change in behavior.

# 10 Discussion-Based Approaches to Teaching Composition

A uthentic discussion can play a significant role in helping students learn to write. According to Vygotsky (1980) and research on writing (Hillocks 1986, 1995), students are able to work at higher levels with the guidance and support of teachers or the collaboration of peers than they can independently. The processes internalized during such guided or collaborative work provide for a new level of development. Engagement in authentic discussion, either with an entire class or in small groups, is one way to support students, enabling them to internalize processes that will allow them to work independently at higher levels. The support provided by this kind of collaboration is particularly effective in helping students learn strategies for writing.

## Using Authentic Discussion to Teach Argument

Using a scenario or case study discussion is a good way to illustrate the elements of an argument and as such is an effective gateway activity for this kind of writing. One example of a scenario for introducing argument is "Necessary Force?"

---

**Necessary Force?**

After Max Burger had had three burglaries at his restaurant, he installed a 220-volt security wiring system to protect his property. He already had an alarm system, security cameras, and a "Beware of Dog" sign that had done little to dissuade thieves. He hooked electrical lines to metal plates at the base of each window to protect his business, located in an industrial district of a midsized Midwestern city. He then put up signs warning that the restaurant was protected by 220-volt security wiring.

Early on a Sunday morning, thirty-seven-year-old Terrence Thug broke a window to the restaurant and tried to climb in. Alerted

---

> to the break-in by the alarm system, police found Thug's dead body on the floor of the restaurant at about 2:30 A.M.
>
> Max Burger has disconnected the wiring system, which violated city building and fire codes. He could face criminal charges for the death of Terrence Thug.

Students are asked to reflect on the situation described in "Necessary Force?" and consider whether they think Max Burger should be convicted of a crime (murder or manslaughter) for the death of Terrence Thug or should only have to pay a fine for a city code violation. They list reasons and evidence for their viewpoint. After students jot down ideas for several minutes, they are divided into small groups to discuss their viewpoints and to see if they can reach a consensus.

The following is an example of the kind of discussion that typically occurs.

*Fatima:* No, no criminal charges. He was just defending himself.

*Matt:* Right, I agree. Nothing worked. What's he supposed to do?

*Marissa:* Well, I don't know. Killing him was pretty bad.

*Matt:* But he had warning signs. It's the guy's fault. He ignored them. *He's* the criminal!

*Kareem:* Right, I agree, it's his fault he was killed, not Burger's. He had warning signs.

*Marissa:* But maybe he didn't believe them. I mean the "Beware of Dog" signs were fake, so maybe he didn't know.

*Kareem:* Well, that's his problem.

*Marissa:* Still, I don't think you can kill someone if they aren't trying to kill you.

*Matt:* How do you know that? He could have killed someone.

*Marissa:* It says, "Early on a Sunday morning," so no one was in the restaurant. It doesn't say anything about a weapon. Look at it this way: if he got caught and put in jail, he wouldn't get death for burglary. But he got a death sentence.

*Fatima:* Well, she has a point there.

*Matt:* I don't think so. I mean what's the guy supposed to do? He's had three burglaries; he spent money on security cameras and an alarm system; the police are useless. He has a right to protect his property. He could lose a lot of money

... that he needs for his kids, to feed his kids. He had
warning signs. The guy was stupid.

*Kareem:* Yeah! What if he did have a guard dog, and the guy
broke in, and the dog attacked him and killed him. You
aren't going to say he can't have a guard dog are you? He
had signs, beware of dog.

*Fatima:* Good point. I think that's right.

After the groups discussed for ten or fifteen minutes, the class recon-
vened to continue the discussion as a whole class. The focus turned to
whether a person has the right to kill someone who is not directly threatening anyone's life. Some students argued that there are circumstances
which should allow this, including clear warning signs, the use of other
deterrence methods first, the inability of law enforcement to stop burglaries, and so forth. Others argued that the security system was unjus-
tified because it was illegal and/or too extreme.

## Illustrating Key Elements of an Argument

The teacher can then use ideas generated in the discussion to illustrate
some key elements of an argument: claim, evidence (data), warrant,
backing, counterargument, and rebuttal (Toulmin 1958, Hillocks 1995).

CLAIM: Burger was justified in killing Thug because he warned him of
the dangerous security wiring.

EVIDENCE (GROUNDS): "He put up signs stating that the restaurant
was protected by 220-volt security wiring."

WARRANT: People are responsible for heeding clear warning signs.

BACKING: Warning signs appear in many dangerous places (e.g.
"Warning: Do not swim alone in pool"). If a person decides to ignore a
warning sign, then it is the victim's responsibility if he or she is injured
or killed. The person who posted the sign has identified the danger and
fulfilled his or her responsibility in communicating that danger to others.

COUNTERARGUMENT: The sign was not believable because the "Beware of Dog" sign was apparently fake. Thug could have been aware
of the fake "Beware of Dog" sign. Also people frequently post false signs
as a scare tactic. They don't want to go to the expense of actually in-
stalling security cameras or a security system.

REBUTTAL: It is Thug's problem if he did not believe the sign. Thug took a chance that the sign was false, and he was wrong. Burger gave fair warning.

Finally, the class can identify other claims that were made in the course of the discussion, the evidence, the warrants, the counterarguments, and the rebuttals.

## Sequencing Discussion Activities

Through engaging in authentic discussion of the "Necessary Force?" scenario, students rehearse orally the processes involved in developing an argument. Clearly, such a discussion will enable students to write a more effective argument concerning whether Burger is guilty of a criminal act. But also, creating a sequence of these kinds of activities will help students internalize a process that they can apply when they examine a different issue. They will be aware that they need to support claims with evidence and warrants and to anticipate counterarguments and respond to them (Hillocks 1986, 1995).

A next step is to have students work in small groups to evaluate brief arguments. Students focus on the following questions:

- What claim(s) does the writer make?
- What evidence is provided?
- To what extent does the evidence support the claim(s)? Explain.
- What is the warrant for the claim and evidence?
- What counterarguments could be raised?
- To what extent does the argument respond to possible counterarguments?

---

**Arguments for Discussion and Evaluation**

1. Ten years ago, Middle Border State University began requiring that at the end of each course, all students be given an opportunity to evaluate the teaching effectiveness of their professors. Since that time, overall student grade averages have risen by 30 percent. Obviously the policy has led professors to assign higher grades in their classes. Potential employers must believe that students are not deserving of higher grades because the number of students who get jobs after graduation has dropped by 10 percent in the last five years.

---

> To help its graduates secure better jobs, Rockridge State University should discontinue the policy of having student evaluations of professors.
>
> 2. A recent study has shown that the number of vegetarians in Grand City has increased by 20 percent. Currently, there are no city restaurants that specialize in vegetarian dishes. Moreover, the average family in Grand City is a two-income family. A nationwide study has shown that such families eat out at restaurants more often than they did a decade ago. Therefore, a new Grand City restaurant specializing in vegetarian dishes will be successful.

As students discuss these two arguments in small groups, their collaboration results in their engaging orally in the strategies involved in writing effective arguments. For example, in discussing the first argument, some students typically say that the claim that professors are giving higher grades as a result of the evaluation policy is supported with the evidence that the grade average has risen by 30 percent. They say the evidence shows that professors are giving higher grades in order to get students to give them higher ratings. But other students will usually suggest that other reasons may explain the rise in grade averages—better students or maybe professors who do a better job of teaching since they know students will be evaluating their teaching. They also point out that the drop in the number of graduates getting jobs may be the result of fewer jobs being available rather than because employers feel that students are less qualified.

## Additional Activities for Teaching Argument

Another way to engage students in the kinds of discussions that teach strategies of argument is having them respond to a letter to the editor. The teacher can select an actual letter from the newspaper or create one. The activity works most effectively if the letter has some flaws, such as a lack of evidence for claims, questionable interpretations of evidence, missing warrants, etc. We created the letter below. We purposely made it an argument that many students agree with upon first reading it. But as they begin critiquing it as an argument, they usually find that it has weaknesses.

---

**Letter to the Editor**

Dear Editor:

The problem of prison overcrowding and the cost of building more prisons is not a difficult one to solve. This problem could be solved if everyone who is given a life sentence without parole were executed instead of kept in prison. Additionally, no prisoners should be held on death row for longer than one year. This would save a lot of money.

This is a good solution to the problem because people would be deterred from committing a violent crime because they would know that they would most likely be executed. The crime rate would go down. With the most violent prisoners removed from the prison population, the prisons would be safer places for both guards and inmates. This would also save money. The inmates who are released from prison would have a better chance of being rehabilitated and not returning to a life of crime because they are exposed to less violent offenders while in prison.

There are virtually no problems with this solution. Of course, some people may argue that there are prisoners on death row by mistake and that executing more prisoners could lead to more mistaken—and irreversible—deaths. But overall there are few mistakes made when executing offenders, and that is just the small price we pay for solving our prison problems. After all, anyone who is convicted of a violent crime can't be completely innocent anyway. And spending a life in prison is no better than being dead. So why not expand the use of the death penalty? It makes sense.

John Q. Public

---

Since students have already worked on evaluating arguments in previous activities, we ask students to read the letter to the editor and write a letter to the editor in response to it. They are encouraged to do the following as they create their letter of response:

- Provide a brief summary of the original letter and writer's viewpoint.
- Determine whether the writer's claims are supported with evidence.
- Determine from a "fact check" whether the claims are valid.
- Evaluate whether the evidence given supports the claims made.

- Explain any ideas with which they agree and why.
- Explain any ideas with which they disagree and why.

---

### Student Response to John Q. Public

Dear Editor:

John Q. Public recently wrote a letter about a solution to the problem of overcrowded prisons. With the nation's prison population surpassing two million in 2002, there is definitely a problem in our prisons. In some prisons, such as those in Arizona, the inmates have to sleep in tents on prison grounds because of lack of space at the prisons. John Q. Public's solution to this problem is to execute all those sentenced to life in prison without parole, instead of keeping them in our overcrowded prisons. He believes this to be a good idea because future criminals would be deterred from committing crimes and this would save the taxpayers money. Although this seems like a logical solution to the problem of overcrowded prisons, there are few facts to back up what John Q. Public says.

John Q. Public states that criminals would be deterred from committing a crime if the death sentences were enforced more. This statement is questionable. Eighty-four percent of the country's top academic criminologists reject the notion that the death penalty acts as a deterrent to murder, and there are facts to back up why they think that way. For example in a fifteen-year period in California, an execution was carried out every other month from 1952 to 1967. During this time in California, the murder rate increased 10 percent annually. Then between 1967 and 1991 when there were no executions in California, the murder rate only increased 4.8 percent annually. In fact, nationwide, the number of people on death row has steadily grown since reinstating the death penalty, from 420 people in 1976 to 3,625 people in 1999. In 2002, the South accounted for 80 percent of all executions and also reported having the highest murder rate. The Northeast in 2002 accounted for less than 1 percent of executions and reported having the lowest murder rate in the nation. It appears as though the death penalty encourages murderers rather than deters them.

John Q. Public also states that it would save the taxpayers money to execute convicted murderers, instead of keeping them in jail and allowing them numerous occasions to appeal their cases. This statement is true. If Florida were to punish all first-degree murderers with life in prison without parole, it would cost $51 million a year. Also true though, is the fact that executions are not cheap. Since 1976, Florida has carried out forty-four executions, each one costing $24 million. Each execution costs about six times the cost of imprisoning a person for life in Florida without parole. John Q. Public's solution might end up costing the taxpayers more money.

The majority of police and criminologists in our country believe that the death penalty does not deter crime, so why does John Q. Public think it will? He only stated generally that criminals would be deterred because they would be scared to be executed. This is not true; with the reinstatement and enforcement of the death penalty, more criminals committed murder. Also while true that the nation would save money if they did not hold prisoners on death row for longer than a year, if the nation were to execute all those sentenced to death row, taxpayers would be paying the same or more than they are now. John Q. Public's solutions to overcrowded prisons will not deter crime or save money, so what will they do? Will his solutions encourage criminals to commit murder and cost taxpayers more money? The answer is "yes."

Sara S.

After students have completed their own letters in response to the letter to the editor, we have them work in small groups. Each group member reads his or her letter to the group. Each group is asked to put together the best ideas from each group member's letter and report to the class on the strengths and weaknesses of the argument presented in the original letter to the editor.

## Putting It All Together

After engaging in this kind of sequence of discussion-based activities, students are given information such as "Junk Food Ban" and asked to write a composition arguing whether the policy instituted at Dewey Middle School should be implemented in their own school, or as another option, at all schools—elementary, middle, and high school—in the United States. Or students can find another issue that they are interested in researching and arguing.

## Junk Food Ban

John Dewey Middle School has recently removed all junk food from the school cafeteria and vending machines. All unhealthy food has been replaced with healthy choices. The school eliminated soda, chips, burgers (58 percent fat), chicken wings (61 percent fat), and hotdogs (77 percent fat).

Students were surveyed about their favorite healthy foods. Based on the survey, the school added items such as sushi, deli sandwiches, baked chicken with rice, homemade soup, salads, and fruit desserts. All drinks with added sugar were eliminated, including those in vending machines. They were replaced with water, milk, and 100 percent fruit juice.

The school even declined to sell low-fat chips. The chair of the Parent Teacher Student Association (PTSA) Student Nutrition Committee said, "What difference does it make if the chips have fewer calories if these calories are still empty? It is not enough that our food be less bad for the kids. We want the food to be good for them. Our turkey and roast beef sandwiches are made with lots of fresh lettuce and tomato. The homemade soups are loaded with vegetables. No matter what kids buy for lunch, they are getting something healthy."

Although many feared the school's food service would lose money, it ended the year with a profit of $6,000.

After Dewey Middle School got rid of junk food, teachers and administrators reported that student behavior after lunch improved and that that there was less litter.

Why these changes? A study conducted by the United States Department of Health and Human Services found that approximately one in every three adults in the United States is obese. According to the U.S. Centers for Disease Control and Prevention, approximately 15 percent of children and teens are overweight. Research has found that most obese adolescents remain obese as adults. The cause of the overweight and obesity problem is generally attributed to people eating more calories and not exercising enough.

The director of the Center for Food and Nutrition Policy at a major university says that data in their studies "indicate that getting off the couch—not watching TV or videos—was far more predictive of whether a child was going to be overweight than any of the other dietary components."

> Also of relevance to this issue is the fact that schools have gen-
> erated more than $750 million each year from the sale of junk food
> through vending machines in the school. Some high schools have
> made as much as $100,000 a year.

Engaging students in these kinds of discussion-based activities
enables them to internalize strategies for writing argument. A sequence
such as the one described above prepares them for assignments in which
they are asked to identify issues they are interested in and write compositions supporting their position. Through rehearsing strategies in a
sequence of discussion-based activities, students develop skill in using
them in other situations.

## Using Authentic Discussion in Teaching Other Kinds of Writing

Discussion-based activities also serve as an effective method for helping students write extended definitions. For example, engaging students
in the kinds of scenario activities described in Chapters 3 and 6 prepares
them for writing extended definitions of justice or heroism. Johannessen,
Kahn, and Walter's *Designing and Sequencing Prewriting Activities* (1982)
presents a series of discussion-based activities that prepare students for
writing compositions that use criteria, examples, and contrasting examples to define an abstract concept.

For teaching students to write effective descriptions and narratives, Hillocks's (1972, 1986, 1995) sequence of "observing and writing"
activities involves students in discussion in order to teach them how to
use specific detail and figurative language. For example, in one activity, small groups of students each develop a description of a seashell.
As groups are creating their descriptions, there is a great deal of interactive problem solving among group members ("Does this part of the
shell look more like a chipped tooth or a mountain peak?")

Throughout this book, there are a number of suggested compositions that students might develop as a follow-up to various discussion activities. For example, after students have developed criteria defining justice through discussing scenarios, they might write an analysis
of whether justice is served in a particular literary work or incident
within a literary work.

## Moving from Discussion to Writing

To focus on specific writing strategies and the processes involved in putting ideas generated in discussion into clear, coherent, organized pieces of writing, teachers will most likely need to develop additional activities such as the following.

After students have engaged in an activity such as the fishbowl discussion explained in Chapter 7, the teacher could distribute a sample composition, such as the following one, written in answer to the question, "Who is the greatest Greek mythic hero?"

---

### The Greatest Hero

The greatest hero is Atalanta.

Atalanta defeated the giant wild boar without any help from the gods. She and Meleager accomplished the task on their own. Perseus killed a fierce monster, Medusa, but he received winged sandals from Hermes that enabled him to fly. Without these sandals he couldn't have defeated Medusa.

Theseus, another great hero, also had help from the gods. His father, Poseidon, gave him the power to breathe underwater so that he could prove to King Minos that he was the son of a god. The gull sent by the gods also taught him a trick that enabled him to defeat his enemies and the Minotaur: to use his enemy's strength against him. Also, Theseus was one of the warriors involved in hunting down the Calydonian boar, but he was unable to kill it.

Atalanta is truly the greatest hero because she and Meleager killed the huge boar without help from the gods. In fact, in her case the gods were actually fighting against her. The goddess Artemis sent the giant boar to ravage the countryside to get revenge against Atalanta because of her great skill in hunting.

---

Students are divided into small groups of three or four to discuss the composition and identify its strengths and weaknesses. If students need specific guidelines, questions such as the following can be provided:

- What is the writer's thesis?
- What evidence does the writer include to support the thesis?
- What makes the evidence convincing or unconvincing?

- Is there any evidence that could be raised to contradict the writer's thesis? What is it?
- To what extent does the writer include an effective introduction and conclusion to the composition? How could they be improved?
- What other suggestions do you have for improving the composition?

Following a class discussion of this composition, students could write their own papers defending their choice for the greatest Greek mythic hero.

Authentic discussion promotes the development of writing skills and strategies because students are able to work at progressively higher levels with the guidance and support of teachers and the collaboration of peers. The processes internalized during such guided or collaborative work provide for new levels of development in written communication.

# 11 Cultivating the Talking Curriculum

In previous chapters, we have shown the ways that discussion supports students through individual lessons or a limited sequence of lessons. Discussion is especially powerful when it permeates an entire curriculum. When driven by the force of key questions, or clearly identifiable points of inquiry that capture student interest and relate to students' day-to-day lives, the impact of discussion on student engagement and learning is formidable. Entertain, for the moment, the idea that students might engage in an extensive, multiweek inquiry into the notion of social responsibility or equality, a term that is freely used every day but not, perhaps, too thoroughly investigated. Or, amidst the current wave of public discussion about the need for character education, imagine a different setting where students, during the formative years of school, might pursue a deeper understanding of ideas such as identity and maturity and the impact these ideas have on motivating students to develop a rich appreciation of what it means to be a person of character. Helping students construct a more thorough understanding of these concepts, and any related questions that arise when considering such concepts, is a solid foundation upon which to base a curriculum. Careful nurturing and planning are at the heart of the undertaking, as is the reliance on the idea that in order to arrive at a fuller understanding of abstract considerations, such as equality or character, students must have the time, means, and opportunity to talk with each other about important issues and ideas that arise during the inquiry.

This practice of placing concepts at the heart of inquiry is a relatively modern undertaking and is a point of debate among many English teachers. Most teachers have become acclimated to the notion of assisting students in identifying and discussing issues related to the universal themes that are at the heart of much of the literature we study. Many teachers would argue that "teaching themes" has been at the heart of English education in secondary schools for a significant period of time. A review of most secondary school curricula, or even a cursory review of the vast array of textbooks published to support secondary school English, offers abundant examples of the theme-based approach to English instruction. Poems, short stories, movie titles, and excerpts from longer works, as well as suggestions for both narrative and persuasive writing assignments, may be found in several commercially produced curricula listed under headings such as "The Golden Age," "Awakenings," or "The Dogs of War." The various texts, regardless of origin or author intent, are grouped together for the purpose of helping students connect the content, style, and meaning of each work to the specific theme.

In his excellent methods textbook on *Teaching English through Principled Practice*, Peter Smagorinsky (2002) identifies a theme as "an idea or motif that ties together the texts, activities, and discussions of a unit" that "often refers to a set of experiences, ideas, concepts, or emotions shared by people within and often across cultures." Citing Illinois English teacher David Anderson, Smagorinsky goes on to identify conceptual units as units "designed to organize students' learning around a particular emphasis" which "must focus on a set of key concepts that students engage with over time." Within the realm of the conceptual unit, Smagorinsky notes, students "have an active role in constructing new knowledge through their engagement with the unit concepts." The difference between the practice of teaching students to identify and discuss themes, then, and the practice of placing students in a position to construct more complex understandings about important concepts, like "What responsibility does a person have to the society in which he or she lives?" or "What is equality?" or "What does it mean to be a person of character?" is significant and worth establishing clearly, especially when attempting to consider the impact that talking in class can have on the curriculum. A clear observance of the distinction between the two approaches engenders greater understanding that while teaching themes is something that can be teacher-centered, inquiry into complex concepts is an endeavor that can be attained only with the careful planning and facilitation of student dialogue. In the latter situation, the teacher really must become the "guide on the side" that is so often invoked at teacher inservice meetings, rather than the "sage on the stage" that is the most common manifestation of teacher presence in American classrooms, particularly English classrooms.

A case in point might include the consideration of W. T. Jewkes and Northrup Frye's (1973) oft-used and much-cited book, *Man the Mythmaker*. Those familiar with the book can recall the archetypal distinctions that Jewkes and Frye rely upon to categorize various world myths. The categorization of the myths by archetype ostensibly serves the purpose of helping students develop a keener understanding of the specific archetype associated with each myth. In this sense, each myth studied helps students develop a greater understanding of each archetype. Within a conceptual framework, however, students might take this process several steps further. In addition to working to understand each archetype and understand how each myth contributes to their understanding of each archetype, students engage in the additional process of inquiring into the way that the pursuit of understanding archetypes and myths assists them in constructing a deeper understanding of a concept that is related to their understanding of the world in which they live. For example, how does an understanding of Jewkes and Frye's "God-Teacher" archetype, and a close reading of the Greek myth about Prometheus, contribute to a student's ability to suggest whether or not all people deserve to be treated equally, or, perhaps, how does a student's understanding of these texts contribute to his understanding of the role that schools should play in the lives of the youth of America? Although both are valid undertakings, the complexity of the latter questions demonstrates the need for sustained, carefully wrought inquiry that is nurtured over time. The unifying concepts of a conceptually based curriculum provide the guidance English teachers need to plan and facilitate meaningful discussion.

In one setting, a school term's worth of inquiry might include an investigation into the benefits and limitations of equality, while in another, students might inquire into the notions of identity and maturity and investigate what these concepts suggest about what it means to be a person of character. Regardless of the conceptual foci of the inquiry, teachers are more likely to achieve desired learner outcomes by giving students the opportunity to navigate their ways through the inquiry by engaging in conversation with each other.

In order to demonstrate how a well-designed conceptual inquiry can be aided by the opportunities for involvement in substantive discussion, one might consider an engaged and sustained pursuit of investigating the rights and responsibilities of individuals. Within such a framework, students would be encouraged to explore the ideas of community, tolerance, and, ultimately, social responsibility. Validation of this type of pursuit stems from the consideration that many students, regardless of developmental age, are not aware of it, but the freedoms they enjoy today were born in the ideas and actions of generations preceding them. Although the role of the individual in society has been the subject of debate, discussion, and deliberation for ages, it is not presumptuous to assume that many students, when confronted by such considerations, would be engaging in this type of discourse for the first time. In *The Social Contract*, Jean-Jacques Rousseau (1968) states that "[m]an was born free, and he is everywhere in chains." Although presented as a rhetorical flourish to introduce his treatise on the nature of freedom, Rousseau's sentiment is worth revisiting in a modern context: Are citizens today free yet bound by constraints? By investigating this question, a teacher might hope that students will develop more complex ideas of who they are and where they fit into the world around them. This premise begins with provincial considerations, such as inquiring into the difficulties of navigating the tumultuous world of schooling, to more global considerations, such as investigating the nature of human rights. In general, the pattern of inquiry suggested here might focus on issues related to becoming a part of a community, investigating issues related to tolerance and exclusion, and subsequently determining the extent to which an individual bears the responsibility to serve the community in which he or she exists.

In order to pursue the conceptual inquiry further, a series of key questions would serve to guide the inquiry and assist a teacher in planning and facilitating the types of discussions that would assist students in generating more thoughtful and more complex understandings related to the inquiry. Such a series of questions might look like this:

I. What is community, and where do I fit in?
  - What does it mean to be a part of a community?
  - How does a person overcome the difficulties of fitting into a new community?
  - To what extent, if any, should a person change in order to accommodate community expectations?

II. How do communities determine whom to include and whom to exclude?
  - What is equality, prejudice, and discrimination?
  - What are basic human rights?
  - How can individual prejudices lead to the loss of human rights?
  - How do victims of intolerance respond?
  - Can we judge who should rule and who should be ruled?
  - Are we ever justified in discriminating?
  - Should we try to make everyone equal?

III. To what extent does an individual have a responsibility to serve the community?
  - What does who we are suggest about what we should do?
  - The Hero Archetype: How should the aspiration to heroic behavior influence the way we live?

In this outline, we see the vast opportunity to engage students in pursuit of both the development and testing of working hypotheses that will enable them to generate more thoughtful and more complex understandings of the conceptual framework at the heart of the inquiry. This sample framework suggests to a teacher a pathway of inquiry that will enable him or her to plan a desired sequence of activities, readings, writings, and other learning experiences that will facilitate student inquiry. The example shown here can be used with such works as Sandra Cisneros's *The House on Mango Street*, Lorraine Hansberry's *A Raisin in the Sun*, H. G. Wells's *The Island of Dr. Moreau*, and *The Odyssey* by Homer. At the heart of such a framework is the promise that students will be placed in a situation where they can construct ideas and test them out by discussing matters with their peers.

## Facilitating Discussion That Corresponds to Inquiry

The suggestion that teachers need to actively seek out ways to prepare students for the discussion of important ideas in class is a tenet of English instruction. Louise Rosenblatt (1995) suggests that "[a]n atmosphere of informal, friendly exchange should be created" and asserted that "[t]here is no formula for giving students the assurance to speak out." Rosenblatt posited the belief that "[s]uch a liberating atmosphere will make it possible [...] to have an unself-conscious, spontaneous, and honest reaction" (67) to the texts and ideas discussed in class. Hillocks, McCabe, and McCampbell (1971) assert the importance of introductory activities, or what today might be called "prereading activities," to introduce students to important ideas or concepts that assist them in making subsequent substantive connections to the literacy activities in which they engage (see examples in Chapter 6). In his later work, Hillocks (1995) asserts the importance of "gateway activities" when he expresses his belief that "[t]heories of discourse, inquiry, learning, and teaching are useless if we cannot invent the activities that will engage our students in using, and therefore, learning, the strategies essential to certain writing tasks" (149), a pedagogical skill extending to the related language arts tasks of reading, listening, and speaking. Several examples of inquiry-based discussion activities, related to the inquiry surrounding the notion of social responsibility itemized above, demonstrate how the strategic planning of substantive discussion opportunities can establish the conducive speaking atmosphere advocated by Rosenblatt while providing students the gateway to inquiry asserted by Hillocks.

We discussed the use of prereading and "gateway" activities in earlier chapters to encourage the authentic discussion of specific works of literature. Here we examine using these activities for extended inquiry. The following narrative inquiry into issues related to gender equity, tolerance, and authority would provide students an opportunity to explore issues suggested by our sample conceptual framework.

### Is She a Victim?
### What's the Difference between What Is Acceptable and What Is Crossing the Line?

*The Problem*

Jenny Tone's first year at Market High School was going swimmingly. Jenny walked into English class with a happy grin, as usual. Jenny always had a happy grin. That's the kind of person she was. Her first semester had gone extremely well, and she was looking forward to the spring. She was already enjoying her second semester classes and most of them were filled with other ninth graders she knew and liked.

After the bell rang and all of the students settled into their seats, Jenny's teacher, Mr. Ross, began with a few general announcements. Mr. Ross then went on to introduce a student who had just been added to the class. "Everyone, please give a rousing round of applause to Larry Starenko. He's joining us today and will be with us for the rest of the semester."

As soon as Jenny processed the name, a cold sensation ran throughout her body. She turned around and looked at Larry, who was smirking and waving nonchalantly to all of the students who were paying attention to him. He obviously enjoyed the limelight. When his eyes met Jenny's, he winked at her and, when he thought most of the class had gone back to their own business and was no longer paying attention to him, he mouthed some words in Jenny's direction. She thought the words he mouthed were "I love you," but she wasn't exactly sure. But she was absolutely positive that almost in the same moment, he pursed his lips together to fashion a kiss and made a suggestive nod in Jenny's direction.

Jenny couldn't believe it.

Beatrice Buck, Jenny's friend who had sat next to her all during first semester whispered, "Do you know that guy?"

"Uh . . . n-not really," Jenny stuttered.

Jenny sat in a daze while class went on. Mr. Ross described a writing activity that would find the class using one of the school's computer labs to work on a story and then edit it later. She passively listened but found her thoughts straying to Larry Starenko and how it greatly displeased her to find him in her English class. It didn't seem fair. The class had gone well all first semester, and now he would ruin it all. It didn't seem fair.

Jenny was being poked by Beatrice.

"Let's go, girl," Beatrice said.

Jenny bolted upright and started following everyone else out of the room, into the hallway, and down to the computer lab. Out of the corner of her eye, she spotted Larry Starenko. He seemed to be speeding up around a corner of desks to get closer to her, but she stepped in front of two boys and headed out the door well ahead of him.

Beatrice lost her breath trying to keep up with Jenny. When they finally made it down the stairs and into the computer lab, Jenny and Beatrice occupied two machines next to each other at the end of a row in the middle of the room. To her displeasure, Jenny noticed Larry sitting down at the computer directly across from her. She couldn't bear to look directly at him, but she could feel him leering at her as he slowly settled into his seat. The two were now facing each other with only two computer monitors separating them. Jenny was startled to see Larry's face peep over from the side of his computer.

"How are you, Jenny?" he whispered.

Jenny hid her face behind her monitor, turned her computer on, and blankly stared at the screen.

In the meantime, Mr. Ross was busily scurrying about the room getting his students settled at their computer stations.

"Come on, Jenny! Get started," he said, as he walked down the aisle to the end of the row. "You, too, Larry. There's no time to waste."

Mr. Ross noticed that Jenny appeared to be more subdued than she usually was but didn't think much of it. He strolled around the lab several more times in the next ten minutes monitoring the progress of various students who had settled in to work.

"Larry, could you move your legs please?" Mr. Ross asked. Mr. Ross had noticed Larry's legs stretched all the way under the table to the point where they were in contact with Jenny Tone's feet directly opposite. Larry immediately drew his legs back to his own space. Jenny looked up with a shocked look on her face.

Mr. Ross settled in to the teacher station at the front of the room and started to look through some papers. He occasionally looked up to remind students about an aspect of their assignments and to save their work every ten minutes or so.

"Larry, is everything all right over there?" Mr. Ross asked. Mr. Ross could see Larry through a space between the several computers that separated them. He noticed that Larry's lips were continually mouthing words, and now and again, he would break out in a strange chuckle. Mr. Ross probably wouldn't have thought much of it, but at the same time he noticed Jenny Tone slumping her shoulders and looking down. She was shifting in her seat uncomfortably and generally seemed to be upset. Mr. Ross had the impression that Larry was bothering Jenny.

"All right, everyone," Mr. Ross bellowed. "Time to pack up. Don't forget to save your work before shutting down your machine, and everyone remember that we'll be meeting here for class tomorrow. Do not go up to the classroom. Got it?"

His students voiced various degrees of understanding as the bell rang, and they began leaving the room.

"See you later, Mr. Ross," Larry Starenko chimed, walking to the door. "I really enjoyed class today. It's going to be a great semester."

"See ya, Larry," Mr. Ross said.

As Mr. Ross gathered his things, he noticed that Jenny Tone was still packing up to leave. "How did it go today, Jenny?" he asked.

"You don't want to know how it went, Mr. Ross," Jenny replied.

"Sure I do," Mr. Ross said. "Speak!" he demanded.

Jenny giggled and began telling him everything that happened. "Last summer, Mr. Ross, this kid Jared came over to my house. I had met him a couple days before at the mall, and I gave him my number. He seemed like a nice kid. My parents were gone when he came over, and he brought along his friend, Larry Starenko, who I had never met before. The whole thing was a real mess because Jared and I never really got to talk or anything because this kid Larry was being a total jerk. He just kept saying a bunch of weird, embarrassing things. I think even Jared thought he was weird."

"What kinds of things did he say?" Mr. Ross asked.

Jenny turned a bit red and looked down. "He just said a bunch of things. And I finally ditched both of them and didn't see Larry again until the beginning of school. I got off my bus for the first time and almost ran right into him. He was just standing there, as if he were waiting for me, or something. And then he just started talking trash again, like he did when he came over to my house over the summer."

"Okay, Jenny, I can tell you're a little upset by all of this. Just take it easy. What were some of the things he was telling you?"

Jenny was definitely getting more upset. "Just a lot of nonsense. Embarrassing things, Mr. Ross. And it's happened a couple other times when I've run into him in the hallway. But I do my best to avoid him most of the time. If I see him in the hallway or something, I'll go the other way, or something, just to get away from him. And now . . ." Jenny's voice broke a little, ". . . and now he's in our class, and he's doing it again!"

The warning bell for the start of the next class sounded, punctuating the end of Jenny's statement. Mr. Ross could see that Larry Starenko was having a visible effect on her. "Jenny, I know you have to go to your next class," Mr. Ross said, as he began scribbling out a pass for her. "What exactly is he doing again, Jenny? What has he done that has gotten you so upset?"

"It's weird, Mr. Ross. But he was talking about me, and he says other things. Really low, like. Sometimes I'm not even sure that I'm hearing him correctly, but I know I am. Even today, when he was talking, he was disgusting me, but Beatrice was sitting right next to me, and I don't think she heard a thing. At least she didn't say that she did."

"Did you ask her?" Mr. Ross asked, handing the pass over to Jenny.

"Well, no, Mr. Ross. This isn't an easy thing to talk about."

"All right, we do have to go, but we'll look into this, Jenny."

The two walked out of the computer lab and were immediately swallowed up by the rushing crowd of students and teachers busily scurrying through the hallway.

Immediately after reading this case study, students might develop an empathic response and clarify their thinking by writing out a first-person narrative from the perspective of the teacher, Mr. Ross. An example of such a response looks like this:

If I was Mr. Ross, after I finished talking to Jenny I would set up a meeting with Larry so I can hear his side of the story. After I talked to Larry, I would set up a meeting with both of them, then they could talk and tell each other what is wrong. I would do this because then I could hear both sides of the story, and they could tell each other how they feel. If Larry keeps pestering Jenny, then I would call his and Jenny's parents so they could talk to their children and find out what's happening. Then if this still happened, I would have to suspend Larry or get him changed to a different English class.

Students share their writings and discuss the various empathic views. Students then continue the inquiry by investigating the situation further by discussing what, exactly, they judge should be done in this situation. Students might consider such possibilities as whether or not Jenny Tone is a victim of sexual harassment or whether it is possible that Larry Starenko could be unjustly accused of sexual harassment. To facilitate the inquiry, students are given a standard sexual harassment policy to help them categorize and evaluate the various incidents in the narrative. One such policy, taken from the York High School handbook in Elmhurst, Illinois, provides students with language like this:

1. Prohibition of sexual harassment: Employees and students are prohibited from sexually harassing other employees or students.

2. Definition: In the case of sexual harassment of a student or employee by a student sexual harassment means:

    - Any sexual advance by a student toward an employee or another student.

    - Any request by a student to an employee for sexual favors from the employee.

3. Sexual harassment prohibited by this policy includes verbal or physical conduct. The terms intimidating, hostile and offensive as used above include conduct which has the effect of humiliation, embarrassment or discomfort.

4. Complaints: Complaints alleging a violation of this policy should be brought to the attention of the appropriate school officials as soon as possible after the alleged incident of sexual harassment.

5. If sexual harassment occurs in the classroom:

    - Student tells the harasser to STOP.

    - Student keeps record of any further incidents: time, place, actions, words, and witnesses.

    - If the harassment continues, student reports the incident to the teacher.

- Teacher tells the harasser that a complaint has been made and the harassment must stop.
- Teacher files a sexual harassment report with the dean and an investigation begins.
- The victim should report any further incidents to a counselor, social worker, or dean.
- The victim will be asked for a written statement of the occurrence(s) and parents will be notified.

Armed with specific policy language to guide their analysis of the situation between Jenny and Larry, students are properly placed in an environment where they are authorized to inquire into the nature of the possible infraction and weigh a variety of hypotheses against the facts they have and specific policy language to guide their judgment. In this authorized environment, students typically engage in the types of conversations illustrated in the following excerpt from a small-group discussion.

*Teacher:* Once you have read through the policy and thought about things that are pertinent to helping you decide whether Jenny is a victim, answer the three questions I provided you. Use the policy, both sides of it, use whatever language you think is useful, tell me whether she is a victim of sexual harassment, whether Larry was unjustly accused, and whether or not the teacher is in a position to determine anything. Let's have a conversation for about fifteen minutes. Answer those questions to the best of your ability. This is a time when you may want to make a CLAIM, provide some EVIDENCE and then EXPLAIN it briefly in your notes. Does everyone know what they should be doing? Good luck!

*John:* All right. Do you guys think that, uh, she was a victim?

*Ben and Angela:* Yeah.

*John:* So then the claim would be . . .

*Angela:* Jenny is a victim.

*John:* Yeah. [Writes in his notes.] Evidence . . . let's see. This, we could use this one . . . "he pursed his lips together to fashion a kiss and made a suggestive nod in Jenny's direction."

*Ben:* Yeah.

*John:* Cause she says she wasn't sure about the words, but she was absolutely positive . . . in that same moment he did that, so . . .

*Ben:* Explanation.

*John:* The explanation would be the, um, the rule in this . . .

*Ben:* The warrant. It would be the warrant.

*John [to the teacher]:* I have a question. Um, for the explanation, 'cause these are rules, you know, but that doesn't have to be the warrant, though, right?

*Teacher:* Doesn't necessarily have to be the warrant . . .

*John:* That could be the explanation . . .

*Teacher:* Could be. Whatever's useful for you.

*John [to Ben]:* See.

*Ben:* All right. So what are we gonna put?

*John:* Hold on . . . [leafs through text] . . . dang, I lost it. What you should put is, like . . . The explanation is the rules say, like, "any conduct of a sexual nature by a student directed toward another student," you know, when such a time that, blah blah, blah . . .

[Angela laughs. They all write.]

*John:* Are you writing that whole thing for the explanation?

*Ben:* Ah . . . no, I'm shortening it up a little.

*John:* Yeah. Let's see. Here, we'll do this. Such . . . here, this one right here. The second sentence . . . "such conduct has the obvious result of creating an intimidating, hostile or offensive school environment for the student." So . . .

*Ben:* For the warrant put, Jenny is obviously upset by what Larry said and did.

*John:* It's got to be a rule, though. Um, um, it should be, like, mmm . . . [pause] we could say, like, when a person makes a sexual reference that the opposing person is not comfortable with, is considered sexual harassment.

*Angela:* Are we supposed to just make one argument?

*Matt:* When a person makes a sexual reference . . .

*Ben:* Next question . . .

*John:* Larry is not . . . falsely accused?

*Ben:* Larry is sexually harassing Jenny?

*John:* That's not evidence.

*Ben:* Yeah it is!

*Angela:* You have to find a fact.

*Matt:* Yeah, Larry doesn't even say one thing to her. All she says is that she's been . . . read it . . . there's not one thing that says he harasses her sexually. You know what I mean? All it says is "How are you doing, Jenny?"

*Ben:* How about, Larry makes Jenny feel uncomfortable? That's evidence.

*John:* We'll say there are many situations. . . . There are many situations where Larry makes . . .

*Ben:* Yeah . . .

*John:* There have been . . . situations . . . in which Larry . . . has created . . . an uncomfortable environment for Jenny.

The dialogue recounted here demonstrates a high level of engagement among the group participants. Introduced to an open-ended point of inquiry and given a framework in which to explore ideas, the students present ideas and challenge each other to refine their thinking. In addition to providing students the chance to engage in, and enhance, critical thinking, the point of the inquiry is also consistent with the conceptual framework that guides inquiry throughout the entire sample curriculum. While establishing whether Jenny Tone is a victim of sexual harassment, students are also reflecting on the obstacles individuals face when attempting to fit into a particular community, in this case, a classroom community. Establishing this gateway for understanding further prepares students to evaluate similar situations and ideas that might be the subject of a variety of other texts they might read during the course of the unit.

The teacher's job, then, becomes one of sustaining and managing this extended inquiry through subsequent points of inquiry. Again, the strategic utilization of gateway activities can assist in achieving this curricular continuity while offering students the continued opportunity to talk about issues that are important to them. After implementing a case study approach and establishing some notion of the challenges of fitting into a community, as demonstrated through the "Is She a Victim?" inquiry, students might investigate several other scenarios that assist them in establishing criteria that they can use to test out beliefs about tolerance and diversity—two concepts that are at the heart of several of the key questions in our sample unit sequence. By attempting to establish identifiable criteria that illuminate these issues, students talk their way to greater understanding of these issues. The discussion-based activity below extends the students' thinking about the critical questions of the unit and suggests another discussion framework that assists in facilitating discussion.

### Can You Say, "You Can't Play"?
### Etiquette for the Twenty-First Century

Vivian Paley, a kindergarten teacher in a Chicago school, posted a sign in her classroom: "You can't say 'You can't play'." She did not want to see any student excluded from any group. The students, of course, complained, insisting that the rule was impossible and unfair. Ms. Paley remained firm. She hoped to inculcate in her five- and six-year-olds a standard of etiquette and conduct that would guide them as adults in the twenty-first century. Anyone who lives in the United States recognizes that the country's diversity and increased awareness of cultural and gender bias have provided a number of awkward situations. It is sometimes difficult to know the right thing to do. Existing guides to etiquette fail to account for the unique situations that will continue to occur in the twenty-first century.
Here is what you can do to help:

1. Meet with two or three other class members to study and discuss the following situations. Read one situation at a time and discuss how you would respond to the problem.

2. Note any unresolved disagreements that remain within your group.

3. List the rules of etiquette that apply in each situation.

4. After you've examined all the cases and listed new rules of etiquette, answer these questions:

    a. To what extent should a person be willing to change beliefs, attitudes, and behavior in order to be included in a group?

    b. To what extent should a group (i.e., club, class, organization) be willing to make accommodations in order to include a new member?

1. Adam and Danae Raspworthy recently moved into the Utopia Hollow subdivision in the suburb of Random Falls. A group of neighbors invited them to dinner to welcome the Raspworthys to the community. It appeared that all of Adam and Danae's new neighbors were of the same ethnicity. At the dinner party, the neighbors served braised eel in apricot chutney, poached octopus in curry gravy, boiled lamb kidneys, sage dumplings, and bone-marrow soup. Adam and Danae, who are very conservative in their eating

habits, almost gagged when they saw and smelled this unfamiliar food. Although they did not want to offend anyone, and they wanted to become accepted members of the neighborhood, they would find it very difficult to eat the food that they were expected to eat. What should Adam and Danae do?

2.  Bella Ardor, a clever and highly respected electrical engineer for the Bassho Electronics Company, was recently reassigned to work at the Company headquarters in Tojo, Japan. Now, each day at work at Bassho in Japan, all the engineers take a tea break at 2:30 P.M. At tea time, the oldest and most revered engineer prepares tea, while everyone else watches. The old engineer is very precise and deliberate in his preparation. The ritual of tea preparation takes precisely twenty minutes every day. No one rushes the old man, and no one talks during the ceremony. After the ceremonial brewing of tea, everyone slowly and quietly sips the refreshment. The elaborate procedure is very frustrating to Bella, who is distracted from her work for nearly an hour. She is more used to popping a tea bag into hot water and going back to her desk. She could propose setting an electronic tea pot on a timer so that the tea would be ready precisely when the workers want it. It seems foolhardy to Bella that a modern company that specializes in state-of-the-art technology would waste time by engaging in a daily tea brewing ritual. Should Bella interfere to try to change the traditional practice? Why, or Why not?

3.  In Azure-Camala, the land where Lanya Lapp grew up, the main business is hog farming. In Lanya's homeland, hogs are prized above all other commodities. The people of Azure-Camala appreciate hogs for their looks, their intelligence, their affection, and their loyalty. The image of a hog graces the national currency, the presidential seal, and the Azure-Camala flag. This year, Lanya has come to the United States to attend college at Middle Border State University. At the university, Lanya has begun dating a boy named Parker Grimhouse. Lanya has become very fond of Parker. Often, to express her affection, Lanya refers to Parker, both in public and private, by a variety of endearing appellations: swine, hog, piggy, piglet, etc. Parker is sometimes shocked and often embarrassed. What do you think Lanya should do? Why? What do you think Parker should do? Why?

4.  Recently women have been admitted to the historically all-male Wisconsin Institute of Military Science (WIMS), a college that pre-

pares young candidates to become officers in the United States Armed Forces. Wanda Reinstone has entered WIMS this year. The school has made little accommodation for women. Wanda has felt comfortable with most requirements—even the typically masculine style uniforms. This fall she faces a dilemma. She is expected to attend the institute's important and elegant Harvest Ball. Although it is not *required*, in the past all of the WIMS cadets have worn the school's formal dress uniform. This is a military style suit, with white pants, dark gray jacket, white shirt, and black bow tie. The cadets customarily wear a military hat and white gloves, which they remove upon arrival at the ball. Wanda could do several things: stay away from the ball, wear the traditional uniform, wear a female variation of the uniform, or wear an elegant, nonmilitary dress. What should she do? Why?

5. A generous scholarship from the League of Convenience Store Operators has allowed Cliff Dweller to leave his working-class community in Milwaukee and attend the prestigious and exclusive Catherine Lane College in Chilblains, Minnesota. The move to Catherine Lane was quite a shock for Cliff. Although he enjoyed his classes, he found it difficult to fit in with the other students. In Cliff's dormitory, it seemed that everyone dressed alike: men wore corduroy slacks, plaid shirts, V-neck sweaters, and loafers; women wore plaid wool skirts, pullover sweaters, knee socks, and loafers. Cliff often felt out of place in the athletic warm-ups and running shoes, which he typically wore. Cliff also found the local slang a bit baffling. The other Catherine Lane students had their own unique speech style. They referred to eating as "slurping sustenance" or S2 (pronounced s-two). Instead of studying, they "pondered print," or P2. "Bolt the beacon," or B2, meant "turn off the light." A "hygiene hiatus," or H2, was a shower. Parties focused on the drinking of CL punch, an obnoxious combination of port wine and mint flavored iced tea, and featured line dancing to country music. Cliff quickly realized that if he were to have any kind of social life at college, he would have to become more like the other Catherine Lane College students. Without any kind of social life, Cliff would likely become lonely, depressed, and challenged to succeed in his studies. What should Cliff do? Why?

6. When eight-year-old Stephen accompanied his mother to his aunt's house, he had hoped that he would have an opportunity to

play with his three cousins—Melissa, Calpurnica, and Jezibel. While Stephen's mother worked with his Aunt Tabetha in the kitchen to plan the family's holiday meal, Stephen was left to join in play with his female cousins in the family room. Before Stephen's mother closed the door to separate the children from the adults, she said, "As usual, I expect you children to settle your own disputes. You are old enough and creative enough to find solutions by yourselves." Melissa, Calpurnica, and Jezibel were eager for Stephen to join them in playing "tea party." They had an elaborate plastic tea set laid out on the floor of the family room. Their dolls sat beside them. The girls dressed in elaborate costumes from the dress-up box. Stephen's cousins appealed to him to don a dress and apron and play the part of Miss Sophonsiba, an elderly and extravagantly wealthy guest at the fashionable gathering. If Stephen were to play with other children this day, he would have to play the game that the three girls already selected. What should Stephen do? Why?

7. Nathan Dupree enrolled this year in second grade at Douglass Elementary School in Blanche Features, Indiana. Initially, Nathan felt a bit uncomfortable at being the only African-American child in the class. One morning during the third week of school, Ms. Blander, the second-grade teacher, instructed the students to open their readers to a story called "Little Bambali." The story, set in India, features a dark-complexioned child who narrowly escapes being mauled and eaten by several tigers. Bambali outwits the tigers, who subsequently turn into a pool of butter as they chase each other around a tree. The story and the Bambali character are clearly intended to be comical. The children, including Nathan, laughed as they read the story aloud. As Nathan looked up from his book, he saw other students looking at him. Nathan began to wonder what was funny, and he felt very uncomfortable. What should Nathan do? Should he tell the teacher he was upset? Should he laugh along with the other students when the class reads similar stories? Should Nathan protest? Should Nathan refuse to read similar stories?

Students are given the opportunity to investigate each of these scenarios and provide a rationale for their beliefs. The outcome of their discussions provides them with a list of criteria, or warrants, that will be useful to them as they continue their prolonged inquiry into community, tolerance, and social responsibility. In response to the scenarios they investigate together, students develop a list of criteria that provide them with a working list of principles that they can later test out against subsequent reading and writing activities. In response to the scenario about the couple who arrive at the home where the exotic foods are served, students generate warrants like, "People should be open-minded and willing to try new things." In response to the scenario about the tea ceremony held during lunch hour, students assert that "people need to be aware of traditions and customs and be willing to go along with them sometimes, even if it's not always personally convenient." With the expression of these principles, students tap into a body of knowledge and experience that they can subsequently use to evaluate the behaviors and actions of characters they read about or behaviors they have seen in film. The sustained inquiry of a conceptually relevant curriculum, enhanced with the reliance upon student-to-student discourse, places students in the position to engage with texts at an advanced level.

Sustaining the conceptual inquiry of the classroom throughout the year requires constant attention to placing students in environments where they construct their own understandings and test their ideas out against reasonable viewpoints suggested by their peers. In pursuing an advanced understanding of the conceptual framework from our sample curricular outline, having investigated the notions of community and tolerance suggested by previous activities, students are allowed to build on the procedural knowledge they've constructed and are provided the opportunity to develop their ideas further. Allowing students to discuss meaningful subject matter that is relevant to their classroom inquiry provides them the additional scaffolding they require to develop their understanding further.

---

### Does "We Can" Mean "We Should"?

*Directions:* Read and discuss each of the following situations with members of your group. Weigh the positive and negative aspects of each situation and then try to come to some resolution of the issue. Write a brief rationale that explains your position. Your rationale should be written in the form of a rule, or criteria statement, that helps to define your position regarding genetic engineering or genetic tampering.

**Case 1. Three Cancerous Mice . . . See How They Run**
Decatur University has recently been experimenting with laboratory

mice. Researchers there have exposed thousands of mice to a variety of bacteria, viruses, diseases, and stressful conditions to further researchers' ability to study, and eradicate, diseases in humans. After a number of years, and millions of dollars, Decatur has developed and bred mice that easily develop malignant cancerous tumors. The rationale behind this development is to provide special mice that can be used to further cancer research that would benefit humans. In other words, mice prone to cancer will develop cancer and can then be used to study cancer. Aside from these benefits, Decatur University is pleased about the potential market for these special mice. They applied for, and received, a patent for the mice they developed. They now own the rights to the mice and can produce and sell them to universities and laboratories around the world. The university will receive all of the profits that emerge from the creation and sale of the cancer-prone mice.

*Question:*
Should Decatur University be allowed to profit from the development and sale of mice they've created which are prone to cancerous tumors?

**Case 2. I'll Take That One!**
For the past two decades, prenatal screening for fetal defects at Pontchartrain Hospital has become a standard part of nearly every pregnant woman's medical care. The most common tests in use include ultrasound imaging, which produces a picture of the fetus, and amniocentesis, a procedure in which a needle is inserted into the uterus and withdraws a small amount of amniotic fluid for cell analysis. Tests conducted during pregnancy are designed to detect a wide range of genetic and other disorders, and to give women the option of obtaining abortions if defects are diagnosed. Some people regard these developments as a breakthrough in the age-old war against disease. Others regard it as a tool to improve society. Prenatal testing, these people say, offers a system of quality control. For the first time in history, parents are able to customize, in limited ways, the kinds of children they bring into the world. Dr. Melvin Baronne agrees with this way of thinking. "Prenatal genetic screening is a positive thing because it gives prospective families freedom of choice," he says. "These tests enabled parents to fulfill their personal expectations with respect to raising a healthy family. This is

especially important for parents who have a known risk of bearing a child with an inherited disorder," he says.

Samantha Prytania, another doctor on staff at Pontchartrain disagrees. "Many of these tests are not even safe," she says. "They're only used because many doctors and hospital administrators are under pressure not only to achieve improvements in health but also to reduce soaring health care costs. Widespread prenatal screening, followed by abortion for fetal defects accomplishes both of these objectives," Prytania says. "I mean, we're asking parents who undergo prenatal testing to make life-and-death choices about what kind of life is worth living and what kinds of disabilities are too costly to society. It's painful to see parents who are told that their baby will be born with Down's syndrome deal with this. And we don't even know where this could go in the future. Will there be a government agency that determines which babies with certain characteristics can be born and which must be aborted? This could lead to a form of discrimination that is too horrible to consider!"

*Question:*
Should Pontchartrain Hospital continue to use prenatal genetic testing on pregnant women?

**Case 3. Our Crops Are Saved!**
Dauphine ADM Genetics Corporation has developed genetic engineering technology to help farmers produce heartier and tastier fruits and vegetables. By altering plant genes, scientists at Dauphine can also create bug- and herbicide-resistant cotton and plants that produce biodegradable plastics and human proteins for medical treatments. Dauphine ADM has a number of other projects, as well. Dauphine is currently trying to keep potatoes from rotting by using genes from chicken embryos and insect immune systems. Learning that the Arctic flounder makes an antifreeze to protect itself against winter chills, Dauphine plans to inject the antifreeze gene into strawberries, so they can make their own antifreeze and protect themselves from unexpected frosts that can wipe out entire strawberry crops. "We've got a million ideas," says corporation founder, Otis Dauphine. "Tinkering around with genetics allows you to do just about anything," he says. "We can feed the world!"

Wayne Audubon thinks that Dauphine's talk about saving the world is "a bunch of malarkey!" "You'll never see the 'antifreeze strawberry'," Audubon claims. "The only thing you'll ever see come out of Dauphine's labs and into farmers' hands will be varieties of corn, soybeans, or wheat that are able to withstand higher doses of one of Dauphine's best-selling and most powerful herbicides, Skeedattle," he says. Audubon believes that coming up with the herbicide-resistant grains will boost worldwide sales of Skeedattle, a product on which Dauphine managed to extend its patent, by $500 million a year. Besides Dauphine's self interest in the herbicide business, Audubon believes there are other, more important concerns. "Most of these herbicides aren't even safe," he says. Supporting Audubon's position is the fact that traces of herbicides like Atrazine have been found in the groundwater supplies of twelve different states and the herbicide 2,4-D has recently been linked to non-Hodgkin's lymphoma, a type of cancer, in farmers. "This idea of genetically developing herbicide-resistant crops so we can use stronger herbicides to kill pests and weeds doesn't work, anyway," Audubon says. "After a while, the weeds get used to the poison and don't die anymore. Then we use a new, more-toxic poison, and they eventually get used to that too . . . it's a vicious cycle. As the grains become herbicide resistant, so do the weeds and the pests! What's the point? It's not worth the cost and the human lives. Plus, the only people coming out ahead are Dauphine employees," Audubon says.

Otis Dauphine thinks that Wayne Audubon is crazy. "I can understand the concern that people have about tampering with the genetic makeup of food," he says. "But because of the initial public fears that 'monster' plants or runaway weeds would be created, the release of these types of plants and herbicides has been rigorously controlled by scientists and a combination of federal agencies: the Environmental Protection Agency, the U.S. Department of Agriculture, and the Food and Drug Administration. There's absolutely nothing to worry about," Dauphine says.

*Question:*
Should Dauphine ADM Genetics Corporation continue to research and produce genetically engineered plants that are resistant to herbicides and pests?

**Case 4. BST . . . It Does a Body Good!**
Tchoupitoulas Foods uses genetic engineering methods to alter farm animals so that they can produce more milk and eggs and better

quality meat. The company's "Superior Chicken" subsidiary developed a breed of chicken with an enormous breastbone, thereby ensuring that chicken farmers who raised this type of chicken would have plenty of breast meat to sell. Tchoupitoulas's "Magical Dairy" subsidiary implements another technique. Scientists at the dairy inject a hormone, bovine somatotropin (BST), into dairy cows to increase their milk production. This bovine growth hormone is a genetically engineered version of a cow's naturally occurring growth hormone. Cows injected with BST in Tchoupitoulas test herds produce an average of 10 percent to 25 percent more milk. "BST is a safe, healthy, and effective way to increase milk production," says second generation company owner, Terry Tchoupitoulas. Tchoupitoulas believes that increasing the productivity of dairy cattle and other farm animals is important for the world to be able to feed its growing population. "Scientists in academia, government, and industry have conducted more than two thousand scientific studies of BST throughout the world," Tchoupitoulas says. "These studies have clearly shown the efficacy, safety, and benefits realized by integrating BST into dairy production," she states. Tchoupitoulas also cites studies that show that BST does not adversely affect the health of treated cows and that show that the milk and meat derived from BST treated cows are safe for human consumption.

Sal Carondelet disagrees. Carondelet also has data from the Tchoupitoulas test herds that shows that cows injected with BST experienced a marked increase in animal health problems. "This means vet bills for dairy farmers, money needed to replace cows, and consumer concerns about possible excessive use of antibiotics to treat sick cows," Carondelet says. Carondelet believes that BST is an enemy to dairy farmers. He believes this type of genetic engineering undercuts the confidence that people have in the dairy industry. "Moms don't want their kids drinking BST milk and eating BST ice cream," he says. "They're afraid of what might happen." Carondelet also disagrees with Tchoupitoulas's claim that BST is tested and safe. Carondelet points to a 1990 Congressional study that found that more than half of the drugs approved by the Food and Drug Administration over a ten-year period were later found to have "serious post-approval risks" for consumers. "There's no mistake about it," Carondelet says; "the only benefit to BST is the increased profit to Tchoupitoulas Foods."

*Question:*
Should Tchoupitoulas Foods be allowed to continue the process of injecting dairy cows with bovine somatotropin (BST)?

The sample activities presented here provide students a framework through which to develop a more complex view of issues related to equality and tolerance suggested by our sample sequence, as well as placing students in a position to discuss their emerging understanding of social responsibility at a higher level. In response to the scenario concerning the creation of mice that are prone to cancerous tumors, students generate a number of criteria that suggest the animals should not be treated in a cruel or particularly unusual way in order to benefit humankind. In response to the scenario concerning prenatal testing, students often develop criteria that suggest such testing is vital and important; however, there should be set limits depending on the nature of the testing. Any one of the scenarios opens up an inquiry into the ever changing scope of the dialogue and provides students with a series of frameworks through which to develop their understandings of these important issues even further. This approach also prepares students to read a variety of literatures that question the extent to which humankind should interfere with nature, a theme reiterated in texts as commonly used as *Frankenstein*, *The Island of Dr. Moreau*, or even more recent nonfiction works such as *Fast Food Nation*. The discussion framework provides students an additional opportunity to develop and apply their emerging knowledge.

# 12 Discussion and Critical Thinking

Some learning standards expressed by state boards of education or by professional education organizations like NCTE prompt teachers to help students to develop critical thinking skills. Any number of activities could require critical thinking: from selecting a reliable used car at the best price to writing an analysis of a poem. While various sources (e.g., Paul and Elder 2001; Paul, Martin, and Adamson 1989; Halpern 1996, 1997) describe different conceptions of critical thinking, inevitably, critical thinking will involve logical reasoning and the assessment of options, whether these options are courses of action or critical positions. Although not a necessary condition, the purposeful interaction with other thinkers will support critical thinking. To illustrate an interactive process of critical thinking, we draw an example from the media and describe a variation on the critical thinking procedures in the classroom.

It is always a pleasure to listen to National Public Radio where Legal Affairs Correspondent Nina Totenburg reports the proceedings of the U.S. Supreme Court. Regular listeners to Totenburg's reports will recognize this format: First Totenburg introduces the case by succinctly relating the events that have raised the critical issues. She then notes the essential question before the Court. As the report continues, Totenburg recounts the arguments made by the petitioner. Typically the arguments are lucid, evidentiary, and persuasive on first face (prima facie). The justices then ask a series of questions that test the reasoning of the spokesperson. There is a kind of Socratic sense to the questioning. While the petitioner might begin with a firm position, the justices ask him or her to apply general claims to other situations, to explain how the desired decision would be consistent with previous rulings by the Court, and to express the legal principles that should guide judgment. The respondent argues the opposing position. The justices ask probing questions of this speaker, testing the general applicability of the claims, challenging the logic, demanding consistency.

---

An earlier version of this chapter appeared as an article in the *Illinois English Bulletin* 86(3). It is reprinted here by permission of the Illinois Association of Teachers of English.

The cases before the Supreme Court are tough ones, which is why they have progressed through the court system. Take, for example, the case of a woman in California who wanted access to a supply of marijuana to ease the symptoms of a debilitating illness. On first face, it might appear to a reasonable listener that the woman's use of marijuana is medically necessary and clearly beneficial. For the government to thwart her suppliers and to threaten them and the patient with arrest and prosecution seems unwarranted and even cruel. However, the questions from the justices raise some doubts: Doesn't the government have a responsibility to control the quality standards for the production and use of drugs? Will recreational drug users claim a medical need in order to use controlled substances with impunity? The attorney for the government then makes a case for restricting the marijuana user. The listener might be persuaded by these arguments. The justices, however, raise doubts again by asking tough questions of the second attorney. A dialogic and dialectical process influences the justices in making their decisions and challenges Totenburg's listeners to move beyond the possible news headline, "California Woman Appeals for Drug Use," and judge the case through a dynamic process to develop what could be called critical thinking.

The dialectic involved in a Supreme Court session is the kind that Kapp (1942) attributes to Aristotle:

> It consists in either arguing about a proposed problem—any debatable problem—from probable premises, or, if one is attacked in argument, in avoiding self contradiction. For this kind of philosophic exercise, there are always two persons required, plus a problem; one person has the part of questioner, the other person the part of respondent and opponent. The questioner first proposes a problem, the respondent chooses his position, and then the questioner has to take as his view that side of the problem which was repudiated by the respondent. Now the questioner must continue questioning and try to draw a conclusion, or we may say, get a syllogism in favor of his view from such answers as he is able to elicit from the interlocutor. The part of the respondent is more passive; but he has to be on his guard against concessions as will enable the questioner to get his conclusion. For if the questioner gets his conclusion, the respondent is obviously the loser, since he will be forced to deny what at the beginning he asserted, or vice versa. (12)

Rarely do any citizens exhibit the kind of critical thinking evident in this process. In schools where the dominant mode of instruction features the transmission of information and regular recitation to check for recall of the information, there will be little evidence of the kind of classroom discourse that promotes critical thinking. It is possible, however, to move classroom instruction into a discussion-based mode that has many features of Aristotelian dialectic and has students engaged in the kind of critical thinking that characterizes a Supreme Court session. Movement in this direction means exposing students to the kind of problems that engage their thought and that connect conceptually with themes and questions in the literature. Teachers would also need to provide for the organizational structures that invite purposeful peer interaction.

The activity that follows comes from a unit of study that includes work with Conrad Richter's novel *The Light in the Forest*. The activity is potentially useful as preparation or extension for thinking about other literature that depicts clashes among cultures (e.g., *The Color of Water, Things Fall Apart*). In Richter's novel, a source of conflict between whites and Native Americans is a basic lack of respect for each group's way of living. Whites dismiss Native Americans as savages, claiming that their language, manner of dress, and general demeanor reveal a primitive nature. For their part, the Native Americans denounce whites as barbarians who know nothing about living an honest, honorable, and healthy life. The criticism on both sides challenges the reader to find some way to decide objectively the merits of the criticism: Is there ever a time when a person can judge by objective standards that one culture is wrong and should conform to the standards of another?

Daily frays into the culture wars today include one group's insistence on respect, while the offender advises that others be less sensitive. It won't take a teacher or student long to find contemporary news stories about clashes between cultures and the expressed hopes for tolerance and respect. Apparently these conflicts are not easy to resolve, or they wouldn't remain controversies. One persistent and representative debate focuses on the use of Native American images and symbols for athletic teams' logos. Teams that claim names like the *Braves*, the *Indians*, the *Warriors*, the *Redskins*, and the *Seminoles* face criticism and protest. Simply stated, the criticism on the one hand charges that the team or school negatively stereotypes one racial group and callously misuses symbols and customs. A typical response from the other camp is that hypersensitive political correctness defies good sense and threatens freedom of expression.

By looking at a representative modern case, students form arguments to offer a rational basis for their own positions, and they are confronted with opposing views that they must account for in an attempt to resolve the dispute. The study of a particular case fosters the development of the specialized language of argument and equips students with analytical thinking strategies that they can subsequently apply to the reading of a related novel.

## Gateway Activity: "The Floodrock Braves"

Gateway activities tap pertinent content knowledge and engage students in thinking processes that can transfer to related learning. The following activity requires student involvement in several stages. First the teacher introduces the basic conflict and background for the case. Students then independently study the related artifacts (Figures 12.1–12.4), which include testimonies from various perspectives. Then the students engage in small-group discussion about whether or not a school should change its controversial logo and mascot. The following materials offer directions for using the activity and provide the related data sets that should serve students in their discussions about the case. Several exhibits of the students' work with the problem reveal the thinking that is required in meaningful small-group and large-group discussion, and the transfer of this thinking into a subsequent written analysis.

---

### The Floodrock Braves

*Background.*

For eighty years the Floodrock High School athletic teams have been referred to as the *Braves*. Even the girls' athletic teams have borne the name "Lady Braves." At halftime of home football and basketball games, a student who dresses up as "Chief Whompum," the team mascot, entertains the crowd with his or her interpretation of the "Whompum War Dance." Chief Whompum's costume is a fanciful imitation of the clothing worn by members of the Sioux nation, a tribe who lived on the North American Plains. The teams' uniforms bear a logo with a cartoon rendering of the face of an Indian in war paint under which can be found crossed tomahawks. At all games, the cheerleaders encourage the crowd to chant "Scalp 'em! Scalp 'em, Braves!"

This year a group of North American Indians from several tribes in Illinois, Missouri, and Wisconsin have petitioned the school to change the name of the sports team and end what they call "the offensive and stereotypical representation of Native Americans." The men and women who signed the petition are not residents in the school district. Many graduates of Floodrock High have a sentimen-

---

tal attachment to the Braves name and mascot. They claim that the school must honor tradition and keep the name. Some residents believe that the school has a right, protected by the Constitution, to use the name even when some persons might be offended.

*Questions for Discussion.*
The school officials would be interested in hearing your advice about whether or not they should change the teams' name or somehow alter the way Indians are represented by the school. They would be especially interested in your responses to the following questions:

1. Does the school have a constitutional right to use *Braves* as the name for their athletic teams?
2. Can the school's use of the name and accompanying Native American symbols *really* hurt or offend anyone?
3. How important is it to uphold school tradition?
4. Do people who do not even live in the Floodrock community have a right to criticize the school representatives and advise them on how to behave?
5. What would be gained by changing the name?
6. In the final analysis, what do you recommend?

*Artifacts.*
Before you make any decisions, prepare for discussion by examining the attached artifacts [Figures 12.1–12.4]. The artifacts will provide some information that you can use in supporting your claims. The four artifacts include: (1) a reproduction of a newspaper account of the controversy, (2) a letter of complaint from a community resident, (3) a letter from Floodrock's athletic director, and, (4) a brief history of Native American tribes in southern Illinois (from a handout composed by Mr. Steinhouse's eleventh-grade U.S. History class).

*Related Research.*
A class that discusses the case of the Floodrock Braves will not be the first group that examines tough questions about retaining or eliminating certain team mascots. Debates about athletic teams' use of Native American symbols, customs, and images recur in many communities throughout the year. A reader can find reports of such debates in new stories and on websites. An Internet search using terms like *Braves*, *Indians*, *Chiefs*, and *Warriors* will yield abundant sources of information and representations of the arguments on both sides of the controversies. In preparation for a classroom discussion

*continued on next page*

and written analysis of the case, it will be useful to complete a search and see how other thinkers have made judgments and expressed their arguments.

*Procedure for Discussion.*
You will follow several steps in thinking about the case:

1. First examine the artifacts and answer the Questions for Discussion individually.

2. After you have prepared your position, join two or three other students in a small-group discussion about the case. In each group, the desks or chairs should be situated in a way that allows everyone to look at everyone else in the group easily. Allow each person an opportunity to speak and take notes on the claims and ideas of all the participants. Select one person as the group spokesperson to report to the whole class what the group has decided.

3. Participate in a large-group discussion. The focus of the discussion will be the attempt to resolve the problem in a way that is fair, understanding, and legal: **What should the School Board at Floodrock High School do about their school mascot?**

*Written Response.*
After participating in discussion and taking careful notes, prepare a written response to the case. Write your response in the form of a letter to the President of the School Board of Floodrock High School. In your letter, you will do the following:

1. Remind the reader about the problem and the central issues. Then advise the reader what to do.

2. Provide a complete rationale for your recommendation. This part of your composition will include claims that you support with specific evidence that you have drawn from examining the artifacts and from taking notes during discussions. You might also draw support from the research you may have completed online or through print sources.

3. In a controversy like this one, obviously other thinkers will not agree with you. Explain as objectively and fairly as possible what other persons have to say about the case. Evaluate the merits of the opposing views.

4. Summarize your position and conclude your thoughts.

5. This is a formal letter to a school board official. The letter should be typed, carefully proofread, and neatly presented.

---

### THE CHIEF IN THE NEWS AGAIN*

by Holly Fargo

A gun sounded to signal halftime of the Floodrock-Jonesboro football game on Saturday night. Under the stands, Hendron Reeves, this year's Chief Whompum, warmed up for his performance. The tradition remains unbroken: the Whompum War Dance since 1917; the small chorus of boos since 1994. Chief Whompum is at the center of controversy again this year.

"The dance is a time-honored tradition at Floodrock," reports Harlan Granville, Recording Secretary of the Braves Boosters. "This tradition has been going on for as long as I can remember. There is value in tradition. No one should interfere with our right to follow our own traditions."

Florion Calvert, a visitor from Jonesboro, contributed to the chorus of boos this year. Calvert notes, "This Whompum character has nothing to do with Indian tradition. It is a mockery. No Indian from these parts dressed that way or danced that way. They are taking a symbol of a rich cultural tradition and making a mockery of it."

Sissy Beaumont, a tenth-grader at Floodrock finds that the critics are being too serious. "Come on," she said, "when

Detail of hallway mural of "The Chief"

are we going to see that Whompum is just a costume character, with no intention of insulting anyone? It is just like dressing up for Halloween. If you are not really a witch, can't you dress up and act like one just for fun. The dance is intended to inspire school spirit. It doesn't hurt anyone."

Not everyone agrees that the school ritual is fun. "Ask a Native American if it is fun," observed Burleigh Steinhouse, veteran history teacher at Floodrock. "A Native American is the only true judge. If someone is offended, can we deny that the dance is offensive?"

There are several games remaining this year, and many opportunities for opponents to debate the legitimacy and sensitivity of the War Dance.

---

*Reprinted from the *Fanfare*, the official school newspaper of Floodrock High School

**Figure 12.1.** An account of the Floodrock High School "Braves" controversy from the school's newspaper, *Fanfare*.

October 3


Dr. Stavros Denton, Superintendent
Floodrock High School
1111 Thomas More Parkway
Floodrock, Illinois 62901

Dear Dr. Denton:

Once again this year I am offended by the despicable spectacle of a white student
of your high school making a mockery of Native American tradition and culture.
I urge you to drop the use of the Braves logo and mascot and immediately stop
the practice of a "Whompum War Dance" at halftime of athletic events.

The use of the Braves logo is offensive. First of all, as a depiction of Native Americans from southern Illinois, the costume and dance are all wrong. Your Chief
Whompum wears the garb of the Sioux tribe, who never lived in southern Illinois. The idea, then, that the mascot honors the rich Native American tradition in
this area is ridiculous.

Second, the dance constitutes mockery, not honor. Native Americans consider their
dances as part of sacred rituals. To invent some stereotypical imitation of Native
American ritual dance as a half time entertainment is tantamount to sacrilege for
those Native Americans who identify certain dances as part of religious ceremony.
Such a practice is comparable to allowing students to enact an imitation of a Ro-
man Catholic mass for the edification of a stadium crowd.

The logo and mascot promote the stereotype of Native Americans as savage, bel-
ligerent, and comical. We have enough trouble with ignorance and bigotry in our
society without the public schools promoting these problems. I ask you again to
drop the team mascot and ban the Chief Whompum dance.

Sincerely,

*Clyde Faner*

Clyde Faner, D.D.S.

**Figure 12.2.** A letter of complaint from a community resident about the
Floodrock High School "Braves" controversy.

**Floodrock High School**
**Home of the Braves**
**1111 Thomas More Parkway**
**Floodrock, Illinois 62901**

FHS

**Athletic Director**

Scalp 'em!

October 30

Dear Parents,

Once again this year, protesters who are not associated with Floodrock High School have chosen to challenge the appearance of our team mascot at half time of football games. You've probably heard the boos and cat calls if you've been in the stands at Kruppke Memorial Stadium recently. I want to respond to some of the criticism so that you'll know that the school and the Athletic Department bear no animosity toward Indians.

The Brave logo and Chief Whompum have been associated with Floodrock athletic teams for over eighty years. The name derives from the fact that many years ago several Indian tribes inhabited our region. We see the use of the logo and mascot as a means for preserving the cultural heritage and celebrating the influence that Indians have had on the region. We recognize the Brave and Chief as time-honored symbols, with authentic roots in our region. We respect the North American Indian as a figure of courage and honor; that's why we want our teams to be associated with the image. The continued use of the Braves logo and the presence of the mascot underscore the importance of celebrating our heritage without interference.

When outsiders protest against our team mascot, they fail to see the ramifications of any change. First of all, it would be quite distressing for alumni of this fine institution to see the symbol of their school torn away and replaced. Anyone who is aware of the Floodrock tradition will automatically associate the school with the Braves. Any change to the team name would result in a significant financial burden for the school, as we would have to change the floor of the main gym, reprint a number of publications, and purchase many new uniforms.

In the end, few persons in the Floodrock community protest against the Braves symbol. The few critics have come from outside our community. With so much support for the mascot, why would we change? The last time I checked, this is America, where majority rules.

Sincerely,


Will Hurdle, M.S.
Athletic Director

**Figure 12.3.** A letter to parents of Floodrock High School students from the athletic director.

U.S. History
Mr. Steinhouse
Fall Semester
Handout #27


### A Brief History of Native Americans in Southern Illinois

The Muskhogean peoples of Illinois had formed a highly developed civilization hundreds of years before the appearance of white settlers. The Indians, who lived mostly in an area around the present day towns of Cahokia, Collinsville, and Belleville, were accomplished craftsmen whose system of commerce extended throughout the Midwest. Excavation of the mounds in southern Illinois reveals sophisticated pottery for utilitarian and artistic purposes. Remnants of their pottery have been found as far north as Minnesota and as far east as Indiana. Clearly the tribe used a vast system of waterways to transport goods and to trade with tribes throughout the Midwest.

The Natchez tribe descended from the earlier Muskhogeans. The Natchez mastered the production of ornamental and utilitarian pottery. The surviving examples of their pottery reveal bold designs, a variety of shapes and sizes, and a range of uses. The Natchez society focused endeavors on agriculture, especially on the production of maize, a staple in their diet. The Natchez continued the Muskhogean practice of building burial mounds. Several of their mounds remain at Cahokia, where many other artifacts reveal the sophistication and peacefulness of the Natchez society.

The Shawnee tribe is associated with the Algonquians of northern Illinois and southern Wisconsin. The Shawnee were also an agricultural society. Maize was a staple, yet they supplemented their diet through hunting and gathering. The Shawnee relied on bow and arrow for hunting and for combat. The Shawnee were not a warlike people, yet the Shawnee were brave and accomplished in battle.

The Natchez and Shawnee began to be displaced from southern Illinois with the incursions of French settlers in the seventeenth and eighteenth centuries. Later arrivals of settlers from the eastern United States during the late eighteenth century and throughout the nineteenth century displaced the tribes to such an extent that few Native Americans remained in southern Illinois by the 1880s.

**Figure 12.4.** A brief history of Native American tribes in southern Illinois (from a handout composed for Mr. Steinhouse's eleventh-grade U.S. History class).

## Small-Group Discussion

The following transcript records the discussion among four ninth graders in a class considered "lower ability." The small group consisted of three boys and one girl. This was one of six groups in the class. Although the members of the group were not assigned roles, one participant assumed a leadership position and prompted the others to begin the discussion. The materials for the case study prompt the students to respond to several questions as they study the material.

*Derek:* Did you guys do your questions yet?

*Alejandro:* No.

*Derek:* Do they have the constitutional right to use Braves as the name for the athletic team?

*Michelle:* I think they do. I don't know. Freedom of speech and the freedom of press. It's kind of like the newsletters and stuff.

*Gerardo:* Yeah, but they are not just writing it down and talking about it. They are dancing and dressing up like Indians.

*Michelle:* That's true. It is kind of crude what they are doing, but I mean the constitutional rights say they can. It's not like they are actually doing "Ha Ha! See me!"; they are just doing it to entertain everyone. Just entertainment.

*Derek:* Yeah. So what do you guys want me to write down? Should I just write . . .

*Michelle:* Yes, they have the freedom of speech to use.

*Derek:* OK #2. Wait a second . . . freedom of speech and freedom of the press. Something like that.

*Michelle:* Can the use of the name and the images really hurt or offend anyone? I don't think it really can. It's just like, they, the Indians, are just sitting at home doing nothing.

*Gerardo:* How do you know they are sitting at home doing nothing? They see this . . . they don't think they have the right to do it. That's why they are saying that. They already said that . . . how he doesn't even dress up or dance like his people here and like they seem to be the people that really get bothered by it.

*Michelle:* They want to change it, but it's like expensive to change it.

*Alejandro:* Yeah, they have to change the team name.

*Gerardo:* Yeah, but I think in a way it really depends on the person. If it could hurt someone or not . . .

*Alejandro:* Yeah.

*Derek:* No. How important is it to hold up? . . . I think it is very important. . . . It depends on the school and. . . . It's like a few years . . . it is a big deal though . . . many different schools think that it is important . . . eighty years is important.

*Michelle:* Also it is important to them because if they were to lose they would have all that money to change . . . it is very important. We have to change everything. School is probably not going to afford any more basketball or anything. It makes no sense.

*Derek:* No, it doesn't. You just said if you change it, the school is not going to be able to afford to have any basketball or anything. If you have to change it, change the uniforms, everything. You have to change and pay for everything else.

*Gerardo:* Why would they change the uniforms if they have no basketball?

*Derek:* That's what we are talking about.

*Michelle:* I know, but they will still have to change it all.

*Derek:* Were we going to write again?

*Michelle:* It's very important. These people are not living in the Floodrock community, and they think they can talk to school representatives and advise on how they behave. Pay attention to the old schools in their own areas. If they are not involved in the school and really have no idea what they are talking about anyway, because it doesn't pertain to them and they are not the ones that are paying taxes to put their kids in the school. They should worry about the schools in their own area, 'cause they probably won't realize how much it would cost to . . .

*Gerardo:* What would you gain by changing the name? Nothing really.

*Alejandro:* Yeah. Except for like it might gain the Indians a little pride or something like that. School would gain nothing. In the end, they would get what they want. They just want to be left alone and not criticized.

*Gerardo:* Yeah, but they are not really being criticized, maybe a tiny bit.

*Derek:* I don't see enough there that really hurts anyone. I'm still on the other one. The school will gain nothing, and Native Americans will get what they want. They want to be left alone and not criticized. In the final analysis, what do you think?

*Michelle:* I think that they should keep the name 'cause it's just their right, and if they feel like changing it they can.

*Gerardo:* But they also have the right to protest. 'Cause every
time the guy goes out there, and they try to make . . . they
have the right to do that, but I just like the music out of the
way.

*Derek:* They should be able to keep the name because it is their
right. Is that it?

*Alejandro:* Yeah.

Michelle begins the discussion by claiming that a school has a
constitutional right to select any team name and mascot it would like.
To Michelle, this is a clear case of freedom of expression. Gerardo notes
a difference. He suggests that the popular chant and the ceremonial
dance go beyond the use of an Indian name. He notes that a Native
American might find the dance disrespectful because "he doesn't even
dress up or dance like his people here." In this observation, Gerardo
reminds the group that the student who dances as half-time entertainment does not wear the clothing common to the Native Americans who
lived in the region. Gerardo's challenge to Michelle is that the school's
freedom to choose a mascot ends when the appearance of the mascot
seriously offends or dishonors other citizens.

Michelle then raises an economic point. She expresses concern that
the school would incur significant expenses if the many instances of the
team name and logo had to be expunged from the building, the uniforms, the stationery, etc. In a way, Michelle is doing a cost-benefit analysis, believing that the dubious benefits of changing the policy do not
warrant the costs of the change.

Derek invokes tradition. He extends the discussion by claiming
that it is important to continue to follow the practices that have had been
in place for eighty years. The importance of tradition seems intangible,
but Derek notes that for many schools "it is a big deal." Derek's recog-
nition of a pattern of many schools' respecting tradition serves as a
warrant to interpret the significance of a practice that the school has
followed for eighty years.

Michelle returns to the economic issues. She notes that the opposition to the Braves mascot comes from people who live outside the
school district boundaries. At first she seems to resent the idea of "outside agitators" interfering with law abiding citizens governing their own
lives in a way they see fit. Her argument becomes an economic one when
she notes that citizens who live outside the school district are demanding changes that will have a financial impact on only those persons who
live within the school district. In other words, as long as the name and
mascot are not *too* offensive, the citizens who pay taxes to support the

school should have uncontested license to do what they want with the school and its symbols.

In the end, Derek notes that he doesn't see enough offense to hurt anyone. Michelle agrees and claims that the school should have a right to choose the name and mascot that it prefers. Gerardo cautions, however, that protesters retain the right to criticize the school for names and symbols that they find offensive. Through the small-group discussion process, the students have revealed their opinions and subjected them to the scrutiny of others. In the discussion, the participants remind each other of exceptions, and identify rules and general tendencies to support their analyses. The discussion involves the process of refinement of each person's position.

## Large-Group Discussion

In a small group, the participants can influence each other to agree to a particular perspective. Expanding discussion among the entire class extends thought by exposing a variety of perspectives. In the example below, the teacher serves as the discussion facilitator and prompts the participants frequently to explain, to support, and to test their ideas.

> *Teacher:* Brian, what did you decide the school should do in this case?
>
> *Brian:* Keep the name and the mascot the same. They've had them for eighty years, with no problems. There is no right for people outside of the school district to change the name. It's fun and doesn't cause any problem.
>
> *Michelle:* I agree with Brian.
>
> *Teacher:* What does it matter that the school has had the name and mascot for eighty years?
>
> *Michelle:* Traditions are hard to change. They'd have to repaint, change floors and uniforms; it would be a real hassle. I agree that people outside of the school district should have no say in the choice of names and mascot.
>
> *Teacher:* Why can't someone from outside the district have something to say?
>
> *Michelle:* It doesn't pertain to them.
>
> *Teacher:* Here in Illinois, a school called Pekin High used to call its teams the "Chinks." This was an offensive name to many Chinese Americans. Do citizens outside of that community have some reason and right to criticize?
>
> *Michelle:* It is not right to call people that, but they aren't associated with this case.

*Javier:* If people in the school aren't offended, what's the big deal? Other people are called *Chinks*, too, who aren't Chinese.

*Teacher:* Then the name is less derogatory if people accept it?

*Javier:* Yes.

*Derek: Chinks* is more slang and derogatory than Braves.

*Javier: Chinks* should be changed if it represents a Chinese person rather than a chicken for a mascot.

*Teacher:* Apparently the school made the connection between Pekin, Illinois, and Peking, China. The name referred to Chinese.

*Javier:* Change it then. I don't know.

*Joe:* They were just trying to have fun (in using the *Braves* name and mascot). No one should be offended.

*Teacher:* How about the chants and the dance? Would you change them in any way?

*Joe:* The chant is not appropriate. "Scalp 'em" is too violent and says that the Indians are all violent.

*Teacher:* They are suggesting that the native Americans are a violent culture? Can you enforce a rule that says they can't chant "Scalp 'em, Braves"?

*Joe:* Yes, but you really can't force people to change.

*Teacher:* Does anyone really get hurt by the name, the mascot, the chant, or the dance?

*Gerardo:* Yes. The dance can be offensive to a lot of people.

*Teacher:* What would you do about it?

*Gerardo:* Get a new dance.

*Teacher:* How would you change it? Would you make it more authentic?

*Gerardo:* Yes, and show more respect.

*Javier:* Don't change it at all. They aren't making fun of the Indians. The chief is there to lift school spirit. As for the violent chant, the Indians were in violent wars, so it is representing something real.

*Julio:* They are honoring a tribe by choosing them.

*Derek:* Someone is always going to have a problem with anything.

*Teacher:* The NBA team in Washington, D.C., changed its name from the *Bullets* to the *Wizards* because the original name seemed to glamorize violence in a city that had a lot of violent crime. Does that seem legitimate?

*Derek:* It's not because of the team name that there's violence. The name doesn't hurt anyone.

*Teacher:* Is the claim that the school "honors" Indians a valid argument for using the Braves name and the chant and the dance?

*Heidi:* Yes.

*Teacher:* Does the funny looking picture on the stationery "honor" Indians?

*Heidi:* It's just a drawing.

*Derek:* The mural drawing looks like it honors Indians.

*Teacher:* Does the school need to change anything?

*Michelle:* If it keeps getting more controversial, it should ease up on the dance. I wouldn't change the name. Just tone down the dance.

*Teacher:* Tone down the dance?

*Michelle:* Yeah. I see someone yelling and screaming and running around. Not as much of that.

*Joe:* But the dance is a highlight at games.

*Michelle:* They can do it in a less offensive way.

*Joe:* That's a major thing, though, and you don't want to change the tradition.

*Derek:* Change the "Scalp 'em" chant.

*Javier:* Where does the myth of them scalping everyone come from?

*Teacher:* Does the chant suggest that all Indians are violent?

*Nick:* I think they should change the name. It's offensive. The dances make fun of the Indians. The outfit isn't even authentic. They aren't honoring anyone.

*Ruben:* There's a lot of Indian named teams, like the Atlanta Braves. If it's OK for them to do, then it's OK for the school.

*Teacher:* Is anyone offended?

*Ruben:* It's been around for awhile.

*Joe:* This school has had this for eighty years.

*Michelle:* Someone has to be offended.

*Derek:* A high school is easier to attack than a pro team.

*Teacher:* In his letter, one critic said that the dance is like making fun of Catholics by imitating one of their rituals as part of the halftime entertainment.

*Gerardo:* It's not the same. They should make it less offensive, though.

*Derek:* Make the chief more legitimate. Change the chant. Say something like "Go, Braves" instead of "Scalp 'em."

*Teacher:* Brian, do you still agree with your original position?

*Brian:* Yeah. Get rid of "Scalp 'em" and say "Go, Braves," and make the dance more real.

Obviously the teacher plays a major role in this large-group discussion by posing questions to ask students to consider exceptions to their general observations or to consider additional details from the case. The discussion does allow students to sort through the various aspects of the case and refine their positions. For example, Brian begins and ends the discussion, and his position changes after he has heard other perspectives. Initially, Brian claims that no one has a right to recommend any change for the school, and everything should remain the same. After approximately twenty minutes of discussion, Brian still embraces his original assumption that the school should be able to call its teams the Braves, but he adds, "Get rid of 'Scalp 'em' and say 'Go, Braves,' and make the dance more real."

The challenges and the tests that participants offer during discussion assist the students in refining ideas. Michelle would like the school officials to call their teams anything they want; however, she recognizes that some names may very well be offensive and inappropriate. As the students continue to talk, the question becomes whether or not the Braves name and the accompanying symbols are offensive enough to change. Javier points out, "They are honoring a tribe by choosing them." Some students have doubts that the Chief Whompum dance, the logo, and the popular "Scalp 'em" chant serve to honor Native Americans. Nick points out: "It's offensive. The dances make fun of the Indians. The outfit isn't even authentic. They aren't honoring anyone." Even Michelle has some doubts. Although she would retain the questionable Chief Whompum dance, she would consider "toning it down" so that it angers fewer persons.

## Written Responses

After the discussions, the students wrote to the Floodrock School Board to advise the members what should be done about the teams' name and mascot. The discussion prepared the students to produce their written arguments by supporting claims and responding to opposing views. In discussion, the skepticism and the challenges are apparent. The students experience the demands for them to support their claims with evidence and explain what the evidence means. The students also know that they will face opposition. It is reasonable to think that students can represent the ideas of others when they have heard a variety of views as the class talked about the case. The students recognize the context for offering their proposals; and through oral discussions, they have practiced developing their own arguments and responding to the challenges of others. As active participants in discussions, students refine ideas and judge whether there is anything of merit offered by other thinkers. Without engaging in the conversation, exposing one's ideas to the scrutiny of other participants, and honestly and fairly assessing the ideas of others, any student's position remains superficial and represents a form of prejudice.

In working with the Braves case, the ninth graders from this class interacted in several ways, all of which can be labeled discussion. But all discussions are not the same activity, as Walton (1998) explains in his exploration of a new dialectic. As a first phase, the learners study the case and the related data sets independently in order to form their own arguments. If there is discussion here, it is the internal *dialogue* that the reader conducts with the case. In the small-group discussion that is represented in the transcript above, the students discuss in the sense of an initial probing and testing positions. As they look toward producing a written report that represents the thinking of the group, the students attempt to achieve consensus in a process that could be properly called *deliberation*. In the deliberation, the members of the group might express opposing views, but they attempt to achieve some unity of position on policy. In the subsequent large-group discussion, students engage for a time in *debate* as opponents attempt to influence the thinking of each other and influence other listeners. All phases of the discussion—dialogue, deliberation, and discussion—contribute to the students' critical thinking about a significant issue and prepares them to write a meaningful response, and in a larger sense readies them to engage in the civil and rational discourse that is a valuable function of a community.

## Summary

Johannessen (1999) encourages teachers to search for new metaphors to represent the roles of the teacher, the student, and the classroom environment. The new metaphors would offer images that are consistent with the dialogic goal suggested by Nystrand (1997) or the conversation model described by Applebee (1996). Chapter 9 explores the contrast between the conduit and toolmaker metaphors as communication frames and their impact on classroom practices. The class inquiry into compelling problems, based on the Supreme Court analogy, allows for the conversation that honors many voices and perspectives, that prepares students to deliberate rationally about the immediate problem, and that provides means for discussing and assessing related themes and issues in the literature that the students read. As Flanagan (1998) contends, instead of conforming to scripted recitation, students who engage in inquiry-based activities join conversations that include challenges, doubt, and attention to multiple perspectives. Relatively simple cases like "The Floodrock Braves" do not produce in students the same intellectual rigor that one would expect among Supreme Court justices and those who argue before the bench; but in the long term, the frequent immersion into various phases of dialogic and dialectical exchanges associated with the discussions about the case trains students to be able to think critically in the variety of situations that are part of their academic world and their daily lives.

# 13 Generating and Evaluating Discussion

Good morning class. I'd like to begin today by examining Huck's decision not to turn Jim over to the men who are hunting for escaped slaves in Chapter 16. What is his moral dilemma, and why does Huck conclude that he 'had done wrong'? Was his decision wrong? Why or why not?"

Most experienced teachers can probably remember a few times when they have started class with a question like this about Mark Twain's *The Adventures of Huckleberry Finn* (1965) or some other equally challenging work of literature with the hope that most or all of the class period would be filled with lively, sensitive, and thoughtful discussion. However, most experienced teachers can probably recall more than a few times when starting a class in this manner turned into a total disaster. That is, after asking what many teachers would regard as a provocative question for students to discuss, the class sits silently staring back at the teacher, or worse, after a long silence a student raises his or her hand and says something like, "I don't know. I guess he's right, sort of." And this comment is followed by a very long silence. Often the teacher either ends up telling the students what Huck's decision might mean or abandons the whole lesson and moves on to something else. Most experienced teachers have had days in which the planned class discussion failed miserably or seemed to fail miserably. This chapter considers two important questions: What strategies, in addition to those that have already been presented, can a teacher use to stimulate discussion in difficult situations when all else seems to have failed? And, how can a teacher evaluate the effectiveness of class discussions, especially for the purpose of improving them?

## Isn't It Just a Matter of Asking the Right Question?

As we work with preservice and beginning teachers and watch them struggle with trying to plan and manage class discussions, we are constantly reminded that one of the enduring myths about teaching is that all a teacher needs to do to have lively class discussions is ask a question and twenty-five to thirty eager young students will immediately raise their hands and engage in an animated class discussion for forty to fifty minutes. The strength and power of this myth is perhaps best exemplified by one young student teacher who continued to go back in the classroom each day and ask whatever question struck him at the moment as intellectually stimulating, and each day the response was silence. When his cooperating teacher asked the young student teacher if he had thought about trying some other strategies to get his students engaged in discussion, he asked, "Well, isn't it just a matter of asking the right question?"

Christenbury and Kelly (1983) maintain that creating engaging classroom discussion through questioning involves more than just asking a stimulating question. They suggest using a logical system as part of an overall plan. What follows is a series of strategies and techniques that a teacher might use as a comprehensive approach to purposeful classroom talk.

## Engaging Students as They Walk in the Door

One strategy we have employed with success is to plan a set of twenty to thirty questions ahead of time. The questions should be a mixture of literal or low-level questions and inferential questions or critical thinking questions. Next we put each of the questions on a slip of paper so that each student will receive one question to answer. As students enter the classroom at the start of class, we hand each one a question and tell them they should think about a response to the question and be prepared to discuss it in a class discussion. We have also found it helpful to have these directions written on the board or on an overhead so that students know what they are to do. Once class starts, we give students a few minutes to think about their answers and then begin the class discussion by either calling on someone to answer their question or asking for volunteers.

This strategy can be very effective with groups of students who are reluctant to speak up. The fact that students can think about their answer before they are called on to speak also allows them to prepare what they are going to say. Often, after one or two students have responded to their questions, other students will be less reluctant to speak up. In other words, this strategy often provides a kind of jump start for a reluctant group of students. Even if students are still reluctant to speak up, students have prepared answers for their assigned questions, and so there is a reasonable assurance that there will be a good class discussion.

## Using a Small-Group Report Format

Another strategy we have used to stimulate discussion with students who are reluctant to speak up in class or sometimes just for a change of pace is to employ the Small-Group Reports format. We assign students to small groups of three to five students and assign each group a set of questions to consider. Sometimes, especially if we have a number of questions, we might divide the questions up so that groups are paired and two groups are answering the same set of questions. We tell the groups to discuss their questions and be prepared to respond in a whole-class discussion. We also tell the groups that each student in a group must say something in a whole-class discussion. We give the groups time to discuss the questions, decide how they will answer them and determine who will answer which questions. We then have the groups begin their reports. Again, after one or two groups give their reports, students are often more willing to contribute in the class discussion. We move around the room, having each group give their reports, and then ask if any other students have anything to contribute to what the group has reported. Often, students will begin adding to the discussion.

This strategy encourages participation because through the small-group discussion, students rehearse their ideas and refine their answers and are less apprehensive about participating in the whole-class discussion. In addition, they have a stake in the response that their group has discussed, and they have the support of the other members of their small group. As a result, we have very often had productive class discussion utilizing this strategy.

## Silent Discussion Strategy

Wilhelm, Baker, and Dube (2001) suggest an interesting strategy for encouraging students to participate. They call it the silent discussion activity. The way the strategy works is to have all students sit in a circle, giving each a blank piece of paper. The students then write out two questions about the text in discussion. One of the questions may be a literal question about the text, but at least one must be a question that will promote discussion and require an inference or focus on critical thinking about the text. Students are then told to pass the questions that they have written out on a piece of paper to the student on their right. The authors then suggest having each student write an answer to one of the questions and add a new question to promote discussion. Students then pass their papers to the right again, write an answer to one of the questions, and add a new question. Students once again pass their papers around the circle. The next step is to ask students to read every-thing on the paper they now have, answer one question, compose one more question, and pass the paper once again. On the next turn, the students read everything on the paper, answer one question, and respond to one of the answers, providing either an agreement and support, dis-agreement, or a follow-up question. Wilhelm et al. (2001) indicate that students should take four to five turns. At the conclusion of the turns, students report one interesting thing from the paper they have in their hands.

The value of the silent discussion is that it gently nudges students into vocal discussion by allowing them to participate without placing themselves publicly on the line. They are merely reporting what other people wrote on the piece of paper they have in their hands, and it is not necessarily what they think. This takes considerable pressure off of students who are reluctant to speak up. This strategy also gives them adequate time to think about what they are going to say before they have to speak in front of the whole class. The approach is a good first step for groups of students with little or no experience in classroom discus-sion.

## Three-Index-Card Strategy

When the problem is one of an imbalance of gender or some other fac-tor such as race or class that affects class discussion, Wilhelm, Baker, and Dube (2001) recommend another strategy. In order to promote more balance in class discussions, these authors recommend a strategy they found in NCTE's quarterly publication *Classroom Notes Plus* "Teacher's Notes" called the "three-index-card-discussion." The way the activity works is that each student is given three blank index cards as he or she enters the classroom. Students then move their desks into a circle, and the teacher informs them that for each turn they take speaking in the discussion they are to throw one card into the center of the circle of stu-dents. In addition, all students must use all three of their cards, but once they have used their three, they are done.

This activity is very effective at increasing the participation of all students. More important, it can also result in discussions that are richer and more focused because students who enjoy talking must use their cards wisely and be careful about what they say since they have only three turns. Those who often do not participate seem to become more comfortable after a number of these discussions as they see that no one is allowed to dominate the discussion. This activity also has an impact on student listening because students must concentrate on what is being said in order to plan when and how they will participate in the discussion.

## Basic Discussion Techniques

We have been tempted at times to blame general adolescent apathy for uninspired and unproductive classroom discussions. We have to look, though, at our own behaviors as teachers to understand students' responses to our prompts for discussion. Christenbury and Kelly (1983) offer some insights about how the teachers' preparation, initiation, and support of discussion affects its quality. For example, they point out that when students seem unable to answer a question, it could be because the question the teacher has asked is unclear. They point out that sometimes teachers ask vague questions that confuse students. In a discussion of Mark Twain's *The Adventures of Huckleberry Finn*, a teacher might ask, for example, "In Chapter 1, what does the Widow Douglas do to Huck?" A clearer framing of the question might be, "In Chapter 1, what did the Widow Douglas do to try to 'civilize' Huck?"

Another problem that teachers, especially new teachers, sometimes have, is the problem of asking multiple questions. This can confuse a student or, as Christenbury and Kelly (1983) indicate, it can cause a student to hesitate or freeze up over a response. For example, a teacher might pose the following two questions back-to-back, "In Chapter 1, why wouldn't the Widow let Huck smoke?" and "What is hypocritical about why she won't allow Huck to smoke?" One solution to the problem is to separate the questions and allow students to answer the first one before asking the second one. In fact, in this instance, the answer to the first question—because it is a "mean practice" or uncivilized—may help students answer the second question. The first question is a lower-level question, and the answer to it lays the foundation for answering the second, which requires critical thinking or interpretation of the text.

Sometimes students may have difficulties answering certain questions because they have not been prepared adequately to answer the questions. After students have read the first three chapters of *Huckleberry Finn*, it is probably not a good idea to start a class discussion with the question, "What are the targets of Twain's satire in these chapters?" Most students will need some preparation before they will be able to answer a question that asks them to make an interpretation. As Marzano (2004) reminds us, sometimes it is a matter of students' lacking the relevant background knowledge to be able to understand what the question demands. It might be more productive to start a discussion by focusing on a single scene or incident and attempt to determine what Twain is ridiculing in that scene before asking students to draw conclusions based on a number of scenes or incidents in the first three chapters. We would start a discussion by asking students, "In what way is the Widow hypocritical in her attempts to get Huck to conform to society's standards? How do you know?"

These questions encourage students to focus on interpreting a single scene. The answers to these questions help to inform students' understanding of what Twain is satirizing in the novel. We would follow up these two questions with others focusing on specific scenes in Chapters 2 and 3 and what Twain is attacking in those chapters. Now, armed with a good understanding of the targets of Twain's satire in the opening chapters, students are prepared to tackle the more complex question that asks them to draw conclusions based on their understanding of the satire in the first three chapters.

Sometimes when students do not respond to a question, it may be that they did not hear the question or did not understand it. We have found that it is sometimes helpful to repeat the question a second time or rephrase it. Sometimes teachers make the mistake of repeating the question or rephrasing it before allowing students enough time to respond. As we discussed in Chapter 5, teachers need to provide appropriate wait time (at least three to five seconds) for students to answer complex questions (Rowe 1974). Research indicates that when teachers learn to pose a question and then wait at least three to five seconds before calling on a student to answer, students tend to give longer answers; more students are likely to participate, ask questions, and volunteer appropriate answers; student comments involving analysis, synthesis, inference, and speculation tend to increase; and the students generally appear more confident in their answers and achieve at higher levels on tests (Berliner 1987; Stahl 1994; Tobin 1987). In addition, these same authorities indicate that there are benefits for teachers when they learn to increase wait time; teachers tend to talk less, repeat questions less often, ask fewer lower-level questions, ask more probing questions, and repeat student responses less frequently. In fact, Orlich, Harder, Callahan, and Gibson (2001) suggest that based on the benefits of wait time, teachers should make the decision to pause or wait "not only once, but twice, even three times," if students are actively engaged and interacting (254).

Teachers sometimes encounter difficulties managing student interaction when students give short answers. Christenbury and Kelly

(1983) suggest that often it is the teachers who cause students to give short answers. As they indicate, without being aware of it, many teachers may start talking before a student has finished her or his response, thus ending the response. Teachers may also break eye contact with the student responders or unconsciously turn away from them. These actions may also result in decreasing the length of the student's response, as students will not continue to talk if they do not believe they have an attentive audience for what they have to say.

To lengthen student responses, Christenbury and Kelly (1983) suggest using positive reinforcement. They recommend some common-sense suggestions to lengthen student responses, including, nodding and asking a student to clarify or expand an answer. Statements such as, "I am not sure I understand what you are saying; could you say that again?" or "Could you give us an example of what you are talking about?" can be very helpful in getting students to lengthen their responses.

Maybe the most difficult problem to deal with is handling wrong or misguided answers. The use of criticism (as well as praise) cuts off discussion; however, if a teacher gives the impression that every student answer is correct or good, then this can create the wrong classroom atmosphere and may lead to some unproductive discussions. Using uptake, found in Chapter 7 (pp. 80–82), is one effective strategy in this situation. In addition, this same chapter (p. 78) describes another useful strategy, polling the class. Still another approach is that a teacher might offer, "I'm not sure about that. What do the rest of you think?" Or, the teacher might say, "That could be the case, but I wonder if others in the class see this differently?" Christenbury and Kelly (1983) indicate that when a student answer is misguided, mistaken, or only partially correct, there is often contrary evidence available. We suggest asking the class if they see any contrary evidence to the student speaker's misguided comment. For example, if a student were to make the argument that Tom Sawyer and not Huck Finn is the hero of *Huckleberry Finn*, we would suggest that a teacher might say something like, "I can understand that you think that Tom Sawyer might be the hero, but does anyone see any evidence to the contrary?" Finally, as we suggest throughout this book, we agree with Christenbury and Kelly (1983) that asking students questions that require them to explore options or values, weigh differing opinions, practice critical thinking, or make inferences from data or a text are preferable to literal level and fixed-answer questions.

## Managing the Discussion-Based Classroom

We have maintained throughout this book that it is vitally important for teachers to make students feel that they can take risks in the classroom. The students need to know that even if they give a wrong or misguided answer, they will not face disapproval or ridicule. When teachers establish a classroom atmosphere like this—one that encourages students to participate—it is likely that student answers will be more frequent, longer, and more in depth.

One basic practice that every teacher can follow is to arrange the room so that it is conducive to classroom discussion. Having students sit in rows, where all they can observe is the back of others' heads, makes it difficult, at best, to encourage discussion or lively interaction with anyone but the teacher. Teachers should consider putting students in a circle or horseshoe arrangement of desks in which students are facing one another. For extremely large groups of students, we would suggest having a double circle or horseshoe as an alternative to rows.

It is important for the teacher to make the students feel comfortable. Christenbury and Kelly (1983) suggest that the teacher encourage an unhurried and unpressured environment that gives students an opportunity to think and respond. Questions that are not presented in a challenging manner or in a rapid-fire fashion can help create an unhurried but businesslike atmosphere. Christenbury and Kelly recommend that teachers begin questions with a question word such as *who* or *what* and not with a student's name or a lengthy introduction or general comment. They also suggest that teachers should scan the entire class as the question is being delivered because this may help to foster attentiveness.

A teacher can make a student feel comfortable in class discussion by maintaining eye contact with the speaker while he or she is speaking. This encourages a student to continue to talk. Conversely, when a teacher breaks eye contact with a student, this will often result in ending student talk because the student feels uncomfortable. Head nods and smiles encourage student talk. Turning away from students will tend to discourage further student talk, but turning toward students with arms uncrossed encourages students to continue with their discourse.

## Peer Evaluation Activities

One way to improve class discussions is through the use of peer evaluation or peer coaching. The idea of having a colleague or supervisor

observe and evaluate the effectiveness of discussions can be a powerful tool to bring about improvement in the quality of discussions. While
some teachers believe that they are quite capable of assessing their own
class discussions and activities and are hesitant to use peer evaluation
strategies, we have found that peer evaluation can be a very effective
way to get an objective assessment of what is actually going on during
class discussions. Sometimes an objective assessment from an outside
observer can offer fresh insight into the dynamics of a class discussion,
uncovering strengths and weaknesses and suggesting possible solutions
for weaknesses.

We vividly recall one particular observation early in Larry's teaching career that made clear to him how important peer evaluation can
be. He was teaching a group of "average" eleventh-grade students, and
he was being observed by his department chair. It was an American literature course, and Larry managed what he thought was a pretty good
thirty- to thirty-five-minute class discussion. After class, his department
chair asked him how many times he had responded to student answers
by saying, "Okay." Thinking that he was good at analyzing his own
discussions and knew his strengths and weaknesses pretty well, he
immediately responded by saying, "Oh, I would say five or six times."
His department chair gave him a quizzical look and said, "Really. I
counted thirty-four times. It was annoying to me, and if it was annoying to me, then imagine how your students felt during that discussion."
It was clear to Larry that he had acquired an annoying bad habit—one
that he had to work to overcome then and still works on constantly more
than twenty years later.

## Video- and Audiotaping Discussions

One method of using peer evaluation to improve class discussions is to
have a colleague video- or audiotape a class and/or small-group discussions for later analysis. If students are not use to being video- or
audiotaped, then it is probably a good idea to tape the class for several
days. Some students have a tendency to show off for the camera, while
others may become very shy. We have found that once students get used
to the equipment in the room, most of them forget it is there. Once the
taping is done, it is a good idea to watch or listen to the taped discussion with the observer colleague. We listen and look for patterns that
highlight probable strengths, such as a tendency to encourage student
responses with friendly body language, or weaknesses, like a tendency
to discourage participation by interrupting students when they are re-

sponding. We discuss what we see and talk about strategies for improving the discussion. It is helpful to tape again in a few weeks to monitor one's progress.

## The Flanders Interaction Analysis

One problem that we face when self-evaluating classroom interaction is that we tend to be poor judges of the amount of student interaction that takes place during our own class discussions. Frequently, we believe that many more students have participated in a discussion than actually have. One particularly effective technique to evaluate the amount and quality of student participation is the Flanders Interaction Analysis (Flanders 1965). In using the Flanders analysis system, it is important to establish some parameters for the desired level of student involvement, or, in other words, for what is regarded as a good discussion. We would maintain that if a discussion lasts more than ten minutes or so, then most of the students (say, 70–75 percent or more) should respond at least once. For an extended discussion (half an hour or more), virtually all of the students should respond at least once. Also, the direction of a good discussion should not be repeatedly teacher to student and student to teacher in return. It should also involve student-to-student conversations in which students respond to each other's comments without the prompting or intrusion of the teacher. Finally, the proportion of *teacher talk* in relation to *student talk* should be below about a third of the total talk.

Flanders developed a system of ten categories to describe the verbal behavior of both teacher and students in a class discussion. The first seven of these categories have to do with teacher talk and are as follows: accepts feelings = 1; praises or encourages = 2; accepts or uses ideas of student = 3; asks questions = 4; lectures = 5; gives directions = 6; criticizes or justifies authority = 7. The next two categories are concerned with student talk: student talk in response to teacher question = 8 and student talk initiated by the student = 9. The final category, silence or confusion = 10. Every three seconds, the classroom observer indicates, by recording the number of one of the categories, what type of verbal behavior took place during the preceding three seconds. Consequently, after gathering such data for a class period or a portion of a class period, the peer observer would have several pages with columns of number sequences.

The observer and teacher meet soon after the class and discuss the patterns that emerge from analysis of the columns of numbers. Very often, we discover that during a class period we have talked far more than we are aware. There are often too many fours (teacher-initiated questions) and fives (teacher lecturing) and too few nines (responses initiated by students). With this profile, the teacher can work on strategies for increasing the number of nines and decreasing the amount of teacher talk. The peer observer/coach can often suggest alternate strategies to bring about the desired result. Also, repeatedly using the Flanders Interaction Analysis can help a teacher to become a more objective observer and evaluator of his or her own classroom discussions.

There are other tools peer coaches and observers might use to analyze classroom discussions. More important, there is real value in using a variety of methods to gather data for analyzing the interaction. A peer observer might make a seating chart and record the number of responses given by each student in the class, perhaps making a distinction between responses to teacher questions and responses that are initiated by students. Also, the observer might draw interaction diagrams with lines showing the flow and direction of the conversation. These techniques can reveal some interesting patterns. For example, recording the number of responses given by each student often uncovers whether certain students are responding much more frequently than others. Furthermore, recording the flow and direction of conversation often reveals that certain pockets of students interact with one another much more frequently than they do with the rest of the class. Armed with this information, the teacher and the observer might discuss strategies for encouraging quiet students to speak up and bring about a more-balanced participation in discussions. In addition, they might plan strategies for encouraging a more-balanced flow and direction of conversation.

## Student Evaluations of Class Discussions

In addition to peer observation strategies, a teacher may want to make use of strategies that have students evaluate themselves and their peers in small-group and whole-class discussions. While the goal of these strategies is to improve discussions, they also offer other benefits. For example, such strategies can help to make students aware of their own behaviors and actions in discussions and improve their speaking and social skills. These strategies also help to motivate students. Most important of all, these strategies help students develop their critical thinking skills.

## Self-Evaluation through Journal Writing

Maxwell and Meiser (2001) and Sorenson (1993) maintain that having students do some self-evaluation in their journals after a discussion is a good way to get students to think about their contributions before another discussion. Here is a set of questions to use as prompts which we have adapted from Sorenson:

- To what extent did I contribute to the discussion?
- How did I encourage others to contribute or clarify ideas?
- What would I like to do in the next discussion?
- How can I do this?
- Who contributed the most interesting or valuable comments?
- What made their comments so interesting or valuable?
- Who encouraged me the most in the discussion?
- How did this person [or these persons] encourage me? (44)

Students might write some or all of these questions in their journals. We would also recommend having a class discussion of their responses, focusing on how students might contribute more in discussions and encourage others to participate. Sorenson maintains that having students reflect on their process has a positive impact on helping students recognize the contributions they and others make. In addition, Sorenson recommends that students should regularly reflect on their contributions because, as students become more familiar with reflecting on their contributions, they become better listeners and more skilled at monitoring themselves during discussions, and their contributions are more thoughtful. Most important, Sorenson argues that through this method, students make significant gains in oral and analytic skills.

## Self-Assessment Rubrics

Having students use various kinds of self-assessment instruments that utilize rubrics is another way to get students to reflect on their involvement and behavior during discussions. We use various kinds of instruments, including check sheets, scale rankings, and short writings to evaluate various aspects of student participation. The instrument in Figure 13.1 is an example of a simple check sheet to have students fill out after each discussion.

The first couple of times we have students complete the check sheet, we collect the sheets and give students feedback on their answers.

For example, we might offer suggestions for how to improve participation or listen more actively. Once students become familiar with the process and are more comfortable with discussing their own involvement, we lead a class discussion of their responses. Some students pay close attention when a peer tells them they need to listen to others more during discussions or stop doing their math homework. As with the journal writing method, this means of reflection also encourages critical thinking, oral and analytical skills, better listening, better monitoring of discussions, and more thoughtful contributions.

While the check sheet method is one effective way to have students utilize rubrics for self-evaluation, scales provide another way to get them to do serious reflection about their involvement. The Small-Group Discussion Evaluation form (Figure 13.2) is an example of an

---

**Self-Assessment of Discussion Involvement**
Directions: For the first three questions, check the comment that best describes your participation in discussions. Please write a short paragraph for the last question.

1. Extent of class participation:
\_\_\_\_\_ Participates actively. Is involved in most discussions.
\_\_\_\_\_ Participates about average amount. Volunteers when interested in topic.
\_\_\_\_\_ Seldom participates. Usually has to be called upon to speak.
\_\_\_\_\_ Participates very rarely and only after considerable prodding.

2. Quality of class participation:
\_\_\_\_\_ Contributes sound and original ideas.
\_\_\_\_\_ Evaluates the ideas of others. Often points out what's wrong with others' ideas. May ask questions of others.
\_\_\_\_\_ Makes brief contributions, usually in a few words. Often expresses only agreement or disagreement.
\_\_\_\_\_ Attempts to sidetrack the discussion with humorous or irrelevant remarks.

3. Signs of involvement even when not speaking:
\_\_\_\_\_ Listens actively. Looks at speaker. Leans forward in chair. Takes notes.
\_\_\_\_\_ Sometimes listens actively. May lose interest temporarily in discussion.
\_\_\_\_\_ Shows lack of interest in discussion. Slouches in chair and stares down.
\_\_\_\_\_ Does other activities during discussion. Whispers to others. Falls asleep.

4. How can you become more active in discussions? Consider how you can increase the frequency and quality of your participation and how you can listen more actively.

**Figure 13.1.** This simple check sheet, filled out by students after each discussion, can be a useful self-assessment of discussion involvement.

instrument that uses a scale for reflection about small-group discussion. We adapted this from Orlich, Harder, Callahan, and Gibson (2001).

At the conclusion of a small-group discussion, we would have each student fill out the form; and then to get the group's feelings, have one student call out the number of a statement and have everyone read

**Small-Group Discussion Evaluation**

Group #_____            Your name: _____

Directions: Rate your own participation in your group by circling one of the numbers in the scales (from 1–5) for each topic stated at the left.

| Topic | Very Ineffective | Somewhat Ineffective | About Average | Somewhat Effective | Very Effective |
|---|---|---|---|---|---|
| 1. What overall rating of effectiveness would you give the discussion session? | 1 | 2 | 3 | 4 | 5 |
| 2. How effectively did your group work together during the discussion? | 1 | 2 | 3 | 4 | 5 |
| 3. How effective were the decisions your group reached? | 1 | 2 | 3 | 4 | 5 |
| 4. How effective was the group in considering ideas you contributed? | 1 | 2 | 3 | 4 | 5 |
| 5. How effective was the leader in making it easy for you to participate? | 1 | 2 | 3 | 4 | 5 |
| 6. How effective were you in encouraging others to speak or get involved? | 1 | 2 | 3 | 4 | 5 |
| 7. How effective were you at listening to others without interrupting? | 1 | 2 | 3 | 4 | 5 |
| 8. How effective were you at contributing ideas and comments to the discussion? | 1 | 2 | 3 | 4 | 5 |

**Figure 13.2.** The Small-Group Discussion Evaluation form uses a scale for reflection about small-group discussion.

out his or her assessment. The group is able to quickly hear the number that is different and indicates a concern. Then, they can talk about the areas of concern. It is probably a good idea to have students use the form a number of times so that they feel comfortable evaluating and reflecting on their involvement. Depending on the particular task, it is relatively simple to add or take away questions to make the sheet task specific. This strategy helps students develop their self-awareness and understanding of group process, and this enables the teacher to assist students in working together more effectively.

Finally, Tchudi and Mitchell (1999) offer an interesting approach to self- evaluation of small-group work. They designed a questionnaire with a series of questions for the evaluation of group work. Students are given a series of ten questions, and they must put a check plus if they felt they excelled in that area, a check if they feel they can answer "yes," and a check minus if they feel that it is an area they must answer "no." Here is a sampling of the questions from their questionnaire:

- Did you help keep the group on task?
- Did you suggest helpful ways to approach the task?
- Did you ask relevant questions in your group?
- Did you demonstrate an awareness and knowledge of issues from the novel?
- Did you pay close attention to the views of others? (363)

As with the other instruments we discussed, Tchudi and Mitchell (1999) have students fill out the questionnaire each time they meet in groups. We would add that it is important for the students to get feedback from the other students in their small group and discuss any areas of concern.

The important point to be made about these self-evaluation instruments is that they are effective at helping students become more reflective about their own involvement in small-group and whole-class discussions. Ultimately, students become more aware of their own process, and they develop better critical thinking and analytical skills. They become more involved in discussions and make more meaningful contributions.

# 14 Conventional and Unconventional Modes of Discussion

The technology available to teachers and students has come a long way in a relatively short period of time. The promise that technological innovation will improve American education is not new and is aptly recounted in the work of self-professed Luddite Neil Postman (1995), who speaks out against the reliance on what he calls the "False God of Technology." Postman outlines the promise that various generations held for such technological marvels as the "16-millimeter film, [. . .] then closed-circuit television, then the 8-milimeter film, then teacherproof textbooks [. . .]" and claims that the most recent technological cure for American education is computers. Postman discusses the futility and hopelessness felt by various generations of teachers who felt threatened by technological innovations that could potentially replace them. He charges that ultimately it's "not a new technology" that is at the heart of the arguments that proponents of the cause make to suggest that education is ripe for an infusion of technological improvement, but, rather, "a new species of child" (39) that would be needed to fulfill all of the lofty projections that techno-educators make to justify their claims for innovation. Postman goes on to reprint a poem attributed to a teacher from the 1920s that, although one of the first manifestations of the hopelessness felt in the face of technological innovation, perhaps voices it better than any generation since:

> Mr. Edison says
> That the radio will supplant the teacher.
> Already one may learn languages by means
>     of Victrola records.
> The moving picture will visualize
> What the radio fails to get across.
> Teachers will be relegated to the backwoods.
> With fire-horses,
> And long-haired women;
> Or, perhaps shown in museums.
> Education will become a matter
> Of pressing the button.
> Perhaps I can get a position at the switchboard. (49–50)

Undoubtedly, many new technologies have exacted a positive influence on classrooms, with some, like television, having a more enduring influence than others; however, all teachers, not just English teachers, seem to be continually under pressure in today's schools to find some way of accommodating technology in a useful and productive fashion.

One might argue that some high school teachers have an easier job of it given the infusion of technology in fields such as science and mathematics. It's the rare math teacher, for example, who can even recall the day when algebra was taught without the assistance of the programmable calculator. But along with their math and science counterparts, candidates for English positions at any school will more than likely be asked several questions during an interview about the extent to which they feel comfortable incorporating technology into the classroom, and these candidates are expected to provide responses that demonstrate that they know more about how to incorporate technology than how to discuss the virtues of word processing on the revision stage of the writing process. The ways through which English teachers can incorporate the wide variety of technological innovations in the classroom are many and varied. Teachers are presently working to develop ways of accommodating Internet research, programs that improve reading proficiency and comprehension, and ways of incorporating digital video as a means of enhancing the understanding of narrative, to name a few. The possibilities and the efficacy of such technological inclusion is subject to a great deal of discussion, and rightly so.

Despite the false promises about the role and impact of technology in the past, technological innovations that have emerged in the last few years, particularly those related to Internet and network technologies, have provided English teachers with a variety of ways to effectively engage students in conversation and enhance the discussions that are nurtured in classrooms. Jeannie Oakes and Martin Lipman (1999) note that when "used in the context of authentic and active learning communities, [. . .] technologies can scaffold learners' explorations beyond the bounds of their current knowledge and provide multidimensional routes of investigation." Efforts made to take advantage of these technologies do not threaten but enhance a teacher's role in the English classroom. They help teachers keep conversations going outside of class, help students engage in inquiry more deeply, provide students with the opportunity to reflect on issues brought up in class and build on them, and introduce students to new and exciting ways of learning that help them make greater sense of what is happening in class.

## Brief Review of Discussion Technologies

Since the late sixties, with the initial development of what we now know as the Internet, university faculty paved the way for the communication form so many of us now take for granted: e-mail. It is still one of the primary ways for students and teachers to communicate outside of class, and now many high schools across the nation also are using this as the means for teachers and students to continue school-related dialogue beyond the typical school day. The addition of more advanced technologies such as Web boards (or discussion boards), Weblogs (or blogs), and even interactive capabilities such as "chat rooms" or digital videoconferencing, pioneered by the development of Columbia University's "CU-SeeMe" Internet videoconferencing capability, has propelled teachers and students into a new era of communication that is breaking through the brick-and-mortar school buildings that house them, and bring them closer together in a virtual community of teachers and learners. Many students now have the ability to fulfill high school requirements in a "virtual environment," without ever stepping foot in an actual school building.

In terms of technologies that might assist teachers in developing new ways of discussing important issues and ideas in class, the most common types that are emerging include blogs and discussion boards. These technologies offer teachers and students the opportunity to engage in online communication, both synchronous and asynchronous. Blogs and boards function as "bulletin boards" upon which teachers and students can post and read messages as well as reply to what is posted by others. With both types of virtual conversations, teachers can control the level of interaction and the content that is reflected. Both types also are Internet based and require the author—and for the sake of our discussion, that would be the teacher—to manage the process, although it is entirely possible to imagine students themselves controlling school-related dialogue technologies outside of class. Depending on the manner in which the technologies are used, teachers and students can expand the discourse that begins in class and sustain it beyond the traditional classroom environment.

A number of programs and platforms exist to assist teachers in setting up virtual communication. As of this writing, WebCT, Blackboard, eCollege, Board Nation, Ezboard, and Boards 2 Go are some of the most prominent developers found in schools today, and their services vary in scope and price. A variety of Weblog software products exist (some very modestly priced), and within moments of loading the software, a teacher can set up a board that his or her students can access from the Internet. Resources that help teachers set up blogs include Blogger, LiveJournal, TypePad, and Moveable Type.

In either case, a dedicated space on a server is needed to "host" the virtual communication site. Today, many schools are providing such space for teachers on school-district servers, while many other teachers incur nominal fees themselves to get started on commercial servers. Teachers might create a blog or board that is specific to their educational objectives and technological proficiency and that caters to the specific needs of a particular group of students. For example, opening up the ability to allow students to freely post ideas and writings to a blog or board can be relatively free of obstruction. A student need only register as a known user of a class blog or board, or a teacher may create several levels of clearance that leave control of what is posted on the site to one or two responsible parties (usually the teacher). Once a teacher sets up a site, maintaining the site is relatively easy and straightforward. Blogs and boards can be used for the most mundane tasks, such as informing students (or even their parents, if they register as recipients and users of the site) of homework assignments or other class business. Class assignments, reading guides, or syllabi can be posted for students to reference or print. Blogs and boards may also be implemented in a way that facilitates class discussion about issues and ideas related to reading and discussion that most typically occurs in the four corners of the classroom.

## Continuing the Discussion outside of Class: The Case of Angelo Siempro

Chapter 11 of this text describes the potential for learning within coherent units designed around significant, overarching concepts. Imagine, for example, a sophomore English class that is pursuing a greater understanding of identity, particularly the idea of what people mean when they use the term *identity* and a consideration of all the factors that go into establishing what a person's identity really is. While pursuing a greater understanding of this concept, students engage in the reading and analysis of several texts, continually reflecting on key questions such as the following:

> To what extent do family and friends influence who you are?"

> To what extent does cultural background or family history influence who you are?

To what extent do emotional responses identify how you are perceived?

How does an individual's self-concept compare to how he/she thinks others perceive him/her?

To what extent is your identity defined by gender and other social factors?

To what extent are we judged by how smart we are perceived to be?

Students continually test their emerging definition of identity against thoughts and ideas that occur to them as they read and revisit these questions. A case study like the "Does She Deserve Honor?" case described in Chapter 6 provides students a contextualized opportunity to address these questions. The activity is not only an effective way of engaging students in meaningful inquiry, but it also provides a strong example of how discussion technologies can be used to extend the conversation and provide students an opportunity to generate deeper understanding.

In this chapter, students engage in the inquiry by considering the complicated case of a fictional student named Angelo Siempro. As with the case studies in earlier chapters, this one presents a problem for which there is no simple resolution. Students are introduced to several characters related to the case and know that they will pretend to be one of these characters during a subsequent simulated meeting. In collaborative groups, students study the situation from one of several perspectives that include:

Angelo Siempro, a student

Mrs. Siempro, Angelo's mother

Brad Taggart, a student

Mrs. Taggart, Brad's mother

Dr. Sterling, principal, Floodrock High School

Ms. Amelia Fitzhugh, president of local teacher's union

Mr. Gilmore Copeland, Brad's favorite uncle

Dierdre Cohen, a senior student at Floodrock High School

The teacher coaches the students to think about how the different characters will respond to the events that they become aware of through a narrative description of Angelo's situation and a resulting meeting that will be run by the students portraying the principal, Dr. Sterling. Students are encouraged to imagine all of the reasonable opposing viewpoints to the position for which they are asked to advocate, thus ensuring a lively discussion of the issues.

---

### Angelo Siempro: Honor Student

*The Case.*

Several years ago at Floodrock High School, there was a very popular student named Angelo. Everyone seemed to like him. Angelo was a very attractive young man. He stood 6' 2" tall, with a trim, muscular figure. He had slightly long blond hair, which he seldom combed, making him look like a child who just rose from a nap. His blue eyes were always clear and liquid. Angelo was always cheerful, and he never took offense when teachers and friends teased him. Although Angelo was rather large and athletic, he projected the image of an innocent child.

Although Angelo was not the most brilliant student, he was well liked by his teachers. They enjoyed his sense of humor, and they appreciated the consistent effort he made to understand any particular subject. Angelo often asked questions in class because he really cared to learn. His classmates would sometimes poke gentle fun at Angelo for asking so many questions, but he never got angry.

Angelo was an accomplished athlete, starring on both the football and basketball teams. During his senior year, Angelo returned a kickoff for a touchdown in the homecoming game against Maple Park. Angelo returned the kickoff ninety-eight yards, a school record which still stands today. Angelo was the star of the team, but he felt self-conscious about receiving praise. He always thanked his teammates and insisted that he was nothing without their efforts.

Angelo was a popular classmate, a good student, and a fine athlete. Faculty members and other students began to believe Angelo was a kind of good luck charm, and they enjoyed being around him. Angelo was almost the perfect student, but he had one small problem—he suffered from a slight speech impediment. Occasionally Angelo would stutter. Usually his stutter would go unnoticed, but when he was nervous or excited, he would stutter so badly that he could barely speak at all. For example, if a particularly tough teacher would insist that Angelo answer a question when he had no idea of the answer, he would stutter so badly that the other students would squirm with embarrassment. The teacher would then begin to feel awkward and would quickly call on someone else. Angelo felt this called attention to his problem, and he became even more self-conscious.

No matter how popular a person is, there always seems to be someone out to get him. This was the case with Angelo. There was another student at Floodrock High named Brad Taggart who, for no apparent reason, hated Angelo. Brad was also popular, but in a different way. Brad was kind of a tough, domineering boy, who seemed to intimidate a number of persons into doing favors for him. Brad had a large circle of friends who followed him around and did whatever he said. Many persons at Floodrock High felt that Brad resented Angelo because, without making a great effort, Angelo had become far more popular than Brad.

When Angelo was a senior, there was a rash of fistfights in the halls, in the cafeteria, and in the senior lounge. Some students claimed that these fights were gang related, but this was never determined. During the spring of that year, there seemed to be two or three fights every week. The parents, the teachers, and the administrators became very concerned about the violence at Floodrock High. The administrators decided to crack down on any incidence of violence. At an April faculty meeting, the principal, Dr. Sterling, insisted that any students caught fighting or trying to incite others to fight would be suspended for five days. There would be no exceptions. Dr. Sterling explained that there was a potentially volatile situation in the school, and the fights had to stop immediately.

Soon after the April faculty meeting, Brad Taggart went to Dr. Sterling's office to report that Angelo was responsible for many of the fights that had occurred that semester. He claimed that Angelo was a gang member and that he and his gang were extorting money from students and beating up anyone who even said "hello" to their girlfriends. Dr. Sterling told Brad that these were very serious charges and asked him if he would be willing to confront Angelo with these charges right there in Dr. Sterling's office. Brad agreed to repeat his charges in front of Angelo.

Angelo was called out of class and reported to Dr. Sterling's office. Brad again claimed that Angelo was the cause of much of the violence in the school that semester. When Dr. Sterling asked Angelo to respond to the charges, Angelo didn't know what to say. He couldn't believe that Brad was saying these terrible things about him. When Angelo began to talk, he stuttered uncontrollably. The more he tried to speak to defend himself, the more he stuttered. Finally Angelo's face turned red, and his fists clinched. He couldn't speak, so he lashed out at Brad and landed a powerful blow on his left eye. Brad collapsed to the floor, smashing his head against Dr. Sterling's desk as he fell. Brad was unconscious for about ten minutes, and when he recovered, he insisted that Dr. Sterling do something to punish Angelo.

Dr. Sterling had been willing to dismiss Brad's charges against Angelo, but now he faced a difficult decision. Dr. Sterling witnessed the assault himself, and he had assured the faculty that he would be harsh with all violent offenders. Because of family problems and illness, Angelo had already been absent ten times that semester; and a five-day suspension would cause Angelo to be dropped from all his classes with failures in each. (NOTE: It was the school policy at the time that any student who is absent from a class for fifteen days or more would be removed from the class and assigned a failing grade. The student's classes would then be replaced by a series of study halls.) Without the credits from that semester, Angelo would not be able to graduate in June with his class. Angelo was also a finalist for the Sons of the Civil War Scholarship. With the disgrace of the suspension for fighting, Angelo would certainly lose the scholarship, which he desperately needed if he were to enter college in the fall.

Dr. Sterling liked Angelo very much. He had worked on many school projects with Angelo and had developed a fatherly affection for him. Nevertheless Dr. Sterling felt he had to live up to the standards that he set for the rest of the school. He felt he had to make an example of Angelo, and the infraction must be punished severely.

After reading this case study, and meeting with other students who prepare for the same role, students join in a large group and simulate a school meeting where all of the characters gather to address one central question: What do you think Dr. Sterling should do? Students are allowed to create "facts" that help their case, as long as the facts are consistent with the known facts of the case study. In simulating this meeting and working to arrive at a satisfactory resolution that attends to all of the various perspectives held by those associated with Angelo and Brad, and the issues and ideas generated from the exchange, students are encouraged to consider more deeply many of the key questions that guide their emerging understanding of identity. A typical student-run conversation generates exchanges like these:

*Angelo:* Brad has been after me for a while. I shouldn't be punished for what happened. Besides, he's not a good student.

*Copeland (Brad's uncle):* How do you know that?

*Dr. Sterling:* And what does that have to do with him bullying you?

*Angelo:* Would you rather let a bad kid like Brad complain or believe someone like me? He lies.

*Dr. Sterling:* How so?

*Angelo:* He says I'm a gang member. I'm not a gang member.

*Copeland:* When did he say you were a gang member?

*Angelo (gesturing to the case study):* He said it.

*Mrs. Siempro:* Brad's integrity is in question here. Brad picks fights in the hallways, and Angelo always resists. Why weren't any teachers present at these times? Angelo always shrugs off the attempts. Also, I'd like to say, I've been to sporting events, and I do believe there may be a grudge between the Taggart family and my son. Once during a game the coach switched Angelo for Brad, and the Taggarts freaked out.

*Copeland:* Liar!

*Mrs. Siempro:* This is just an attempt to see their son. . . .There's a certain resentment between the Taggarts and Angelo. Brad often makes fun of Angelo . . . with the stuttering. It's his one weakness . . . this time he has crossed the line. . . .yeah, I think Mrs. Taggart doesn't discipline Brad.

*Dr. Sterling:* You and Mrs. Taggart don't get along?

*Mrs. Siempro:* We've had words. I don't know who wouldn't like my son. He gets good grades, and he's a good kid.

*Copeland:* Brad is the only one who Angelo doesn't get along with.

*Mrs. Siempro:* Brad has friends, but he bullies them.

*Copeland:* There has to be some reason that Brad hates Angelo.

*Brad:* He's not as good as everyone says. He has a darker side. I'm accused of picking on kids, but he does it. I saw him. I saw him take a freshman . . . Angelo . . . and put him in a locker.

*Mrs. Siempro:* My son would never do that. Find the kid that will say he did that. . . . They'll say that Brad did it.

*Angelo:* Were there any witnesses?

*Mrs. Taggart:* My son's reputation is not true. People have failed to mention Brad's clubs and how he counsels kids at day care. These things do not describe a bad kid.

> *Fitzhugh (faculty union rep):* Your policy is not fair. What
> grounds do you have for this policy?
>
> *Dr. Sterling:* We'll talk later.
>
> *Fitzhugh:* We'll talk now. Angelo is not our main concern.

After playing out this meeting in class, students are encouraged to step
away from the roles they prepared and consider all of the various perspectives from which they heard. Although a conversation would likely
occur in class, it is compelling to assess student responses as reported
on a Weblog, an experience that allows them to visually trace what their
classmates are thinking and to build upon their ideas in a significant
way.

Weblogs and discussion boards allow teachers the opportunity
to ask students to respond to classroom inquiry but to do so online.
There, at the teacher's direction, the students respond in staggered shifts,
each charged to demonstrate familiarity with the comments of the student responders before them and to build on those comments in a substantive way. The process encourages students to develop their own
ideas, publicize them through a public forum, and be prepared to respond to other ideas suggested by members of their learning community. By engaging in a process such as this, students are challenged to
confront what many, including Gerald Graff (2003), see as the "lack of
interest in entering the public sphere." Graff makes the case that much
of what students are offered in schools fails to promote genuine discourse but that the "emergence of the Internet, the electronic town meeting, and talk-back radio hold out promise" for assisting students to realize that their thoughts, and how they express them, are worthwhile
considerations and worth developing. Although the technique described
here is also possible in traditional classroom settings (one envisions a
teacher taking in student submissions and then copying them for subsequent reference, and duplicating that process as many times as
deemed necessary), blogs and boards are a more natural platform for
this type of exchange given the ease with which student submissions
might be posted and the instantaneous access students have to all of
their classmates' opinions. An initial student posting to the Angelo
Siempro case looks like this:

> I think considering Angelo's case, Principal Sterling should re-
> peal the current zero-tolerance five-day suspension policy, and
> replace it with a more flexible policy, involving anger manage-
> ment classes, and community service, in addition to a one- or
> two-day suspension. Even though Angelo is not getting his full
> five-day suspension, he will still be punished with anger man-

agement and community service. Even though it may look like Angelo is getting off easy, he really isn't. My reasons for this are that I think the zero-tolerance policy was unfair to begin with. Also, if Angelo has the five-day suspension, he will fail classes and won't graduate, ruining his future. Another reason is the controversy between him and Brad Taggart. Although Angelo did punch Brad, there are reports of Brad having a grudge against Angelo, and [being] jealous of him. He took advantage of Angelo's speech impediment, his stutter, when accusing him. Teachers report Brad harassing kids in hallways and bullying his own friends. Angelo, on the other hand, is a very hardworking student, and claims made by Brad that Angelo bullies kids and is the cause of the violence in the school have no evidence. Yes, it may seem like zero-tolerance except for Angelo, but this would be changing the rules for everyone, and he would still have other punishments coming, and a possible police report from the assault. Angelo is still not getting off easy.

When posted to a Weblog or discussion board, this initial student response becomes a fertile starting point from which subsequent student contributions can be formulated. In this case, students were encouraged to answer the same question about what they thought Principal Sterling should do but were given the additional task of paraphrasing what a previous student had to say about the case and building off of that argument. Given these requirements, a subsequent response to the case study takes on these characteristics:

I still believe that everyone who said that Angelo should not be punished to the full extent was wrong and is still wrong. Almost everyone said "He should be punished but not to the full extent." What is up with this? Come on, people, we need to think about time efficacy and treat everyone as equals. We can't go around making exceptions to everyone and treating everyone differently. This is one school and there should be one rule for everyone to follow. I agree with the statement that Jess made, "Just because he is a good student, [a] well-liked individual, and well mannered doesn't make him an exception from the rule." This is also what I think and that we can't make exceptions to a "zero tolerance policy." That is why it is "zero tolerance," so if something happens, no matter what, you are going to get punished for it. Almost everyone else thought there should be an exception to the rule. Come on, people. I'm sorry, but I have to say, and ask, why they would make that rule if they knew it was going to be broken? I do think he should be punished to the full extent of the zero tolerance. Pat argues with me by stating, "Mark says that it doesn't matter if someone is a straight A student or a bad one," but I disagree because the straight A student does not need as much straightening out as a delinquent and therefore should not

be punished as harshly. So are you saying that it is all right for a
good straight A student to go around punching people? You could
be a great student, but that doesn't mean you don't or won't punch
or beat someone up. I believe and still believe Angelo should be
punished for what he did and to the full extent of the zero tolerance policy.

This student's response clearly incorporates the thoughts and ideas of
students who responded before. In addressing the arguments of others, even attributing the arguments to specific classmates, the student
is demonstrating an emerging understanding of public discourse at the
highest level: The student takes the time not only to further his own
beliefs, but also to address and refute the thoughts of those who provide reasonable opposition to his position.

An additional positive learner outcome from the utilization of
these technological discussion opportunities includes the effect on learning itself. All English teachers are familiar with the phenomenon of
witnessing a vibrant and meaningful conversation unfold in the classroom only to wonder afterward, what, exactly did we talk about? We
can only imagine, or learn directly, should we take the time to actually
ask students about the efficacy of classroom discussion, how ethereal
the words spoken in class can appear to students who are caught up in
the heat of the moment and later, upon reflecting, find themselves unable or quite limited in their ability to recall with great specificity what
exactly was said. That teachers might even require students to cite the
words of their peers as evidence in an argumentative writing about an
issue or idea in class, is a futile undertaking without the assistance of
some visual manifestation of what was actually said in class. Transcripts
of conversations are excellent tools for such dialogic reflection, as are
the types of good note-taking strategies that teachers have encouraged
for years. But discussion aides like Weblogs and discussion boards pos-
sess vast potential in providing students the means to reflect on the
conversations that teachers nurture in class. One student's reflection on
the efficacy of blog postings while his class considered the Angelo
Siempro case illuminates the point further:

I personally have never heard of such a thing as a blog, but I
definitely think it is one of the most useful tools I have seen in my
school career. It is awesome that I can look over things and compare thoughts out of the classroom with my peers. Without the
site, I feel like I'm missing an opportunity to further my learning
experience and get to do things outside of the school environment. I love being able to look at other's responses and type at
the same time. It's a lot easier than taking notes and it is actually

fun. Overall, I would give the blog an A+ with what it does, and for making English fun. In class, I love having discussions and debates, and I think that is the best thing about English class. I know that the blog will help me out down the road, and prepare me for college too. I know that I have learned and want to learn more about outside of the classroom work and reflecting!

Recent technological advancements, particularly in the areas of Weblogs and discussion boards, demonstrate the potential value of both generating and extending meaningful classroom dialogue both within class and beyond the traditional classroom setting. With relative ease, a teacher can now utilize an elaborate discussion board service or simple software package and assist students in keeping meaningful classroom conversations going outside of class. In doing so, classroom discourse is rendered more meaningful because it is, at once, more visible and more available for continued reflection and analysis. Students are allowed the opportunity to reflect on issues brought up in class and encouraged to refine their thinking and fashion more elaborate responses that take into account the multiple perspectives that can emerge from classroom dialogue. Given the opportunity they provide for students to look over and analyze the ideas and arguments that emerge from classroom discussion, these technologies can introduce students to new ways of learning that help them comprehend classroom discussion at a higher level and create a deeper sense of appreciation for the discourse in which they engage. There is no need to fear, as the teacher in 1920 feared Mr. Edison's newfangled radio, the technologies that might assist the extension of class discussion beyond the classroom. Without the careful planning, lesson sequencing, and innovation employed by English teachers seeking to engage students in the learning process at a higher level, these technologies are useless.

# 15 Discussion, Diversity, and Democratic Ideals

*Any education given by a group tends to socialize its members, but the quality and value of the socialization depends upon the habits and aims of the group.*

John Dewey, *Democracy and Education*

Throughout this book, we have promoted the idea that students should frequently participate in meaningful discussions. For one reason, we understand that the students' active participation will promote their learning of the content of a course. We also believe, however, that the interaction with peers in exploring significant questions involves a process that in itself teaches lessons about how to work with a diverse group of fellow human beings and appreciate them for who they are.

Gary Marx (2002) notes that the United States is becoming a nation of minorities, and schools in the United States will become increasingly diverse in the future. Some teachers can easily identify themselves as teaching in a diverse setting, but everyone who teaches, teaches among a diverse population. And every student who leaves school will enter a diverse community. That being true, an important question for every teacher today is this: How do we prepare children to live as civil, thoughtful citizens in a diverse society?

For some schools, various character education programs promote values like fairness and responsibility, which could be elements that support tolerance and contribute to democratic goals. For other schools, the answer to the question above lies in a deliberate program of exposing students to some aspects of several cultures through formats like Hispanic Heritage Week, Black History Month, and the Multicultural Club. These are all worthwhile endeavors that celebrate the best of many cultures, but the efforts emphasize only one aspect of diversity and focus on exposing students to the diversity of ethnic cultures. Of course, diversity can be found in any classroom and takes many forms: gender, personality, learning style, sexual orientation, socioeconomic status, religion, and political affiliation. Again, the question for any teacher is this: How do we prepare children to live as civil, thoughtful citizens in a diverse society?

## Preparing to Live in a Diverse Society

Here is a deceptively simple answer: In every classroom, provide frequent occasions for students to engage each other in meaningful, content-related conversations about challenging issues that matter to them. This is something that every classroom teacher can do, no matter what subject, without the consent of administrators and without the wholesale endorsement of the rest of the faculty. This practice promotes the learning of the content of specific disciplines. As we have noted throughout this book, this is a practice that rarely occurs in schools. In fact, engaging students in frequent meaningful conversations about significant issues would be a revolutionary school reform.

Our simple answer prompts several complex questions:

- How are such conversations possible?
- How can the active participation in authentic discussions help students to respect and appreciate diversity?
- How does students' involvement in significant conversations with a variety of people help to promote social justice?

To illustrate, consider the English curriculum at Community High School in West Chicago, Illinois. In the school's conception of the English curriculum, a few broad, overarching questions focus the inquiry, and support the unity and coherence among the various language activities. Here are some of the key questions, which derive from the literature that the students study:

- How are all citizens equal?
- What are the factors that shape one's identity?
- What is the balance between individual rights and social responsibility?

These questions focus inquiry for the required English classes and for interdisciplinary classes that integrate English and social studies.

In one way or another, all the required English courses explore concepts related to diversity and social justice. This is most obvious in the freshman curriculum. The team of English teachers who designed the English curriculum for the ninth grade hoped to influence the mastery of essential language skills, but they also intended that the curriculum would promote social justice. The big question for the curriculum is: What is equality? The one big question is ultimately at the heart of most discussion throughout the school year. This big question prompts a series of ancillary questions that emerge from involvement with the literature. Some of these questions are identified in the school's curriculum guide:

> The literature that students have studied in ninth grade shares the feature that all the works explore themes about prejudice, bigotry, and intolerance. The themes appear to be important and persistent ones. In the Declaration of Independence, Jefferson asserts as a "self-evident truth" that "all men are created equal." The document and Jefferson's claim are important cornerstones to American democracy. Of course, Jefferson and other signers of the Declaration were slaveholders and had a narrow view of who could be considered an equal. But we take what they said as a "promissory note," as [Martin Luther] King put it, and continue to explore the broader meaning that all human beings in many circumstances must be regarded as equals. Many influential writers, like John Steinbeck, Lorraine Hansberry, and Elie Wiesel, have represented in their works some distressing instances when the spirit of the claim that "all men are created equal" has been violated. Other writers, like Shakespeare, imply the questions, "Isn't it right and appropriate that some persons hold a position of higher status in a society?" and "Isn't it true that some people are just more civilized and better than others?" Other writers, like H. G. Wells, Daniel Keyes, and Kurt Vonnegut, make us wonder if it would ever be possible to change individual citizens to make everyone "equal" in almost every regard. Furthermore, the reader trembles to think of the resulting problems were such a world possible.
>
> If one is to group a series of related readings because they all explore problems with intolerance, there is the danger of leading students through a superficial catalog of stories in which a character has been the victim of prejudice or bigotry and the reader can feel sorry for the victim and indignant toward the oppressor. The curriculum would take the form of a series of bigotry-of-the-month experiences. Furthermore, treating the topic of prejudice in an inquiry-based mode poses some challenges. After all, isn't prejudice always bad? Will there be students in our classrooms who want to identify themselves as champions of bigotry? So what's the problem? If themes about prejudice and intolerance are going to be rich enough to sustain a yearlong inquiry process, there must be some challenging and significant questions.

This portion of the rationale acknowledges that the students will explore questions that are difficult for adolescents and adults to answer. Each stage of the curriculum prepares students for subsequent stages, as the conversation becomes broader and richer.

Other pages from the school's curriculum guide reveal why teachers determined that the questions that would guide group inquiry over the course of the school year were significant and were appropriate for ninth graders to study:

> Why would it be appropriate to study themes about prejudice and intolerance in English 1? Most students in English 1 will be ninth-graders. They come to the larger high school from a variety of smaller feeder schools. The students have to determine where they fit into the new environment where there might already be several established groups: some based on ethnicity, some based on talents and interests, some based on rejection by other groups. The new high school students must figure out where they fit into the mix and how they will react to students who don't look the same or act the same as they do. The structure of schools historically does much to classify and stratify the population. Will the classification and stratification influence students to accept the idea that some people are naturally the elite and others are the dregs? Can students demand to be included in any group with whom they want to associate? Can any student reject other students? Are students making judgments about the worth of other students based on their appearance, intelligence, or activities? How do students feel themselves when they are judged and/or rejected because of their appearance, intelligence, or activities? In the [United States], we need only look at the sad history of violent attacks in schools to know how grave the consequences are when fresh and eager new students become outcasts. It's tough being new to a large high school, and the students' responses to the crucial questions listed above may stay with them and guide behavior during adulthood.

The guide emphasizes that the questions that students talk about and write about are critical to the conduct of their lives. The discussions, then, are far more than mere assessments of recall. Instead, they are the dynamic investigations of current and perennial problems, and students recognize that how each person responds does matter. Smagorinsky (2000) makes a strong case that authentic discussions are likely to do more than the variety of prepackaged character education programs to help students to understand moral and ethical obligations. It is not enough to recite universal platitudes to guide correct behavior. Instead, students benefit from working with others in figuring out how they and the characters they encounter in the literature should behave responsibly in specific, recognizable situations that challenge their ability to do the right thing.

The curriculum guide for the course provides a developed rationale for what teachers teach and how they teach it. This practice of expressing the need, nature, and complexity of the concepts and goals of the curriculum might be a good practice for any teacher in planning a course of study, especially when teaching in a multicultural environment where one has to reflect upon assumptions and reexamine the needs and interests of students. It is certainly worth the effort to identify the questions that unify the variety of language activities into a coherent whole, and explain, if only to oneself, why these questions are worthy of our attention for any extended period of time.

## Discussing Equality and Social Justice

Where does one begin in engaging ninth graders in a deliberate program of investigation about issues of social justice? Perhaps the first question that Thomas Jefferson prompts us to consider is this: What does it mean to be *equal*? Commentator Abraham Kaplan (1987) observes that discussions of social philosophy often focus on the general question of equality. To attempt to answer the question means establishing guidelines, criteria, or "rules" for the occasions when citizens *must* be treated as equals. At Community High School, West Chicago, Illinois, ninth graders begin their first year of high school English by engaging each other in a discussion about problem-based scenarios that challenge them to figure out the appropriate behavior for citizens who are going to treat fellow citizens as equals. Consider the problems posed by the following scenario:

> While sixteen-year-old Louise Lew was in her bedroom getting ready for her date, her father answered the front door. Mr. Lew opened the door to discover Mitch Reiter, Louise's new boyfriend. Mitch wore faded blue jeans with holes torn in both knees, a bicycle chain around his waist, armadillo skin cowboy boots, and a T-shirt with the slogan, "A Mind Is a Wonderful Thing to Waste!" Mitch's hair was shaved on one side of his head, with the remaining locks dyed with orange and yellow stripes. Mr. Lew told Mitch, "Wait here," and closed the door in his face. Mr. Lew then dashed up to Louise's room and informed her, "You are not going out with that creature." To what extent are Mr. Lew's concerns legitimate?

In small groups, the students will disagree, challenge each other, defend their own positions, attempt to express general rules, imagine exceptions, refine their statements, and invent their own scenarios to support their claims. Here is a typical example of the kind of rules the students express:

1. Private clubs may exclude nonmembers, as long as equivalent clubs are available to the people who have been excluded.

2. No matter how old a person is, he or she should be able to continue to work at a job, as long as he or she can do the job well.

3. We should not prejudge persons on the basis of race or ethnicity alone.

4. People are allowed to practice their own religious beliefs, unless their practices harm others.

5. For jobs that are not politically sensitive, employers should not select people on the basis of their political affiliation.

6. No matter how intelligent or mentally disabled a person is, he or she should have opportunities for education, jobs, housing, and general welfare.

7. You should not judge the value of a person based on the person's physical appearance alone.

8. Citizens with physical challenges should enjoy the same basic rights as all other citizens.

In working with the scenarios, the students are able to express a set of rules for guiding their behavior; more importantly, they had to work collaboratively with a diverse group to be able to negotiate and derive the rules. The process of deriving the set of rules might take two or three days. Although the activity might seem very time consuming, it becomes the foundation for subsequent investigation, and the process the students experience in working closely with each other is as important as the outcome they produce.

The conflicts represented in the literature suggest a series of related questions that can guide reading and serve as the basis for discussion. First one must wonder if there are ever occasions when a person would be justified in prejudging others. In other words, is all discrimination necessarily bad? If students begin with the idealistic assertion that all citizens must be treated as equals and all humans must be accorded basic rights, do they allow any exceptions to the rule? One complication comes when Mr. Lindner in *A Raisin in the Sun* asks the Youngers if it is a right of every citizen to decide with whom he or she wants to associate. Must everyone allow admission to everyone upon every occasion, or is it possible to be exclusive on some occasions? What does the law allow and protect? What does our sense of right and wrong guide us to do?

Easy answers to the central question about equality may elude us, and subsequent encounters with other literature complicate the problem. With *Flowers for Algernon*, for example, Daniel Keyes raises doubts about the ways in which we label and value humans based on their perceived intelligence. While Keyes might influence us to think that all persons, no matter how intelligent we judge them to be, deserve to have their human dignity recognized and respected, the more discriminating among us might reject the preprocedure Charlie Gordon, with a below average IQ, as the surgeon who will remove our life-threatening brain tumor. While we might sympathize with the childlike Lennie Small in *Of Mice and Men*, it is hard to imagine anyone without an obsessive interest in rabbits and other soft things welcoming him as a regular companion to movies, dances, sporting events, and conversations over latte at the coffee shop. Could anyone's rejection of Lennie be justified? While it is easy to condemn those whose prejudices guide cruel mistreatment of fellow human beings, it remains difficult for most adolescents to apply ideal principles of equality in tough situations. Vivian Gussin Paley worked for social justice when she insisted that her kindergarten class honor the rule "You can't say 'You can't play'" (Paley 1993), but can her rule apply universally so that no one can exclude anyone from any association? These gray areas for judgment become the territory for group inquiry. It is important to recognize that this delving into thorny questions, developing critical thinking and essential interpersonal skills, and moving away from recitation formats that emphasize simple recall is uncommon; and if the reader plans to teach in this way, you will be different from most of your colleagues.

## Can You Say, "You Can't Play"?

Another activity requires the students to work together again to refine their generalizations about equality by guiding one's behavior regarding the inclusion or exclusion of any citizen to a group or community. This activity and complete set of scenarios is included in Chapter 11. We reprint one of the scenarios here to illustrate how it leads students to grapple with the issues:

> Adam and Danae Raspworthy recently moved into the Utopia Hollow subdivision in the suburb of Random Falls. A group of neighbors invited them to dinner to welcome the Raspworthys to the community. It appeared that all of Adam and Danae's new neighbors were of the same ethnicity. At the dinner party, the neighbors served braised eel in apricot chutney, poached octopus in curry gravy, boiled lamb kidneys, sage dumplings, and bone marrow soup. Adam and Danae, who are very conservative in their eating habits, almost gagged when they saw and smelled this unfamiliar food. Although they did not want to offend anyone, and they wanted to become accepted members of

the neighborhood, they would find it very difficult to eat the food that they were invited to eat. What should Adam and Danae do?

After deliberating about the set of scenarios, one group of students expressed guidelines upon which they expanded in letters to Ms. Paley. These are the guidelines that the students offered:

1. Be open to new ideas and new ways of doing things.
2. Be respectful toward other people's beliefs and ideas, unless those beliefs are unlawful or harmful.
3. Attempt to understand the intent behind someone's behavior and discuss conflicts.
4. Adjust your behavior to the dominant group, as long as you don't surrender your values.
5. If a person does not feel comfortable with a group, he or she should turn away and join another group.
6. Sometimes, when it is impossible to change, the dominant group should adjust to make the new person feel comfortable.

In the letters to Vivian Paley, the students evaluated the efficacy and reasonableness of Paley's rule and offered their own set of rules, with accompanying examples to illustrate the importance and validity of each rule. One student, whom we will call Chablis, introduced her letter in a personal way:

> In our English class, we have been discussing some rules of etiquette, and our teacher came across a rule that you made up, which is, "You can't say, 'You can't play.'" When I read this rule, I thought that it was the best rule that I have ever heard, and I wish that I was in your class, because it would have made an impact on me somehow. I do remember times when I was younger [when] my classmates would leave me out for unknown reasons. Now the friends that left me out still leave me out sometimes. Not only is it mean, but it hurts; it hurts really bad. When you're left out, sometimes people will join gangs. I'm glad that I have enough sense to realize who my real friends are. When you judge people to be in certain groups, you have to take in some considerations.

The same student wrote six more paragraphs before she summarized her evaluation in this way:

> No matter what race people are or how they act, it shouldn't matter unless they are harming you in some way. It may not only harm you physically, but it may harm you emotionally. People have to accept people for how they are and not try to change them if they are happy with themselves. If people can learn to

include people in activities and groups, everybody would get along a lot better. Soon I hope people will realize that it is better to help than to hurt.

Chablis's letter reveals complex thought that resulted and benefited from her purposeful interactions with her classmates. During the course of discussion, other students disagreed with and challenged Chablis. The structured discussion activity prompted her to search her memory to find means for evaluating each situation. Exposure to multiple and competing views helped her to sort through possibilities and find the ground where she felt most comfortable. By hearing the views of others, Chablis gained insights that expanded her thought. The challenges of others prompted Chablis to express the reasonable grounds for her claims, raising the level of thought from unsupported prejudices to rational and deliberate decisions. Chablis's multiple-paragraph letter, with its framing of the problem of applying Ms. Paley's rules, its expression of a set of her own rules, the description of examples to illustrate the rules, an explanation of the relevance of the examples, and its summary analysis, resulted from involvement in small-group and large-group discussion and the inevitable exposure to a diversity of people and the variety of views they represent. The series of related activities prepared this student and her classmates to judge in a very rational and deliberate way the behavior of the characters in the literature they studied and, just as importantly, equipped them to negotiate their own behavior in the complex of sensitive and challenging situations that are part of everyday life.

Vivian Paley was impressed enough and kind enough to respond to the students' letters, and her comments emphasize the importance of the students' continuing conversations:

> This particular rule evolved mainly in the kindergarten but the inherent concepts of inclusion and exclusion must be reexamined at every stage of our lives. Indeed it would not be excessive were the discussion upon which you base your letters to take place at every grade. As our perceptions in general develop, so does our sense of what is fair and unfair in school life and beyond. Nothing is more urgent in a democratic society than this continuing need to explore who we are and who we want to be.
>
> The recognition that each of you is not powerless to create a school society in which other people's feelings matter comes across in your letters. The more you talk and write about these real events that occur every day to you and others, the more sensitive everyone becomes to those who need support, kindness, and a welcoming hand. Once we are brave enough to say "This is what happened to me, and I think it is unfair and hurtful," then

we are ready to see what is being said and done to others. At this point, rules are not needed since we begin to feel what another person feels.

Ms. Paley encourages us to keep the discussions going, but, as noted earlier, seldom does authentic discussion take place in classrooms. At the same time, other scholars (Applebee 1996; Hillocks 1999; Sizer and Sizer 1999) write convincingly that meaningful interaction among students is crucial to learning the concepts of any discipline. Other important figures in education long ago emphasized the importance of functioning in a classroom as an interconnected community of learners. John Dewey insisted that schools need to prepare citizens for living in a democracy, and that preparation means more than being able to read position papers and feel the obligation to visit the polling place on election day. Here is how Dewey (1944) viewed democracy:

> A democracy is more than a form of government; it is primarily a mode of associated living, of conjoint communicated experience. The extension in space of the number of individuals who participate in an interest so that each has to refer his own action to that of others, and to consider the action of others to give point and direction to his own, is equivalent to the breaking down of those barriers of class, race, and national territory which kept men from perceiving the full import of their activity. These more numerous and more varied points of contact denote a greater diversity of stimuli to which an individual has to respond; they consequently put a premium on variation in his action. They secure a liberation of powers which remain suppressed as long as the incitations to action are partial, as they must be in a group which in its exclusiveness shuts out many interests (87).

In short, Dewey claims that when one lives in a democracy, the actions of individual citizens necessarily touch the lives of other citizens. As much as one might try, it is not possible to completely isolate oneself from other citizens. One's talents, one's industry, one's lethargy, one's drunkenness, one's lawlessness, one's constant piety, all contribute positive or negative effects on the community of citizens. As Martin Luther King (1992) points out, we are all "caught in an inescapable network of mutuality; tied in a single garment of destiny."

Dewey reminds us that schools have an obligation to prepare children to understand and live the experience of an "associated life":

> A society which makes provision for participation in its good of all its members on equal terms and which secures flexible readjustment of its institutions through interaction of the different forms of associated life is in so far democratic. Such a society must

> have a type of education which gives individuals a personal in-
> terest in social relationships and control, and the habits of mind
> which secure social changes without introducing disorder. (1944,
> 99)

Living the associated life in school does not mean functioning as the
passive receptacle for the transmission of information. Preparation for
living productively in the diversity of American democracy necessarily involves frequent, meaningful interaction, with students grappling
together with questions, problems, and issues that have some significance to their lives.

One more example illustrates a way that students extend their
thinking through regular discussions with their peers. If the students
believe that it is essentially good to consider all citizens as equals, how
far would they go to insure equality? Daniel Keyes with *Flowers for
Algernon* and Kurt Vonnegut with "Harrison Bergeron" confront the
reader with the possibility that medical and technological advances
might make it possible to transform everyone to become literally equal
in some sense. So discussion must expand to include judgments about
these possibilities. The following activity extends discussion of the issues related to the literature. The students' participation in the discussion prepares them to write about a critical question. Hearing and sort-
ing through a variety of responses to the problem helps students to
frame the problem for their readers and to advance arguments that include considerations of opposing views.

---

### Designing a Better Human?

*Meet Morty.*
A child named Morty DeFamma lives in a very poor neighborhood
in Chicago. He has a number of physical challenges. He is inordi-
nately small for his age, which causes him to be an object of ridicule at school and in his neighborhood. His hands are malformed,
with gnarled fingers, stubby, painful to bend. Morty's legs are short
and excessively bowed, making it difficult to run or walk rapidly.
He wears old, hand-me-down clothes, which are mostly tattered, ill-
fitting, and soiled. Morty suffers from several allergies and is susceptible to respiratory infection. The several infections and allergies
have caused Morty's facial skin to age markedly. He has bags under his eyes, wrinkles, and an unnatural yellowish cast.

Morty is often absent from school. When he attends school, he
feels self-conscious and finds that his various physical ailments

---

make it difficult for him to concentrate. For all these challenges, Morty still is polite and agreeable with all of his teachers and other school personnel. He is very helpful to his neighbors and to his family. Morty has a great sense of humor and has nurtured several friendships in his neighborhood.

*Now.*

Now, through medical and technological advances, and through grant money available from government agencies, it is possible to change Morty's life dramatically. A program of growth hormone injections will allow Morty to grow four inches over time. Reconstructive and cosmetic surgery could lengthen and straighten Morty's fingers; additional surgery could alter the bowed condition of his legs. Other cosmetic procedures could radically alter the appearance of Morty's face.

*Prescription for Equality.*

If you could change Morty to make him more the equal of other children his age in his community, what would you prescribe? Check from the list below those actions, if any, that you think should be taken to alter Morty.

_____ Reconstructive surgery on fingers and legs

_____ Cosmetic surgery on face

_____ Bleaching skin and other cosmetic facial procedures

_____ Growth hormone injections

_____ Allergy testing and regularly scheduled shots

_____ Haircut and/or hair dying

_____ New wardrobe

_____ Other: _____

_____ Nothing

*Reflection.*

Review the list of actions above that you have prescribed. In a letter to Ms. Aimee Welligan, Director, Department of Progressive Health, explain why each one of the actions is necessary to improve Morty's life or to make him more of an equal in his own community. In each case, then, explain how the change would be better than the way Morty is today. If you have prescribed nothing, write the letter to Ms. Welligan to explain why the actions are not necessary and will not make Morty any better.

Ninth-grade students produced the following two compositions after they participated in discussion about Morty's situation. The compositions reveal that the discussion did not direct the students to repeat the position that the teacher sponsored. The opposing positions represented by the two compositions in Figures 15.1 and 15.2 suggest that the important outcome for the teacher was the students' demonstration of critical thinking, which involves logic, assessment, and attention to a variety of perspectives.

The compositions honor the idea that each individual is unique, and there is danger in trying to define a universal standard and in in-

---

Dear Ms. Welligan:

Morty DeFamma is a child with many physical challenges. Although it is possible to change Morty, some critics question whether we should change him at all.

I don't totally disagree, but I don't totally agree either with these critics. One of the reasons I don't totally agree is because I believe that Morty DeFamma should end up having reconstructive surgery on his fingers and legs. I think he should have this done because that way he would be able to walk and run normally. Also, he would be able to grab onto things easier because he would be able to with his fingers.

Another reason why I kind of agree is because I think Morty should get regular allergy testing and regularly scheduled shots. I think he should get this because he is susceptible to respiratory infection and he is allergic to many things.

A couple of reasons why I don't agree with the critics is because I think the only things that Morty needs to have done are things that would make life a little easier for him. The things that would just change his appearance but not help him out wouldn't be what I think should be done.

In the end, Morty DeFamma has many physical challenges in his day to day schedule. Many things are possible to help Morty out, but there are only two I would agree on. The first is reconstructive surgery on his hands and legs, but also regular allergy testing and scheduled shots. The rest I don't agree on because they wouldn't help him out but would rather change his appearance.

Sincerely,

Juan

---

**Figure 15.1.** Sample Composition 1, in response to the "Meet Morty" activity.

fluencing everyone to conform to that standard. The students' guiding principle seems to be that the individual's health and contentment are of primary importance; surface appearance and fashion are less important if changing these features will change the quality of the person. The discussions with peers provided the means for students to grapple with the issues and find the language to express their positions in written statements.

## Discussion and Social Aspects of Learning

Cognitive psychologists will advise us that meaningful interaction among students is not just a philosophically attractive aspect of school,

---

Dear Ms. Welligan:

Morty DeFamma is a child with many physical challenges. It is possible to change Morty in many ways, but some critics think that nothing should be done at all. I agree with the critics.

God made Morty that way, and God makes no mistakes. If Morty was meant to be normal, then he would not have been born with all of those disabilities.

Another reason is that he is said to be a big help to his neighbors and family. If he is a big help with all of those disabilities, then he does not have to change at all. He already has everything he needs to be a helpful person.

Also, he is a good friend just the way he is. He has a good sense of humor and is a good person without all of those expensive surgeries and shots. He does not have to be like everyone else to have friends. He made friends with all of his disabilities.

Another thing is that if he is happy just the way he is, then don't change him just so he can fit in with all of the others. If he is not happy, then maybe he could get a couple of things done, but then he would not be the same person. He would be totally different.

So please take all of the things I mentioned to you into consideration before you make any drastic changes in Morty.

Sincerely,

Ada

---

**Figure 15.2.** Sample Composition 2, in response to the "Meet Morty" activity.

but is *essential* to learning. Vygotsky (1980) insists that learning is an essentially social activity. The interactions with peers often present those occasions when other thinkers raise doubt, call for support, invite consideration of other possibilities, and ask for reconciliation between assumptions and data. The interactions with others will often raise doubt and lead to new discoveries. This is a kind of definition of *learning*. As noted earlier, Vygotsky (1986) cites Jean-Jacques Rousseau, who describes moments when "the mind bumps up against the wall of its own inadequacy." These moments occur often when one works with others to explore open-ended questions and ill-structured problems. The experience of doubt is an important element in the process of learning. Also important is a deliberate procedure for investigation, which can be supported through work with a diverse group of peers.

Ralph Tyler, in his influential *Basic Principles of Curriculum and Instruction* (1969), recommends that needs assessments from studies of various sources must pass through two filters: a psychological one (what we know about the way humans learn) and a philosophical one (what we value). Learning environments that allow frequent occasions for peers to grapple together with significant questions serve pragmatic ends: The interactions seem to encourage learning, and they are conducive to democratic ends of equity, inclusion, and fairness.

If a school has a majority population of Latino students and in no class do students study the literature, art, culture, and history that represent the students' experience, the school has a problem. If 50 percent of the school population is female, yet no one reads women authors and no one studies the contributions that women have made to government, science, mathematics, and the arts, the school has a problem. But, regardless of the school's culture, each teacher, in almost every subject, can provide opportunities for students to interact with each other in discussing questions that will not have predetermined answers and whose investigation with a variety of peers will serve to develop an understanding of concepts that are key to the discipline. The grappling with certain questions will obviously lend itself to promoting social justice, as is the case with the equality and inclusion scenarios. The work in concert with peers to discuss authentic problems and questions, no matter what the subject, will also promote social justice as students contend with a variety of views that challenge and extend their thinking. Under the management and scrutiny of teachers, students begin to honor some standards of behavior for functioning amidst diversity until, over time, imposed civility becomes internalized to guide behavior in the larger, more diverse society.

Engaging students in meaningful discussions that might promote democratic ideals and foster an understanding of, and interest in, social justice, sounds like a pretty serious endeavor. Although the effort is an important one, this does not mean that the conversations are necessarily grim, stuffy, or rancorous. On the contrary, meaningful discussion about authentic questions infuses lessons with a dynamic energy that makes the lessons fun and engaging. Contrast, for example, listening to someone read a paper aloud, versus engaging a peer in conversation about a recognizable problem. It is not a stretch to imagine students leaving a classroom and continuing the conversation as they pass through the halls or meet at their lockers. After a time and much practice, conversation could become the primary mode of instruction in a teacher's classroom. Ideally, students can develop important habits of mind as they become highly engaged in lessons that foster diverse perspectives and promote social justice.

# References

Applebee, Arthur N. 1996. *The Curriculum as Conversation*. Chicago: The University of Chicago Press.

Applebee, Arthur N. 1999. "Building a Foundation for Effective Teaching and Learning of English: A Personal Perspective on Thirty Years of Research." *Research in the Teaching of English* 33 (May): 352–66.

Applebee, Arthur N., Judith A. Langer, Martin Nystrand, and Adam Gamoran. 2003. "Discussion-Based Approaches to Developing Understanding: Classroom Instruction and Student Performance in Middle and High School English." *American Educational Research Journal* 40 (3): 685–730.

Appleman, Deborah. 2000. *Critical Encounters in High School English: Teaching Literary Theory to Adolescents*. Urbana, IL: National Council of Teachers of English (NCTE).

Atwell, Nancie. 1998. *In the Middle: New Understandings about Writing, Reading, and Learning*, 2nd ed. Portsmouth, NH: Boynton/Cook.

Bakhtin, Mikhail M. 1981. *The Dialogic Imagination: Four Essays*. Austin: University of Texas Press.

Bakhtin, Mikhail M. 1986. *Speech Genres and Other Late Essays*. Austin: University of Texas Press.

Barton, James. 1995. "Conducting Effective Classroom Discussions." *Journal of Reading* 38 (5): 346–50.

Berliner, David C. 1987. "But Do They Understand?" In Virginia Richardson-Koehler (Ed.), *Educators' Handbook: A Research Perspective*, 259–93. New York: Longman.

Bloom, Benjamin S. 1956. *Taxonomy of Educational Objectives: The Classification of Educational Goals*. New York: McKay.

Book, Cassandra L., and Kathleen Galvin. 1975. *Instruction in and about Small Group Discussion*. Falls Church, VA: Speech Communication Association.

Booth, Wayne C., Gregory G. Colomb, and Joseph M. Williams. 1995. *The Craft of Research*. Chicago: University of Chicago Press.

Boyer, Ernest L. 1985. *High School: A Report on Secondary Education in America*. HarperCollins.

Bruner, Jerome Seymour. 1960. *The Process of Education*. Cambridge: Harvard University Press.

Burke, Jim. 2003. *The English Teacher's Companion: Complete Guide to Classroom, Curriculum, and the Profession*, 2nd ed. Portsmouth, NH: Heinemann Boynton/Cook.

Chiesi, Harry L., George J. Spilich, and James F. Voss. 1979. "Acquisition of Domain-Related Information in Relation to High- and Low-Domain Knowledge." *Journal of Verbal Learning and Verbal Behavior*, 18: 257–74.

Christenbury, Leila, and Patricia Kelly. 1983. *Questioning: A Path to Critical Thinking*. Urbana, IL: NCTE.

Cristoph, Julie N., and Martin Nystrand. 2001. "Taking Risks, Negotiating Relationships: One Teacher's Transition." *Research in the Teaching of English* 36 (2): 249–86.

Csikszentmihalyi, Mihaly, and R. Larson. 1984. *Being Adolescent: Conflict and Growth in the Teenage Years*. New York: Basic Books.

Csikszentmihalyi, Mihaly, Kevin Rathunde, and Samuel Whalen. 1993. *Talented Teenagers: The Roots of Success and Failure*. Cambridge, UK: Cambridge University Press.

Delpit, Lisa. 1996. *Other People's Children: Cultural Conflict in the Classroom*. New York: New Press.

Dewey, John. 1944. *Democracy and Education*. New York: The Free Press.

Dickinson, Emily. 2004. "Fame is a bee." *The Collected Poems of Emily Dickinson*. New York: Barnes & Noble Classics.

Elbow, Peter, and Pat Belanoff. 1989. *Sharing and Responding*. New York: Random House.

*Elements of Literature*, Third Course. 2005. Austin, TX: Holt, Rinehart and Winston. 5–22.

Flanagan, Joseph M. 1998. "Using Multiples Perspectives to Foster Civil and Rational Discourse." *Illinois English Bulletin* 85 (Late Spring): 82–93.

Flanders, Ned A. 1965. *Teacher Influence, Pupil Attitudes, and Achievement: Cooperative Research Monograph No. 12*. Washington, DC: U.S. Office of Education.

Flanders, Ned A. 1970. *Analyzing Teaching Behavior*. Menlo Park, CA: Addison-Wesley.

Freeman, Yvonne, David Freeman, and Sandra Mercuri. 2002. *Closing the Achievement Gap: How to Reach Limited-Formal-Schooling and Long-Term English Learners*. Portsmouth, NH: Heinemann.

Freeman, Yvonne, David Freeman, and Sandra Mercuri. 2003. "Helping Middle and High School Age English Language Learners Achieve Academic Success." *NABE Journal of Research and Practice* (Winter): 110–22.

Freire, Paulo. 1970. *Pedagogy of the Oppressed*. New York: Continuum.

Goodlad, John. 1984. *A Place Called School*. New York: McGraw-Hill.

Goodlad, John. 2003. "A Nation in Wait." *Education Week* 22 (April 23).

Graff, Gerald. 1992. *Beyond The Culture Wars: How Teaching the Conflicts Can Revitalize American Education*. New York: W.W. Norton.

Graff, Gerald. 2003. *Clueless in Academe: How Schooling Obscures the Life of the Mind*. New Haven, CT: Yale University Press.

Grossman, Pamela, and Anna E. Richert. 1988. "Unacknowledged Knowledge Growth: A Re-Examination of the Effects of Teacher Education." *Teaching and Teacher Education* 4 (1): 53–62.

Halpern, Diane F. 1996. *Thought and Knowledge: An Introduction to Critical Thinking*, 3rd ed. Mahwah, NJ: Lawrence Erlbaum Associates.

Halpern, Diane F. 1997. *Critical Thinking Across the Curriculum: A Brief Edition of Thought and Knowledge*. Mahwah, NJ: Lawrence Erlbaum Associates.

Hawkins, Thom. 1976. *Group Inquiry Techniques for Teaching Writing*. Urbana, IL: NCTE.

Hillocks, George, Jr. 1972. *Observing and Writing*. Urbana, IL: National Council of Teachers of English/ERIC Clearinghouse on Reading and Communication Skills.

Hillocks, George, Jr. 1980. "Toward a Hierarchy of Skills in the Comprehension of Literature." *English Journal* 60 (3): 54–59.

Hillocks, George, Jr. 1984. "What Works in Teaching Composition: A Meta-Analysis of Experimental Treatment Studies." *American Journal of Education* 93 (1): 133–70.

Hillocks, George, Jr. 1986. *Research on Written Composition: New Directions for Teaching*. Urbana, IL: National Conference on Research in English/ERIC Clearinghouse on Reading and Communication Skills.

Hillocks, George, Jr. 1995. *Teaching Writing as Reflective Practice*. New York: Teachers College Press.

Hillocks, George, Jr. 1999. *Ways of Thinking, Ways of Teaching*. New York: Teachers College Press.

Hillocks, George, Jr. 2002. *The Testing Trap: How State Writing Assessments Control Learning*. New York: Teachers College Press.

Hillocks, George, Jr., Elizabeth A. Kahn, and Larry R. Johannessen. 1983. "Teaching Defining Strategies as a Mode of Inquiry." *Research in the Teaching of English* 17 (3): 275–84.

Hillocks, George, Jr., and Larry Ludlow. 1984. "A Taxonomy of Skills in Reading and Interpreting Fiction." *American Journal of Educational Research* 21 (1).

Hillocks, George Jr., Bernard J. McCabe, and James F. McCampbell. 1971. *The Dynamics of English Instruction: Grades 7–12*. New York: Random House.

Holden, James, and John S. Schmit, eds. 2002. *Inquiry and the Literary Text: Constructing Discussions in the English Classroom*. Urbana, IL: NCTE.

Jago, Carol. 2001. *Beyond Standards: Excellence in the High School English Classroom*. Portsmouth, NH: Boynton/Cook.

Jewkes, W. T., and Northrup Frye, eds. 1973. *Man the Mythmaker*. New York: Harcourt Brace Jovanovich.

Johannessen, Larry R. 1992. *Illumination Rounds: Teaching the Literature of the Vietnam War*. Urbana, IL: NCTE.

Johannessen, Larry R. 1997a. "Enhancing Response to *Romeo and Juliet*." In Ronald E. Salome and James E. Davis (Eds.), *Teaching Shakespeare into the Twenty-First Century*, 154–65. Athens: Ohio University Press.

Johannessen, Larry R. 1997b. "Examining Pedagogical Content Knowledge in Student Teachers: A Study of Six Student Teachers from Two Graduate English Education Programs." Unpublished dissertation. University of Chicago.

Johannessen, Larry R. 1998. "Helping Prospective Teachers Create Active Learning Environments That Encourage Diverse Perspectives." Paper presented at the NCTE Spring Conference, Santa Fe, New Mexico, March 20 (ERIC Document #ED 417 426).

Johannessen, Larry R. 1999. "First Steps in Helping Novice English Teachers Think in New Ways about Teaching." *Illinois English Bulletin* 86 (Winter): 37–50.

Johannessen, Larry R. 2001. "Teaching Thinking and Writing for a New Century." *English Journal* 90 (6): 38–46.

Johannessen, Larry R., and Elizabeth A. Kahn. 1997. "Teaching English Language Arts for a Technological Age." *The Clearing House* 70 (6): 305–10.

Johannessen, Larry R., and Elizabeth Kahn. 2005. "Engaging Students in Authentic Discussions of Literature." In Thomas M. McCann, Larry R. Johannessen, Elizabeth Kahn, Peter Smagorinsky, and Michael W. Smith (Eds.), *Reflective Teaching, Reflective Learning: How to Develop Critically Engaged Readers, Writers, and Speakers*, 99–116. Portsmouth, NH: Heinemann.

Johannessen, Larry R., Elizabeth A. Kahn, and Carolyn Calhoun Walter. 1982. *Designing and Sequencing Prewriting Activities*. Urbana, IL: NCTE.

Johannessen, Larry R., Elizabeth A. Kahn, and Carolyn Calhoun Walter. 1984. "The Art of Introducing Literature." *The Clearing House* 57 (6): 263–66.

Johannessen, Larry R., and Thomas M. McCann. 2002. *In Case You Teach English: An Interactive Casebook for Prospective and Practicing Teachers*. Upper Saddle River, NJ: Prentice Hall.

Kagan, Spencer. 1992. *Cooperative Learning*. San Juan Capistrano, CA: Kagan Cooperative Learning.

Kahn, Elizabeth A., Carolyn Calhoun Walter, and Larry R. Johannessen. 1984a. "Making Small Groups Work: Controversy Is the Key." *English Journal* 72 (3): 63–65.

Kahn, Elizabeth A., Carolyn Calhoun Walter, and Larry R. Johannessen. 1984b. *Writing about Literature*. Urbana, IL: ERIC/NCTE.

Kaplan, Abraham. 1987. *In Pursuit of Wisdom: The Scope of Philosophy.* Lanham, MD: University Press of America.

Kapp, Ernst. 1942. *Greek Foundations of Traditional Logic.* New York: Columbia University Press.

King, Martin Luther, Jr. 1992. *I Have a Dream: Writings and Speeches That Changed the World.* San Francisco: Harper.

Kroll, Barry M. 1992. *Teaching Hearts and Minds: College Students Reflect on the Vietnam War in Literature.* Carbondale: Southern Illinois University Press.

Langer, Judith. 1993. "Discussion as Exploration: Literature and the Horizon of Possibilities." In George E. Newell and Russell K. Durst (Eds.), *Exploring Texts: The Role of Discussion and Writing in the Teaching and Learning of Literature.* Norwood, MA: Christopher-Gordon.

Langer, Judith A. 2001a. "Beating the Odds: Teaching Middle and High School Students to Read and Write Well." *American Educational Research Journal* 38 (4): 837–80.

Langer, Judith A. 2001b. "Succeeding Against the Odds in English." *English Journal* 91 (1): 37–42.

Lee, Carol. 2001. "Is October Brown Chinese? A Cultural Modeling Activity System for Underachieving Students." *American Educational Research Journal* 38 (1): 97–141.

Lortie, Dan C. 1975. *Schoolteacher: A Sociological Study.* Chicago: University of Chicago Press.

Marshall, James D., Peter Smagorinsky, and Michael W. Smith. 1995. *The Language of Interpretation: Patterns of Discourse in Discussions of Literature.* Urbana, IL: NCTE.

Marx, Gary. 2002. "Ten Trends: Educating Children for Tomorrow's World." *Journal of School Improvement* 3 (1) (Spring).

Marzano, Robert J. 2004. *Building Background Knowledge for Academic Achievement: Research on What Works in Schools.* Alexandria, VA: Association for Supervision and Curriculum Development.

Maxwell, Rhoda J., and Mary Jordan Meiser. 2001. *Teaching English in Middle and Secondary Schools*, 3rd ed. Upper Saddle River, NJ: Merrill/Prentice Hall.

McCann, Thomas M. 1996. "A Pioneer Simulation for Writing and for the Study of Literature." *English Journal* 85 (3): 62–67.

McCann, Thomas M. 2003. "Imagine This: Using Scenarios to Promote Authentic Discussion." *English Journal* 92 (6): 31–39.

McCann, Thomas M., and Joseph M. Flanagan. 2002. "A *Tempest* Project: Shakespeare and Critical Conflicts." *English Journal* 92 (1): 29–35.

McCann, Thomas M., Larry R. Johannessen, Elizabeth Kahn, Peter Smagorinsky, and Michael W. Smith, eds. 2005. *Reflective Teaching,*

*Reflective Learning: How to Develop Critically Engaged Readers, Writers, and Speakers.* Portsmouth, NH: Heinemann.

Meier, Deborah. 1995. *The Power of Their Ideas.* Boston: Beacon Press.

Mitchell, Diana, and Leila Christenbury. 2000. *Both Art and Craft: Teaching Ideas That Spark Learning.* Urbana, IL: NCTE.

National Commission on Excellence in Education (NCEE). 1983. *A Nation at Risk: The Imperative for Educational Reform.* Washington, DC: U.S. Government Printing Office.

Nussbaum, Martha C. 1997. *Cultivating Humanity: A Classical Defense of Reform in Liberal Education.* Cambridge, MA: Harvard University Press.

Nystrand, Martin, with Adam Gameron, Robert Kachur, and Catherine Prendergast. 1997. *Opening Dialogue: Understanding the Dynamics of Language and Learning in the English Classroom.* New York: Teachers College Press.

Oakes, Jeannie, and Martin Lipman. 1999. *Teaching to Change the World.* Boston: McGraw-Hill.

Orlich, Donald C., Robert J. Harder, Richard C. Callahan, and Harry W. Gibson. 2001. *Teaching Strategies: A Guide to Better Instruction,* 6th ed. Boston: Houghton, Mifflin.

Padron, Yolanda N., Hersh C. Waxman, and Hector H. Rivera. 2003. "Educating Hispanic Students: Obstacles and Avenues to Improved Academic Achievement." *ERS Spectrum* 21 (2): 27–39.

Paley, Vivian Gussin. 1993. *You Can't Say You Can't Play.* Cambridge, MA: Harvard University Press.

Paul, Richard W., and Linda B. Elder. 2001. *Critical Thinking: Tools for Taking Charge of Your Learning and Your Life.* Upper Saddle River, NJ: Prentice Hall.

Paul, Richard W., Douglas Martin, and Ken Adamson. 1989. *Critical Thinking Handbook: High School: A Guide for Redesigning Instruction.* Rohnert Park, CA: Foundation for Critical Thinking.

Pearson, P. David, and Dale D. Johnson. 1978. *Teaching Reading Comprehension.* New York: Holt, Rinehart, and Winston.

Pichert, James P., and Richard C. Anderson. 1977. "Taking Different Perspectives on a Story." *Journal of Educational Psychology* 69: 309–15.

Postman, Neil. 1995. *The End of Education: Redefining the Value of School.* New York: Alfred A. Knopf.

Probst, Robert E. 1988. *Response and Analysis: Teaching Literature in Junior and Senior High School.* Portsmouth, NH: Boynton/Cook.

Rabinowitz, Peter J., and Michael W. Smith. 1998. *Authorizing Readers: Resistance and Respect in the Teaching of Literature.* New York: Teachers College Press.

Raphael, Taffy E. 1982. "Question-Answering Strategies for Children." *The Reading Teacher* 36: 186–90.

Reddy, Michael. 1979. "The Conduit Metaphor—A Case of Frame Conflict in Our Language about Language." In Andrew Ortony (Ed.), *Metaphor and Thought*, 284–324. London: Cambridge University Press.

Riley, Joseph. P. 1986. "The Effects of Teachers' Wait-Time and Knowledge Comprehension Questioning on Science Achievement." *Journal of Research in Science Teaching* 23: 335–42.

Rosenblatt, Louise. 1995. *Literature as Exploration,* 5th ed. New York: Modern Language Association of America.

Rousseau, Jean Jacques. 1996. *The Social Contract.* New York: Penguin Books.

Rowe, Mary B. 1974. "Wait-Time and Rewards as Instructional Variables, Their Influence on Language, Logic and Fate Control: Part One—Wait Time." *Journal of Research in Science Teaching* 11: 81–94.

Sassoon, Siegfried. 1918. "Base Details." *Counter-Attack and Other Poems.* [Available online] 5 Oct. 2004 http://www.bartleby.com/136/11.html.

Seuss, Dr. 1937. *And to Think That I Saw It on Mulberry Street.* New York: Vanguard Press.

Silverstein, Shel. 1964. *The Giving Tree.* New York: HarperCollins.

Sizer, Theodore. 1984. *Horace's Compromise.* Boston: Houghton Mifflin.

Sizer, Theodore R., and Nancy F. Sizer. 1999. *The Students Are Watching: Schools and the Moral Contract.* Boston: Beacon Press.

Slavin, R. E. 1991. *Student Team Learning: A Practical Guide to Cooperative Learning.* Washington, DC: National Education Association.

Smagorinsky, Peter. 1989. "Small Groups: A New Dimension in Learning." *English Journal* 78 (2): 67–70.

Smagorinsky, Peter. 1993. "Preparing Students for Enriched Reading." In George E. Newell and Russell K. Durst (Eds.), *Exploring Texts: The Role of Discussion and Writing in the Teaching and Learning of Literature.* Norwood, MA: Christopher-Gordon.

Smagorinsky, Peter. 2000. "Reflecting on Character through Literary Themes." *English Journal* 89 (5): 64–69.

Smagorinsky, Peter. 2002. *Teaching English through Principled Practice.* Upper Saddle River, NJ: Prentice Hall.

Smagorinsky, Peter, and Pamela K. Fly. 1993. "The Social Environment of the Classroom: A Vygotskian Perspective on Small Group Process." *Communication Education* 42 (2): 159–71.

Smagorinsky, Peter, and Pamela K. Fly. 1994. "A New Perspective on Why Small Groups Do and Don't Work." *English Journal* 83 (3): 54–58.

Smagorinsky, Peter, and Steve Gevinson. 1989. *Fostering the Reader's Response: Rethinking the Literature Curriculum, Grades 7–12.* Palo Alto, CA: Dale Seymour.

Smagorinsky, Peter, Thomas M. McCann, and Stephen Kern. 1987. *Explorations: Introductory Activities for Literature and Composition, 7–12*. Urbana, IL: NCTE.

Smagorinsky, Peter, and Melissa E. Whiting. 1995. *How English Teachers Get Taught: Methods of Teaching the Methods Class*. Urbana, IL: NCTE.

Sorenson, M. 1993. "Teaching Each Other: Connecting Talking and Writing." *English Journal* 82: 42–47.

Stahl, Robert J. 1994. "Using 'Think-Time and Wait-Time' Skillfully in the Classroom." *ERIC Digest*. Bloomington, IN: ERIC Clearinghouse for Social Studies/Social Science Education. ED 370 885.

Stern, Deborah. 1995. *Teaching English So It Matters*. Thousand Oaks, CA: Corwin Press.

Tchudi, Stephen, and Diana Mitchell. 1999. *Exploring and Teaching the English Language Arts*, 4th ed. New York: Longman.

Tobin, Karl. 1987. "The Role of Wait-Time in Higher Cognitive Level Learning." *Review of Educational Research* 57: 69–95.

Toulmin, Stephen E. 1958. *The Uses of Argument*. Cambridge: Cambridge University Press.

Twain, Mark. 1884/1965. *The Adventures of Huckleberry Finn*. New York: Bantam.

Tyler, Ralph. 1969. *Basic Principles of Curriculum and Instruction*. Chicago: University of Chicago Press.

Vygotsky, Lev S. 1980. *Mind in Society: The Development of Higher Psychological Processes*. Cambridge: Harvard University Press.

Vygotsky, Lev S. 1986. *Thought and Language*. Cambridge, MA: MIT Press.

Walton, Douglas. 1998. *The New Dialectic: Conversational Contexts of Argument*. Toronto: University of Toronto Press.

Wilhelm, Jeffrey D., Tanya N. Baker, and Julie Dube. 2001. *Strategic Reading: Guiding Students to Lifelong Literacy, 6–12*. Portsmouth, NH: Heinemann Boynton/Cook.

Zemelman, Steven, Harvey Daniels, and A. Hyde. 1998. *Best Practice: New Standards for Teaching and Learning in America's Schools*, 2nd ed. Portsmouth, NH: Heinemann.

# Index

# Authors

**Joseph M. Flanagan** completed his BA in English from Augustana College, Rock Island, Illinois, his MAT in English from the University of Chicago, and a Certificate of Advanced Study in educational administration from the University of Illinois, Champaign–Urbana. Flanagan is an experienced high school English teacher. He now teaches at York Community High School, Elmhurst, Illinois, where he serves as the chair of the English department. His articles have appeared in *English Journal* and *Illinois English Bulletin*. He lives in Elmhurst, Illinois, with his wife Nancy, his son David, his daughters Mary and Anne, and his mixed breed hound Ernie.

**Larry R. Johannessen** is associate professor in the Department of English at Northern Illinois University, where he teaches in the English education program as well as literature courses primarily dealing with the Vietnam War. In addition, he currently serves as director of Undergraduate Studies in English. He holds a BA from California State University, Hayward, and an MAT and a PhD from the University of Chicago. He taught high school English and history for ten years. In addition to chapters in books, he has contributed over sixty articles to scholarly journals. With Tom McCann, he is coauthor of *In Case You Teach English: An Interactive Casebook for Prospective and Practicing Teachers* (2002). He is author of *Illumination Rounds: Teaching the Literature of the Vietnam War* (1992) and a coauthor of two popular NCTE publications: *Writing about Literature* (1984) and *Designing and Sequencing Prewriting Activities* (1982). With McCann, Kahn, and others, he is coeditor of *Reflective Teaching, Reflective Learning* (2005). He is listed in *Who's Who Among America's Teachers* and *Who's Who in American Education*. His current research is in the areas of teacher knowledge and thinking, particularly for preservice and novice teachers; secondary school English curriculum and instruction; literacy learning; and the literature and film of the Vietnam War. He has collaborated with McCann on research about the concerns of teachers during their formative years of teaching (*Supporting Beginning English Teachers*, 2005). He lives in Wheaton, Illinois, with his wife, Elizabeth Kahn.

**Elizabeth Kahn** has taught English language arts for twenty-eight years, currently at James B. Conant High School, where she serves as English department chair. She earned a BA in English from Wake Forest University and an MAT in English and a PhD in curriculum and instruction from the University of Chicago. She is a coauthor of *Designing and Sequencing Prewriting Activities* (1982) and *Writing about Literature* (1984). She has published articles in many journals, including *Research in the Teaching of English, English Journal, Journal of Educational Research,* and *Illinois English Bulletin.* With McCann, Johannessen, and others, she is coeditor of *Reflective Teaching, Reflective Learning* (2005). Kahn is a National Board Certified Teacher. She lives in Wheaton, Illinois, with her husband Larry Johannessen.

**Thomas M. McCann** has taught English in a variety of school settings, including eight years in an alternative school. He holds a BA from Northern Illinois University, an MA from Southern Illinois University, an MA from Saint Xavier University, and a PhD from the University of Chicago. He has published articles in *Research in the Teaching of English, English Journal, Educational Leadership, Illinois English Bulletin, The Wisconsin English Journal,* and *California English.* With Peter Smagorinsky and Stephen Kern, he is coauthor of *Explorations: Introductory Activities for Literature and Composition, 7–12* (1987). With Larry Johannessen, he is coauthor of *In Case You Teach English: An Interactive Casebook for Prospective and Practicing Teachers* (2002). With Johannessen, Kahn, and others, he is coeditor of *Reflective Teaching, Reflective Learning* (2005). McCann has taught in four high schools, two colleges, and three universities, where he worked with preservice and practicing teachers in graduate education programs. He has supervised teachers in high school for twenty years. He served for fourteen years as English department chair at Community High School in West Chicago, Illinois, where he taught English and supervised other English teachers. He also worked as assistant principal for curriculum and instruction at Community High School. He is now assistant superintendent for curriculum and instruction for Elmhurst Public Schools. He also serves as adjunct professor of English at Elmhurst College. He has collaborated with Johannessen on research about the concerns of teachers during their formative years of teaching (*Supporting Beginning English Teachers,* 2005). He lives in Elmhurst, Illinois, with his wife Pamela and daughter Katie.

*This book was typeset in Palatino and Helvetica by Electronic Imaging.*
*Typefaces used on the cover were Anastasia and Formata.*
*The book was printed on 50-lb. Williamsburg Offset paper by Versa Press, Inc.*